"This is a must-read for anyone who has spent time in the White Mountains of New Hampshire. *The Last Traverse* provides a very detailed look at the events that turned a day hike into a struggle for survival. Most important, author Ty Gagne provides tremendous insight into the commitment, sacrifice, skill, and courage of the mountain rescue teams and the National Guard UH-60 Black Hawk crew, whose efforts prevented an even greater tragedy."

—Mike Durant, retired CW4 U.S. Army UH-60 pilot and author of *In the Company of Heroes* and *The Nightstalkers.*

"Gagne tells two stories here, first the accident, then the rescue, in a perfect blend of informative, white-knuckle, storytelling. His analysis of the decision-making process will keep newcomers to experts safer on trips to our Northeast mountains' alpine zones in winter. Just be sure you've got a hot, sugary drink at your elbow before you become absorbed into the universe of this tragic but life-affirming story."

—Laura Waterman, author of *Starvation Shore* and *Losing the Garden: The Story of a Marriage*

"Having climbed the White Mountains, and in particular Mt. Lafayette, many times, I found Ty Gagne's book riveting. He has done a great deal of research and demonstrates enormous attention to detail. He brings the people in the book alive in ways that make us feel we know them well. You will feel the snowstorm and the bitter cold as the hikers make their way upward—and you won't be able to put the book down."

—John Lynch, Governor of New Hampshire (2005-13)

"Ty Gagne's latest book is essential reading for hikers. *The Last Traverse* is a compelling, thoroughly investigated, real-life story of a winter hike in the White Mountains that goes awry and the critical lessons to be learned from it. It is also a testament to the heroic efforts of the professionals and volunteers who brave perilous weather conditions to rescue stranded hikers and to the exceptional medical professionals who treat hypothermia victims."

—Kelly Ayotte, U.S. Senator for New Hampsire (2011-16), Attorney General of New Hampshire (2005-09)

"Ty Gagne spent an incredible amount of emotional energy carefully researching and gracefully writing this fantastic story that focuses on risk, trust, service, humility, and—most important—resilience. Highly recommended."

—Jason B.A. Van Camp, founder and chairman of Mission Six Zero, and author of *Deliberate Discomfort: How U.S. Special Operations Forces Overcome Fear And Dare To Win By Getting Comfortable Being Uncomfortable*

The Last Traverse

Tragedy and Resilience
in the Winter Whites

Ty Gagne

The Last Traverse
Tragedy and Resilience
in the Winter Whites

Copyright © Ty Gagne 2020

ISBN: 978-1-7349308-3-2

731 Tasker Hill Rd.
Conway, NH 03818
USA
www.tmcbooks.com

For Debbie, Matthew, Megan, and Tyler

This book is dedicated to all first responders, healthcare workers, and members of the U.S. Armed Forces: those who stand between us and the breach, be it in a small town, a city, an emergency room, a battlefield—or a mountaintop. I am forever grateful for your selfless service.

Contents

"We call it full conditions. It's about as cold and windy as you can withstand. It's not the place to spend the night, so something happened. There was a desperate situation."

—Rick Wilcox, Mountain Rescue Service,
Concord Monitor, Feb. 13, 2008

Prologue

Readers of my previous book, *Where You'll Find Me: Risk, Decisions, and the Last Climb of Kate Matrosova* (TMC Books, 2017), might recall the Prologue, entitled "Full Conditions." It chronicles a series of errors I made before and during my first (and only) winter traverse of the Franconia Ridge in New Hampshire's White Mountains in February 2008. Adverse weather conditions, and my own misjudgments, taught me important life lessons that I've shared with readers and others in hopes that people might reflect on their own decision-making process, whether in the mountains or elsewhere.

In the final paragraph of "Full Conditions," I mention that eight days after my traverse, two hikers from New Hampshire became trapped in a storm during their own attempt of the same ridgeline. The younger, less experienced of the two hikers, James Osborne, was found and rescued. Sadly, his older, more experienced companion, Laurence "Fred" Fredrickson, succumbed to the injuries he sustained in his long encounter with the cold. Both were found on Little Haystack Mountain not far from each other, and both were heartbreakingly close to the safety of treeline, and quite possibly an outcome that would have left this page as white as the winter storm that consumed them on the ridge.

Though I was warm, fed, and sheltered in the comfort of my home some thirty minutes south of Franconia Notch during the search for Osborne and Fredrickson, I felt a strong connection to them and their fate. Later on, as I learned more about the circumstances of their harrowing experience, the distance between us became even narrower. In fact, their story and that of their rescuers stayed in my mind for years. Based on what I knew, I felt there was an important story to tell, and I hoped to do so in a way that might cause others to reflect on and discuss things like risk, trust, service, and humility. So eleven years after the accident, I reached out to James Osborne, hoping he might tell his part of the story that claimed his friend and significantly altered the course of his own life.

James immediately saw the value of sharing his ordeal in an attempt to help others avoid the same fate. We spent many hours talking about his life before, during, and after the accident. He gave me full access to all the medical records that charted his treatment and recovery, and he introduced me to Fred's ex-wife, Bette. She and her sons, Trevor and Kyle, have contributed greatly to this story.

I have also reached out to the nearly three dozen rescuers who were part of saving James's life and recovering the body of his friend. They and other experts have been extremely generous in both the time and information they have shared with me. Their experience, advice, and wisdom will, I hope, provide worthwhile guidance to those readers who venture uphill in any season.

Looking north on the Franconia Ridge Trail on the approach to Mount Lincoln.

I
PENDULUM

"The Edge...there is no honest way to explain it, because the only people who really know where it is are the ones who have gone over."

—*Hunter S. Thompson*

Intensive Care Unit 4 South, Room 15
Dartmouth-Hitchcock Medical Center
Lebanon, N.H.
Tuesday, Feb. 12, 2008
9:00 p.m.

James Osborne is on the precipice, barely holding on to the frayed rope of advanced life support. The hospital's technology and medications are working to protect him from falling into the abyss, but just how long this fragile anchor system can keep him aloft is uncertain. As the life struggle rages on, he swings helplessly back and forth through a spectrum of amorphous dreams and disruptive stimuli. His primitive brain is on alert, working behind the scenes in support of the intervention it senses is being undertaken by forces unknown. This is because his analytical brain, the cortex, did an emergency bailout over a day ago and hasn't been heard from since.

Osborne is being rewarmed because he arrived here dangerously cold. He remains critically ill from the effects of hypothermia and third-degree frostbite on portions of his feet, hands, face, and torso. The immediate threat to his life is the hypothermia, so any comprehensive treatment of his frostbite will have to wait.

Amid the chaos, Osborne is showing subtle signs of brain activity. He shakes his head gently during examination of his face and eyes. At times, he rests his hands on his lower torso with fingers interlaced, an indication of protective posture. In this state, Osborne's primitive brain is detecting sound, smell, and changes in light and touch. What it can't do is process, interpret, or understand what any of this stimulation means. That is the cortex's responsibility.

When his brain swings farthest away from the cortex's reach toward the apex of his primitive brain's activity, Osborne is suspended in a place of situational avoidance. Separating him from any contact with the excruciating reality that awaits him if he regains full consciousness, these big swings are completely out of his control. The longer they go on, the weaker his connection to life will get. The immediate goal of his treatment team is to shorten the distance and duration of Osborne's brain swings through active rewarming techniques. If their intervention is effective, the swings to and from the murky, dreamlike state will slow and eventually stop.

Earlier in the day, there was a flurry of activity around Osborne. Attending physicians, residents, nurses, and clergy discussed, debated, and formulated plans for his care. His mother and stepfather, other family members, and a few coworkers were also present, trying to understand all that had transpired. At this hour, however, a tentative calmness pervades the Intensive Care Unit and the room Osborne occupies. Only a lone nurse on her scheduled rounds remains in his room. The glaring ceiling lights that throughout the day bathed him and his caregivers in brightness and warmth are dim, as are the lights and sounds of the monitors and pumps that hover beside and above his upper torso. Ambient light, generated by the multiple floors of rooms in the adjacent wing, is tempered by the partially retracted shade in the bay window behind and to the right of Osborne's bed. The ICU where he lies occupies just a fraction of this level-one, 396-bed academic medical center, one of the premier hospitals in New England.

During the evening's respite, Osborne's nurse moves with methodical focus from the monitors measuring his vital signs to his chart. She checks his IVs and gently tends to several wound dressings. While she works near Osborne, the nurse generates soft sounds and casts shadows across his closed eyelids. This stimulation triggers a swing toward consciousness. His cortex is making its slow return to the fight, reaching out for awareness. He feels an obstruction in his throat. The cortex is trying to make sense of that feeling. Something is lodged in there like a hard candy swallowed whole. Whatever this is, his cortex is sensing it as a problem.

Slowly, Osborne opens his eyes. He feels lethargic but present. Did he die? Is the afterlife this clinical? As his brain processes the sensory data being delivered by his eyes, he identifies a tube protruding from his mouth and feels it in his throat. It's alarming, but he's too exhausted and confused to do anything about it. Someone approaches him. His cortex infers a hospital room, a nurse—trouble. The nurse leans toward him and rests her hand on his shoulder. The human contact and sound of her voice temper some of the fear and uncertainty he's feeling. She speaks to him.

You're at Dartmouth-Hitchcock Medical Center in Lebanon. Though he doesn't grasp where this is, his brain is processing everything she's saying to him. He's able to imagine and draw logic from her words. He feels relief that he is alive. But all of this is requiring a huge amount of energy to navigate. He acknowledges her with his eyes and a subtle nod of his head.

You were in a hiking accident on Sunday. Do you know that? His heavy eyes remain in contact with hers. He executes another nod, indicating that he does.

You were hiking with your friend, Fred. His body tenses. He's back on the ridgeline with Fred. Then he's present again in the room and back in his bed. His eyes are locked on hers, waiting for more information.

I'm sorry to tell you, he died. When her words connect, he feels grief at the loss of his friend and starts to cry. He is experiencing overwhelming emotional stress. The energy stores he rebuilt over several hours of unconsciousness and treatment are burning up as he struggles to process the information she is conveying.

When Osborne reaches the point of overload, his cortex shuts off again. It's all too much to handle. His primitive brain, sensing significant physiological stress in what is still a marginal recovery, steps into the breach and interrupts Osborne's conscious thought. This part of his brain refuses to allow consciousness to interfere with his body's healing. Osborne's eyes close again as his brain releases its grip on consciousness. He swings back toward the safety of nothingness, far away from physical pain, the nurse's words, and the truth of what has occurred.

II
ORIGINS

"Truly great friends are hard to find,
difficult to leave, and impossible to forget."
—Unknown

Looking south, Franconia Ridge on the upper left, Cannon Mountain Ski Area to the right.

Cannon Mountain
Franconia Notch, N.H.
Sunday, Feb. 3, 2008
Early afternoon

The annual ritual is in progress. Thirty-six-year-old James Osborne watches his friend and coworker, Ernie Brochu, effortlessly carve sweeping turns down the steep slopes of Cannon Mountain (4,080 ft.). It's Super Bowl Sunday, and the two are feeling a lot of good energy, not only because they're out skiing together, as they do on this day every year, but also because the New England Patriots are set to play the New York Giants, and the Pats are favored by 12.

It's not one of those ideal "bluebird sky" days, by any means. The temperature in Franconia Notch is in the low 20s, and winds are out of the west at around 20 mph. At the Mount Washington Observatory, about 20 miles to the east, the weather observer will log a gust of 69 mph later in the day. But that's business as usual at this high intersection of three weather systems. There's thick sky cover hovering over Cannon and the surrounding peaks, but the poor visibility isn't detracting from the friends' enjoyment at being outdoors and doing something they love. Brochu recalls it as a "perfect, perfect day."

On the opposite side of the Notch, a couple of thousand feet above and to the east of Osborne and Brochu, their friend and coworker, 55-year-old Laurence "Fred" Fredrickson, is traversing the Franconia Ridge Trail somewhere between Little Haystack Mountain (4,760 ft.) and Mount Lafayette (5,260 ft.). He's likely moving quickly, as he usually does when hiking in the White Mountains. This is his fourth winter hike of the season. High on that ridge, the weather is roughly the same as it is over on Cannon. Temperatures are in the mid-to-upper teens, and winds are in the 30-mph range. Just like Cannon, the Franconia Ridge and its high summits are socked in.

As anyone who has hiked extensively in the White Mountains knows, the weather, especially in winter, is highly volatile. From one day to the next, conditions can vary from relatively mild to dangerously brutal. For example, had Fredrickson been traversing the Franconia Ridge the day before, he would have encountered the same zero visibility he is experiencing today, but the winds out of the west would have been significantly stronger and the temperature several degrees colder. Throughout the previous day, the Observatory clocked sustained winds in the 80s and 90s, observed a peak gust of 118 mph, and reported that the temperature never breached 9°F. Conditions on the ridge that day were certainly "full." Hikers would have been actively resisting the westerly wind's effort to push them eastward off the ridge and down into the remote Pemigewasset Wilderness.

In years past, Fredrickson has joined Osborne and Brochu on their annual Super Bowl Sunday ski outings. But during the previous winter, he sprained his knee while skiing and vowed never to go skiing again. Not one to sit idle, however, Fredrickson continues to go out and up at every opportunity, just not on skis.

Unlike his two friends, Fredrickson is on his own today. With Falling Waters Trail and the summits of Little Haystack and Mount

Lincoln (5,089 ft.) in his wake, he stands on the summit of Mount Lafayette. He removes his digital camera from his pack and hands it to another hiker he's encountered there. Using Fredrickson's camera, the hiker takes a photograph of him. Thirty-five minutes later, Fredrickson takes three more photos of himself down near treeline and the Appalachian Mountain Club's Greenleaf Hut.

The trail signs at the summit and the krummholz down near treeline are coated in thick rime ice. In each photo, Fredrickson smiles into the camera, his cheekbones set high and frost glazing his

Fred Fredrickson on Mount Lafayette during his Franconia Ridge Traverse hike on Feb. 3, a week before his return to the ridge with James Osborne.

eyebrows and the tip of his nose. His dark yellow shell jacket and red winter hat offer a bright contrast to the dreary opaqueness all around him. An hour later, while descending the Old Bridle Path, he takes three additional photos of himself. He has shed the shell jacket now that he's below treeline and out of the wind and frozen fog. The photos show a man fully present and content.

Meanwhile, over on Cannon, Osborne and Brochu have finished their lunch in the Lafayette Food Court cafeteria and are back on the slopes. As they descend, they're finding similar conditions to what Fredrickson is experiencing higher up. The frozen fog limits their ability to see what's ahead, and ice spreads over the lenses of their goggles. They stop to rub the ice off the lenses and reevaluate. It's a brief assessment. "Let's just go," Osborne says to his companion.

Brochu agrees to end the day, and the two complete their final run. They load their gear in the car and drive to Brochu's house, where they'll watch the Super Bowl with Fredrickson and two other coworkers, Steve Harbert and Craig Middleton. All five work for Concord Coach Lines, a popular bus company in the Granite State.

Fredrickson is the last to arrive at the house, and he's pumped. Osborne recalls his friend's euphoria: "Fred showed up, and he had this crazy story of being up on the ridge when his eyebrows filled up with snow."

Fredrickson's enthusiasm is always contagious to those around him, especially when he talks about his outdoor pursuits. "Fred was animated about that hike" Brochu recalls. "He wore shell pants that allowed him to slide most of the way down Old Bridle Path."

The friends enjoy their traditional Super Bowl meal of Brochu's prized chili and begin watching the game, hoping for a Pats victory. The strong bond the five men feel has been forged by a shared mission at work and a shared passion for hiking in the White Mountains. Osborne is the newest member of the group, having arrived at Concord Coach in 2004. His companions share a longer tenure with the company. Craig Middleton trained and acclimated Osborne to the company ethos. Brochu recalls Osborne's arrival: "When James came on board, we called him the youngest old man in the company, because he was very mature for his age."

Osborne moved to New Hampshire from Ohio in 2002 with his then-wife, Elizabeth Gruber. The couple divorced in late summer 2005. He had attended Kent State University, where he majored in history, and earned a master's degree in elementary education from Antioch. Prior to joining Concord Coach, he worked at a local nonprofit and taught elementary school in East Boston for two years before the commute became too much for him—and for their relationship. Having worked for a bus company in Ohio, Osborne was happy to join Concord Coach, and he readily found new friends there.

Osborne met Fredrickson for the first time in 2004. Still a fairly new driver, he was on a bus run to Boston when he received a call on the bus's cell phone. "I get this frantic call that there's a bus broken down at the Holiday Inn on Route 1, and that I need to drive up there and give the driver my bus so passengers can continue to Portland, Maine," recalls Osborne. "It's 10:00 p.m., and I get a second call that I'm to wait with the broken-down bus for the towing company."

Soon his phone rings a third time. It's Fredrickson, whom Osborne doesn't yet know. "Are you still waiting for the tow truck?" Fredrickson inquires.

"Yes," Osborne replies.

"You're going to be there all night. I'll come and get you," Fredrickson tells him.

As promised, Fredrickson arrives in his bus and picks up Osborne. He expresses his frustration that Osborne has been left stranded. On the ride back to New Hampshire, the two converse about Osborne's experience as a new driver for the company and learn a bit about each other's backgrounds. Osborne talks of his interest in cycling, which Fredrickson shares, and he discovers that Fredrickson is an avid hiker. Osborne is moved by Fredrickson's generosity in picking him up and impressed with his calm demeanor. "He always wanted to take care of the people around him," says Osborne. "He was pretty laid back. He loved to laugh."

The following year, in the summer of 2005, Osborne is on a two-day bus run to Bangor, Maine, when he meets Steve Harbert. Both men have driven buses there from different routes and happen to have an overlapping night's stay. Osborne and Harbert talk for hours, and Osborne realizes he's met another like-minded colleague who enjoys cycling and who shares Fredrickson's love of hiking in the White Mountains. They agree to go into the mountains together sometime. Surprisingly, they also discover they are both alumni of Kent State University in Ohio, and that they both drove a bus on campus while there.

Harbert and Osborne take their first hike together in April 2006 when they summit Mount Hale (4,055 ft.) in Bethlehem, N.H. From there, Harbert suggests they embark on the classic endeavor of hiking the state's 4,000-footers: the 48 mountains in New Hampshire that are at or exceed 4,000 feet in elevation. Osborne was unaware there were that many summits of such height in New Hampshire and immediately signs on to the goal.

The two hike or bike nearly every Tuesday, their mutual day off. Osborne recalls that on one Tuesday, in June 2006, they are slated to go cycling, but Harbert calls the night before and says the weather is going to be spectacular and that they should climb Mount Washington (6,288 ft.), the highest peak in the northeastern United States. Osborne is a bit hesitant to tackle the challenge. "I agreed to go, but begrudgingly," he recalls.

Osborne's reluctance is quickly erased by the experience. "It was spectacular," he says. "We were both in good shape. It was sixty degrees on Mount Washington, and there was almost no wind. We hiked the Ammonoosuc Ravine Trail to Lakes of the Clouds Hut, and summited. On the way down, we left our packs at the hut and ran over to the next peak (Mount Monroe, 5,371 ft.). The sun was going down, and it was one of those moments as a hiker when everything's right with the world." According to Osborne, the Mount Washington trip "solidified us as peakbaggers. This is what we were doing."

They make a few attempts to summit Mount Lafayette on the Franconia Ridge that summer but turn back because of concerns about the weather. During one of their attempts, they encounter heavy rain and severe lightning right at treeline and choose to bail out.

In the summer of 2007, Fredrickson begins to join Osborne and Harbert on their weekly outings, and Middleton occasionally goes along. Brochu recalls watching the group evolve: "These guys got into it really hard-core. I would see them after the weekend. They formed this group: Craig, Steve, James, and Fred. They had a great time doing that stuff."

Among all of these outdoor friends, Fredrickson, who joined Concord Coach twelve years earlier, has the most hiking experience. His son Trevor, who hiked and climbed with his dad from childhood to adulthood, still marvels at his drive and passion. "He loved the outdoors," says Trevor. "He had tagged all the four-thousand-footers in the Northeast and was working on the Hundred Highest. He was near completing that goal."

One father-son trip to Maine's Katahdin (5,267 ft.) stands out in Trevor's memory. "We met in Bangor and drove to Millinocket, stayed overnight there, and hiked the next couple of days," says Trevor. "His plan was not to drive back home with me. He dropped his bike off at one end of a mountain range in southern Maine and then drove to the other end and hiked for a day to do a few other peaks. Then he rode his bike back to his car."

Having climbed, camped, and hiked for most of his life, Fredrickson spent as much time as he could in the backcountry. "Several times during our hikes we'd run into Fred, who was adding mountains to his itinerary before linking up with us," Osborne recalls.

In July 2007, Fredrickson, Harbert, and Osborne decide to climb Mount Carrigain (4,700 ft.) in Livermore, N.H., part of the Pemigewasset Wilderness. They reach the peak, and during the descent, Fredrickson tells them that Mount Nancy (3,926 ft.) is nearby. It's not a 4,000-footer, but it is on the Hundred Highest list. Why not summit Mount Nancy, since they are already there?

"Mount Nancy was a bushwhack," says Osborne. "But Fred decided we'd do that. None of us were remotely qualified to navigate a bushwhack, but we got up there, and we signed the notebook."

Unfortunately, after this unplanned detour, the three are overtaken by darkness during the bushwhack back to their car. "It got dark, and we had one headlamp," says Osborne. "We affixed the headlamp to the top of a stick to illuminate the ground. It was warm, and we ran out of food and water."

For Osborne it is a challenging set of hours. "I remember seeing the car. I had such a sense of euphoria. It was 10:00 p.m. when we got out. I hadn't eaten since 1:00 p.m. and had hit the wall."

They are all tired, hungry, and battered from bushwhacking through thick brush. Brochu recalls seeing Fred in the days following the hike. "He had bug bites and was all cut to hell."

Fredrickson had become well known among his friends and coworkers for maintaining a high level of physical fitness. At about 6 feet tall and approximately 175 pounds, his body fat was reportedly less than 10 percent. In addition to the time he spent outdoors, he would put in many hours at the gym. It was not uncommon for him to arrive in Boston on a morning bus run and, while waiting to drive the return trip in the afternoon, hit the gym. After arriving back in

Concord in the evening, he would often hit the gym again.

In an interview with the *Concord Monitor* on Feb. 13, 2008, Heidi Lessard, the manager of the Concord Coach terminal in Concord, said, "Fred was really into keeping fit and healthy. It was a little infectious in that he attracted other people to do those things."

Fredrickson's ex-wife, Bette, echoes Lessard's comments: "He became so health conscious, almost to an extreme. He had no fat whatsoever. Going to the gym, biking, climbing—he would always be giving me his body fat number, and he always wanted it to go down and down," she says.

But although he was remarkably physically fit, Fredrickson's low level of body fat caused him to get cold easily. Osborne recalls such an occurrence: "There was one July when we had hiked the Wildcats. We came down, all sweaty, but Fred was shivering. It was late afternoon and probably in the seventies."

"Fred was in a different world, fitness-wise," Osborne says. "On our hikes, it was Fred out front, then Steve, then me. Steve and I were closer in distance than Steve was from Fred. There was no keeping up with him. He would wait, and so would Steve. I accepted I was the slowest person out there."

Because he felt he lacked their ability and experience, Osborne deferred to Harbert or Fredrickson on planning and logistics whenever they went hiking together. "Steve did the planning; he was very judicious about it," Osborne recalls. "One of my errors was ceding too much responsibility to them, in general."

According to Osborne, he and Harbert hiked together approximately thirty times between April 2006 and the fall of 2007, and summited thirty-nine peaks. "We added up the hiking miles and the meals we'd eaten afterward. It was pretty staggering to see how much time we'd spent together."

Osborne hiked with Fredrickson more than a dozen times as well, usually with Steve along. They also cycled a few times and skied together. "There was a lot of camaraderie among all of us," Osborne says.

The 2007 hiking season would culminate for Osborne in September when he and Fredrickson hiked the Huntington Ravine Trail on Mount Washington, the most difficult hike in New

Hampshire. It was a beautiful, warm fall day. But despite the ideal conditions, Osborne struggled. "There were some moments I was pretty uncomfortable on that hike," he recalls. "I was out of my element, as I'm not a rock climber."

On one particularly exposed part of the hike Osborne, who is about 5 feet 10 inches tall and 210 pounds, found himself in a difficult spot. "Fred, what the hell did you get me into here?" he recalls saying in jest at one point. "Hand me your backpack, I'll take care of it," Fredrickson replied.

James Osborne on the Huntington Ravine Trail, September 2007.

Osborne gingerly handed the pack up to his friend and completed the tricky set of exposed moves. After topping out, they hiked through the Alpine Garden, one of Fredrickson's favorite spots to sit and have lunch, and then descended the Lion Head Trail. When it was over, Osborne was delighted. The experience of working through the challenges boosted his confidence and served as a fitting end to that year's hiking,

A little more than four months later, as he watches the 2008 Super Bowl with his four friends, Osborne realizes that Fredrickson's enthusiasm about that day's winter traverse has drawn him in. While he has done numerous hikes with Fredrickson and others in the room, he has yet to experience the heightened challenge and jaw-dropping beauty of winter hiking in the White Mountains, especially above treeline—where he loves to be. A winter hike seems like the obvious next step, and the idea will take shape within the next few days.

But before it does, the five friends watch as the Patriots fall to the New York Giants 17-14. So much for the 12-point spread.

Fred Fredrickson on the Huntington Ravine Trail, September 2007.

III
MOVEMENT

"Ponder and deliberate before you make a move."

—*Sun Tzu*

Interstate 93 North
En route to Concord, N.H.
Friday, Feb. 8, 2008
Afternoon

Fred Fredrickson is fully immersed in one of his two passions, driving a passenger bus for Concord Coach Lines, while simultaneously talking about his second passion: winter hiking. He's on his way back to the terminal at the Concord Transportation Center after making a morning run to South Station in Boston. Seated in the first row and engaged in conversation with him is his colleague Abbi Saffian, who works at the transportation center as a customer service representative and ticket agent.

Saffian is returning from a morning commitment in Boston and has carefully selected her return itinerary. "I always choose my travel schedule around my favorite drivers, and Fred was one of them," she says. "He really cared about people working at the ticket counter and at the station. He was a genuine human being. He would get off work and order us pizza, go get it, and come back and eat with us. He was just awesome."

While the bus's diesel engine hums steadily in the background, Fredrickson and Saffian share their plans for the upcoming weekend. He tells her that he and James Osborne are going hiking. Saffian recalls being surprised by this. "It's so cold and snowy! Why would you even do that? You're going to freeze," she tells him. Fredrickson reassures her, explaining that he's an avid hiker and knows how to stay safe.

This isn't the first time one of his coworkers has questioned Fredrickson's desire to hike in winter. "You just have to be smart about it," he would say. He describes to Saffian how beautiful winter hiking is and says it's his favorite time of year to hike. "It's a really different experience," he tells her.

Eastern Mountain Sports
Manchester, N.H.
Friday, Feb. 8, 2008
Early evening

James Osborne snakes around the racks of outdoor gear at Eastern Mountain Sports in search of a couple of important pieces of kit. In less than two days, he's going on his first winter hike, and while he's well equipped for the three other seasons, he needs to gear up for this one.

In the days following the Super Bowl evening, Osborne and Fredrickson have talked on the phone, as they often do several times a week. Winter hiking has become the recurring theme. "The winter hike idea evolved during that week," says Osborne. "We talked about gear: snowshoes and crampons. I didn't have either and had never used them."

In the course of their conversations, the two have made plans to drive to Franconia Notch on Sunday, Feb. 10, and do a traverse of the Franconia Ridge. They will follow the same route Fredrickson did on the previous Sunday, a traverse he has done several times before, in every season. By now, Osborne has also hiked in Franconia Notch on several occasions, including doing the traverse of the ridge, but only in spring, summer, and fall.

"I remember James talking about his excitement at this being his first winter climb," says Ernie Brochu. "He was totally relying on Fred in terms of what to bring, what to wear, all of that. I knew they were hiking, but I didn't know the details. I didn't realize until they were missing that it was the Franconia Ridge."

Osborne locates a pair of hiking pants that are a bit more rugged than the ones he generally wears. There are cargo pockets on each leg that will come in handy for carrying food. He is told that the store has sold out of snowshoes, so he makes his way over to the climbing gear and searches the floor-to-ceiling shelves for a pair of crampons. His eyes finally lock on a single pair of Black Diamonds. He asks the retail associate if these are the only crampons in stock. The associate tells him they are because it's pretty late in the season. He sees that he's gotten lucky with only one pair left, so he grabs them. With pants and crampons in hand, he makes his way to the checkout counter.

Sometime that Friday, Osborne checks Sunday's weather. "As a hiker, you should check the [Mount Washington] Observatory forecasts," he says. "They provide much more useful information. But I checked AccuWeather or the Weather Channel, and nothing looked alarming to me."

Aircraft Hangar
N.H. Army National Guard Aviation Support Facility
Concord, N.H.
Friday, Feb. 8, 2008
Early evening

Staff Sgt. Matt Stohrer of the New Hampshire Army National Guard walks with purpose into the massive hangar. It's fully illuminated by the enormous lights hanging from the high ceiling, and the space is clinically clean. The hangar reflects a discipline and order that is rarely found outside the U.S. military. Stohrer's eyes are immediately drawn to the five Sikorsky UH-60 Black Hawk helicopters lined up, side by side, all the way to the far end of the giant room. The sight of the aircraft in varying degrees of maintenance, repair, and standby never gets old for him.

Born and raised in close proximity to this base, Stohrer developed an early passion for military helicopters. "I used to watch them fly over my house when I was growing up in Concord," he says. As his high school graduation approached, Stohrer had yet to find his path. His grandfather had been in the Navy and fought in World War II. Stohrer found himself leaning toward that branch of the service until his grandfather suggested he join the Marines. His uncle, a member of the National Guard, suggested he look into that branch instead. Stohrer took this advice, and eventually found his way to the New Hampshire Army National Guard recruiting office, where the recruiter encouraged him to become a repairer of utility helicopters, known as UH-1 aircraft, for the Concord-based aviation support unit.

In 1997, at age 18, Stohrer enlisted as a UH-1 repairer for the 1159th Medical Company. After attending Basic Training and Advanced Individual Training, he returned to the unit a year later. At the time of his return, the army was transitioning from the UH-1 Iroquois helicopter, also known as the "Huey," to the UH-60 Black Hawk. Because some of the veteran members of the unit were nearing retirement, Stohrer was given the opportunity to serve as a UH-60 repairer. He recalls this unlikely advancement with gratitude: "It was like I kind of hit the lottery. At 19, I was really young for it."

Stohrer worked in helicopter maintenance until 1999, when he achieved flight status because crew chiefs were needed at the time. One of the primary responsibilities of the crew chief is to oversee the maintenance of the aircraft. This includes diagnosing and troubleshooting mechanical issues during a flight and then talking with maintenance personnel back on the ground. Crew chiefs also conduct visual inspections of the aircraft and perform preventive maintenance daily (PMD), checking fluids and securing parts. When in flight, the crew chief is also involved with mission-specific tasks, such as facilitating troop entries and exits, and helping hoist injured patients into the aircraft.

Stohrer eventually became a standardization instructor for the unit, which involves training other crew chiefs. In 2002, his unit was deployed as a "stabilization force" to Bosnia to provide medevac services in the region. In 2005, he was deployed to Iraq for Operation Enduring Freedom. During that deployment, the insurgency was ramping up, and Stohrer and his colleagues found themselves flying several medevac missions a day for injuries sustained in IED explosions and other casualties of war. "We'd get into our unarmed helicopter, fly into a hostile landing zone, pick up the wounded, and fly to the hospital," he says.

On returning from the war, Stohrer resumed his role in the Army National Guard unit, sometimes flying on search and rescue (SAR) missions within New Hampshire. He and his colleagues are members of C Company 3-238th General Support Aviation Battalion (GSAB), Air Ambulance Aviation Regiment.

By 2008, Stohrer had logged 1,200 hours in the back of a Black Hawk and participated in a dozen SAR missions, most of which were in the White Mountains in winter. "I've been given an amazing opportunity," he says. "I'm born and raised in New Hampshire, and to be able to do SAR missions is really meaningful. I've hiked Lafayette—I used to hike with my parents—and to be able to pull people off the Appalachian Trail to a safe place is very rewarding."

On this February evening, Stohrer is in the hangar to practice a ritual he and the other crew chiefs perform every Friday. He's here to assess aircraft availability and prepare for the possibility of assisting New Hampshire Fish and Game with potential search and rescue operations over the weekend.

Stohrer and his colleagues are members of a partnership that has spanned almost sixty years. The first documented SAR mission in which the New Hampshire Army National Guard (NHARNG) assisted New Hampshire Fish and Game (NHFG) in a rescue was in November 1951, when it deployed sixty guardsmen to participate in a ground search for a missing person in Kilkenny, a township of Coos County. Seven years later, in 1958, the NHARNG would conduct its first SAR mission by air, looking for a missing aircraft in the southern part of the state. "Fish and Game wants eyes above treeline, and we're able to cover so much ground," Stohrer says.

Stohrer walks down the row of idle aircraft, pausing to talk with maintenance personnel in order to choose one that is "flight ready." They identify a good candidate: aircraft 88-26031, or Black Hawk 031 for short. If the 238th Battalion is activated for a search and rescue call, or what is officially known as a State Mission, the Black Hawk will go by the call sign "Guard 031."

The aircraft Stohrer has chosen is a UH-60A weighing approximately 14,500 pounds. It is a four-blade, single-rotor helicopter with twin GE 700 turbine engines. It has two 180-gallon fuel tanks that, when full, add 2,400 pounds of weight to the aircraft. The UH-60 runs JP8 jet fuel that contains anti-icing additives. Under what are considered normal conditions, the helicopter burns 840 pounds of fuel per hour, which provides approximately two and a half hours of flight time. But conditions in the airspace over the White Mountains are rarely, if ever, normal. So burn rates can increase significantly, which decreases time in the air.

Having designated an aircraft, Stohrer walks over to the locker that houses the rescue equipment and begins hauling it out, piece by piece. "I always configure the gear as if we're doing the mission," explains Stohrer. He knows that Black Hawk 031 already has a rescue hoist installed at the rear edge of the right cabin door. The hoist is used when the Black Hawk is unable to land because of terrain and safety concerns. When that happens, the crew chief is lowered to the ground on the hoist, with or without a litter, to assist with a rescue. Stohrer places a hard-plastic basket stretcher, also known as a Stokes litter, on the floor of the rear cabin and secures it with two straps. To the interior rear wall, he installs a bag holding a tagline, a nylon rope that attaches to one end of the Stokes litter and is held by a medic or other crew member while on the ground. The tagline helps control the litter's movement and prevents it from spinning during hoist operations. Stohrer then secures a forest penetrator on the rear wall next to the hoist. The forest penetrator looks like a giant, three-pronged fishhook when its retractable arms are deployed. It is used as a rescue seat to extract patients who are able to sit up, or for other personnel.

UH-60 Black Hawk helicopter.

Next, Stohrer places an AxelCut splice tool next to the hoist and forest penetrator. The AxelCut tool is used to cut the hoist's cable in the event that it becomes caught on trees, rocks, or around the crew chief during rescue operations. Stohrer then uses tie-downs to secure a blanket bag and oxygen tank.

Finally, Stohrer puts a harness and headset with an Integrated Communications Systems (ICS) cord on the back wall. These items are intended for use by the Fish and Game law enforcement liaison, a

Conservation Officer (CO) assigned to the rescue. The harness keeps the CO secured to the aircraft during flight and allows him or her to move about the rear cabin and assist with the rescue operation. The ICS cord permits the CO to communicate with the helicopter crew and search and rescue personnel on the ground through the technosonic radio installed in the aircraft. The harness, headset, and ICS cord are stored in a green bag, matching the color of a Conservation Officer's uniform.

Black Hawk helicopter with crew chief on a forest penetrator and hoist line.

When all the Black Hawk's seats are installed, it can accommodate thirteen combat-equipped troops. For SAR missions, most of these seats are removed to allow space for the rescue operation. Two passenger seats remain along the back wall, one of which is designated for the Fish and Game liaison, and the other for an additional passenger, if necessary. At the front of the cabin are two fixed seats, located directly behind the pilots, one on the left and one on the right. They face away from each other and toward the gunners' windows. For SAR missions, each crew chief looks out a gunner's window to conduct a visual search of terrain and to serve as a rearview mirror for the pilots during flight.

Stohrer recognizes the importance of preparing the aircraft for an urgent event that may not happen. "In medevac, we call it the 'golden hour,'" he says. "You want to be able to launch, retrieve the patient, and get them to a hospital within the hour. We want to prepare as far in advance as possible so we can save time and get that patient to the definitive care."

The main hangar where Stohrer stands is considered "warm storage" because the building is heated. But this isn't where the designated Black Hawk will stay. Stohrer finds the "tug," which looks like a huge automotive jack, and wheels it under the belly of the aircraft. With the hydraulic lift, he raises the helicopter off the ground. It gently sways side to side. Behind him, the enormous bay door slowly opens and, using the throttle on the T-handle, Stohrer backs the Black Hawk out of the hangar. Now outside in the cold winter air, he pulls the aircraft across the tarmac over to the cold storage bay and puts it inside. There, Black Hawk 031 assumes what is known in the medevac parlance as "first-up bird" status. But the members of the 238th have coined a different phrase, one that stresses the symbiotic working relationship between the Army National Guard and New Hampshire Fish and Game during search and rescue operations. For them, it is the "link-up bird."

It has taken just fifteen minutes for Stohrer to ready the "link-up bird" for a possible State Mission during the coming weekend. Before he turns and walks back toward the warmth of the main hangar, he takes one last look at the remarkable machine that has mesmerized him since he was a young boy, and smiles. Time to head home to his family.

Home of Bette Fredrickson
Western New Hampshire
Friday, Feb. 8, 2008
Evening

Bette Fredrickson greets her ex-husband as he walks in the front door carrying pizza and a movie. This is a weekly ritual for the two who, although divorced for four years, remain close. "Fred and I still enjoyed each other's company," says Bette today. "We were best friends. Fred was really the best friend I've ever had." Moving to the living room, Fred gets the movie started while she divvies up the pizza, and they settle in.

The couple first met in 1971 at the Appalachian Mountain Club's Cardigan Lodge in Alexandria, N.H., when Bette was 23 and Fred just shy of 20. Having graduated from Colorado Women's College, Bette was taking a weeklong graduate course in environmental studies offered by the University of New Hampshire and held at Cardigan Lodge. Fred was on the lodge's hut crew. Bette vividly remembers the first time she saw Fred. "He was bringing in a plastic bowl of wax beans," she recalls. "He was wearing denim overalls with a yellow T-shirt, and he was drop-dead gorgeous—long blond hair in a ponytail. I kind of followed him around, I have to admit."

During that summer, one member of the hut crew quit, and Bette's request to fill the vacancy was accepted. The work covered her room and board and allowed her to stay on, which kept her near Fred. On their first date, the pair went rock climbing, and they spent the rest of the summer hiking together in between work hours. "We hiked Katahdin, and I told him there was no way I was going over the Knife Edge," she says. "So we turned around. It was very gentlemanly of him." On a later trip, they would return to the Knife Edge, and this time Bette managed to "crawl across it."

At the end of the summer, Bette returned home to Farmington, N.H., and Fred went back to his sophomore year at Rensselaer Polytechnic Institute in Troy, N.Y., where he was preparing to become an astrophysicist. "Fred was the closest that you could come to an academic genius; he was so bright," she recalls.

On weekends, Bette traveled back and forth to New York to see Fred. They'd hike, ride bikes, and talk. Fredrickson found his second semester to be much more difficult academically than the first, and he decided to leave school at the conclusion of the semester and return home to Massachusetts. Because of his driven nature, the decision to leave had to be difficult for him, Bette says. "Whenever he did anything, he did it to the best of his ability. He always pushed himself. He was extremely competitive with himself, to a fault. He was an incredible perfectionist."

Bette and Fred married in June 1972. For their honeymoon, they climbed Mount Marcy (5,344 ft.) in the Adirondacks, the highest summit in New York. "We ran to get above treeline because the black flies were so bad," Bette recalls.

That year, the Fredricksons moved to Stoddard, N.H., and Fred decided to resume his studies at Keene State College. From 1973 to 1980, attending college classes off and on, he worked at the High Lawn Tack Shop near their home. Using his engineering talent, he started to design and make equipment for handicapped equestrians. "He loved working with his hands," Bette says.

The cabin they were renting was rustic. Fredrickson installed gas heat, constructed a bridge over a stream to improve access to the home, and built a bed. On weekends the couple headed north to the White Mountains to hike and camp. They completed the Franconia Ridge loop together half a dozen times, and often went winter camping as well. Bette recalls that Fred often over-packed just to challenge himself. "We carried half of the house on our backs," she says. "We were always very prepared."

In 1980, Bette gave birth to twin sons, Trevor and Kyle. It was a stressful time, because the infants arrived home weighing only four pounds each. "Fred was incredible with them," Bette says.

As the boys grew, the Fredricksons included them in their outdoor endeavors. "We loved to take them out and do stuff together," says Bette. "We'd go with other people, and sometimes Fred would take them alone." In 1981, when Bette ended her maternity leave and went back to her teaching job, Fred worked part time and took care of the boys. At one point, he spent time as a teacher's aide and drove a bus for the Kearsage Regional School District. "He clearly enjoyed working with kids," says Bette.

When the boys were three, Kyle broke his leg. Fredrickson took an old pack frame and built a seat on it so he could carry Kyle on

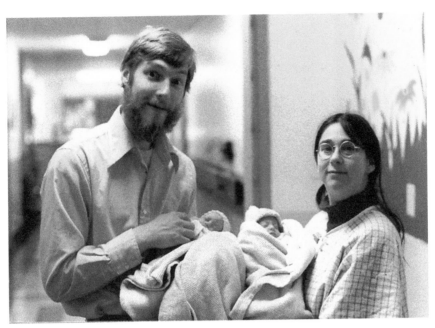

Fred and Bette Fredrickson in 1980 with their three-month-old twin sons.

hikes of Mounts Kearsarge and Monadnock. Trevor recalls that time fondly: "When my brother was three, he shattered his femur and there are pictures of him in a full-body cast. My dad converted a steel frame backpack, and we hiked."

Over time, Bette and Fred gradually grew apart and eventually decided to separate. The couple divorced in 2004 but maintained their friendship. "He would still come to the house to help," Bette recalls. "I really feel bad that he never found what his real passion was. He loved driving buses, and he enjoyed the people. But I think working with children and teaching was his true calling." When talking to those who knew Fredrickson best, it becomes clear that he chose to turn a great deal of his physical and mental energy and skill into outdoor pursuits.

The twins have fond memories of their dad and enjoy sharing anecdotes about their times hiking and canoeing with him. Of the two boys, it is Trevor who has developed an avid interest in the outdoors that closely mirrors his father's. He and his dad spent a lot of time in the backcountry well into Trevor's adult years. "He was never trying to push it with me," says Trevor. "He was perfectly willing to hike within the limits of the people he was with. He did

Fred Fredrickson with his two sons on Mount Kearsarge.

hike alone, but not a lot. He liked people with him."

On a hike to Bondcliff, Trevor and his father attempted to do the long loop over Franconia Ridge, but Trevor grew tired and didn't believe he could complete it. Without pressure or debate, Fredrickson immediately turned them around so they could return to their campsite. Trevor says his father always used a measured approach to risk in the outdoors. "He attempted to do the Presidential Traverse on three separate occasions, ran out of daylight each time, and called it," he says. "He wouldn't knowingly take a risk when he wasn't prepared for it."

On this Friday evening, Bette and Fred enjoy their evening of pizza and a movie, but most of all, they relish the companionship and easy conversation. At one point, Fred mentions he's taking one of his coworkers on his first winter hike over the weekend. He doesn't provide her with a lot of details about their plan, but she concludes it's likely happening on Sunday and that they're going to do the Franconia Ridge traverse. She knows Fred is a highly experienced four-season hiker and that he knows the mountains intimately. So she just offers her best wishes and a caveat: "Stay warm and be careful."

The following evening, as she does any time she knows Fred is going into the mountains, Bette checks the Mount Washington Observatory's website. She becomes somewhat concerned when she reads the forecast for Sunday. "I knew there was a storm coming in, but Fred said they'd be done in four to five hours, and they were going to leave early in the morning," she recalls. So she doesn't call Fred to see if he's seen the forecast.

Home of James Osborne
Southern New Hampshire
Saturday, Feb. 9, 2008
6:00 p.m.

James Osborne is a little anxious. Throughout the day, he's been on and off the phone with the operations manager at Concord Coach Lines. Two years earlier, Osborne was promoted to general manager of Boston Express, a sister company of Concord Coach. He's now responsible for the management of this growing service. One of his drivers, scheduled to work the following morning, is going to be away on vacation in Daytona Beach, Fla. That wrinkle leaves the 5:30 a.m. to 2:30 p.m. shift empty. With Boston Express still in its infancy, Osborne has told the operations manager he will step in and fill the shift if no one else is available to do it. He mentions that he has plans to go hiking, but that he'll do it if needed.

At some point on Saturday, Osborne calls Fredrickson to inform him of the work situation. "I've got to make sure I have a driver before I can commit to the hike," he tells him. Characteristically, Fredrickson avoids pressuring his friend. He understands the nature of the job.

"Fred, why don't you just take the shift, and we'll hike another day?" Osborne says, only half-jokingly. "Nope, I'm going hiking tomorrow," answers Fred.

At 6:00 p.m., the time the operations manager is scheduled to go home for the day, Osborne's phone rings. "I found a driver for you, James," he says. Osborne is excited by the news and mentions he'll be able to go out hiking the following day. The operations manager signs off, heading into a two-day break on Sunday and Monday.

Osborne immediately calls Fredrickson to say he'll be able to go with him the next morning.

"Did you go to EMS and get crampons and snowshoes?" Fredrickson asks.

"I got crampons," Osborne replies.

"Good, I'll see you tomorrow."

When Osborne asks Fredrickson about the weather for Sunday during one of their phone calls, Fredrickson replies, "Everything will be fine."

"I probably thought, 'Oh, yeah that's good enough,'" Osborne recalls. The two agree to meet at Einstein Bros. Bagels at Fort Eddy Road in Concord at 7:00 a.m. Osborne decides he'll gather and prepare his gear for the hike when he wakes up in the morning.

In what he calls "a quirk of fate," Osborne acknowledges that if the empty shift had not been filled at the last minute, "there would have been no hike that day for me."

IV
FORECAST

"The weather always goes to shit in the afternoon.
The sun makes clouds and wind."
—Rick Wilcox, former president of
Mountain Rescue Service

Mount Washington Observatory Weather Station
Mount Washington Summit
Sargent's Purchase, N.H.
Sunday, Feb. 10, 2008
Between midnight and 4:00 a.m.

Stacey Kawecki, a weather observer at the nonprofit Mount Washington Observatory located on the summit of the Northeast's highest peak, sits at an L-shaped desk in the weather room and stares into her computer screen. The fluorescent lights overhead have been dimmed to minimize eye strain for those who work the overnight shift. Before dark on a clear day, if Kawecki were to turn 180 degrees and look out any one of the five large Lexan windows, she would see the remote peaks of the Northern Presidential Range and the full expanse of the Franconia Ridge 20 miles to the west. On rare, completely clear days, she would be able to see even farther west, all the way to the Green Mountains of Vermont. On this dark night, however, freezing fog and blowing snow are limiting her visibility to only 250 feet.

Like all twelve-hour shifts at the Observatory, Kawecki's is task rich. She continually monitors weather radar and a myriad of analog and digital charts and instruments lining the walls before her. Once an hour, she dons her winter gear, climbs one flight up the steel spiral staircase of the weather tower, and walks outside onto the observation deck, where she records the weather as she experiences it at that moment. Kawecki and her colleagues do this twelve times per shift for a total of twenty-four times per day, 365 days per year. Variables like extremely high winds and lightning might keep the observer closer to the doorway of the tower, but no weather condition ever gets in the way of these hourly recordings.

At 12:30 a.m., Kawecki walks out the front of the building to collect the "precipitation can." Located about 100 yards away, the receptacle allows her to measure how much snow has accumulated. Before she is able to reach it, however, she is met by blowing snow and a 3-to-4-foot drift in front of the door. With the deep snowpack on the summit and winds at 30 mph blowing it around, Kawecki must add shoveling of the front door and emergency exits to her task list.

Every other hour throughout her shift, Kawecki climbs the weather tower stairs to the second-flight landing and ascends a ladder leading to the platform at the top of the tower. With the summit in the clouds, rime ice forms on the anemometers that measure wind speed. They must be de-iced by carefully selecting a spot on the post that holds the instrument and banging on it with a steel bar. Chunks of ice fall away with each impact. When winds are really high, the sheared ice becomes a dangerous projectile. The sound radiates down through the tower and into the staff and volunteer living quarters below ground level.

Thanks to the instrumentation in the weather room, the equipment outside, and her observations in real time, Kawecki is able to collect data every hour on temperature, wind speed and direction, visibility, barometric pressure, precipitation, and sky cover. She then

Weather observer removing snow from weather instruments on the Observatory tower.

submits the information to the National Weather Service (NWS), which uses it and data collected from other locations to run multiple weather models that meteorologists use to determine their forecasts.

The Observatory is the only point in the eastern United States that provides the NWS with continuous observational data from 6,000 feet. "This adds a lot of value to our station in that we can provide a sample of atmospheric properties from an area where data normally wouldn't be collected," says Tom Padham, a weather observer, meteorologist, and shift leader at the Observatory since 2013. "Air at this level does have implications for the ground below."

Sometime after midnight, the NWS posts the newest weather model data, which allows Kawecki to begin putting together the forecast for the day. Just before 4:00 a.m., she updates the Observatory website's weather page, Current Conditions, 24-Hour Statistics, and the accompanying Forecast Discussion. Her first order of business is to get the word out to those down below who are up early packing outdoor gear and imbibing high doses of caffeine. At the top of the page, in bold letters and framed in a box, Kawecki posts a warning of things to come:

Windchill warning in effect 7 p.m. tonight through tomorrow

Visitors to the website who are planning on a short Sunday outing might be undeterred by this alert. The real concern lies in the text of the Forecast Discussion, which projects brutal weather beginning later in the day and into Monday:

As the powerful low moves east, it will sweep an arctic cold front through the region late this afternoon, plunging temperatures into the subzero range tonight. A shortly lived lull in the winds will occur today, as the center of the low passes overhead. However, as the strong high pressure forces its way south, and the powerful low continues on its eastern track, moving up into the Canadian Maritimes, the pressure gradient will tighten significantly, and winds will increase quickly and drastically. Overnight, winds will shift to the northwest, and that icy air will filter swiftly into the region, especially on winds sustained at 70-100 mph, with gusts well over the century mark. Tomorrow, precipitation will be mainly upslope snow showers, as moisture is pushed up and over the mountains. Winds will sustain at 70-100 [mph] tonight and tomorrow. In combination with temperatures in the mid-teens below zero, a windchill warning will be in effect for the higher summits between 7 p.m. through the forecast period. Strong winds, plenty of snow, and freezing fog will produce whiteout conditions on the summits through the forecast period.

Padham believes the Forecast Discussion is critical information for anyone planning to visit the higher summits of the White Mountains: "It's important to read the Forecast Discussion we put in there because it has a lot of information we can't physically fit into the small block that has specific details on the day's temperature and wind speed."

In looking back at the Forecast Discussion for Feb. 10, 2008, Padham notes its complexity: "If you look at that discussion, you can see that we were talking about snow squalls. There were going to be some heavier rounds of snow and gustier winds when those rounds of precipitation moved through. It was a pretty unusual and complicated system."

An important variable with weather is timing. "One of the more frequent questions we get is, 'What time is the precipitation going to start?'" says Brian Fitzgerald, director of Science and Education at the Observatory. "If we're going to give anything, it's going to be a time range, because we don't like giving people specific times that will then become the key decision-making factor in their turnaround or stop times. Even within a forty-eight-hour forecast, it's very difficult to pinpoint exact times when we know drastic changes are going to happen."

Given the expansive footprint of the White Mountains and the distance between Mount Washington and other summits throughout the region, Fitzgerald says, "As a general rule of thumb, if you know there are storms arriving—that there is going to be precipitation and/or a dramatic increase in winds—the timing will depend on your location and the speed of the front. It could arrive where you are before hitting Mount Washington, at around the same time, or later. There are also localized effects dependent on terrain, such as notches and ravines."

The information the Observatory provides is an important public service. But these experts are right to stress the unpredictable nature of weather in the White Mountains, especially for the higher summits. Their forecast is meant as only one piece of information hikers and skiers can use in deciding what to do: go, not go, or alter the itinerary. "We can't tell you what decision to make as far as whether or not you should hike or the gear that you'll need," says Padham. "That's still your decision, and hopefully you'll make your most educated decision based on the potential conditions you're going to be putting yourself into."

V
ANTICIPATION

"Despite all I have seen and experienced, I still get the same simple thrill out of glimpsing a tiny patch of snow in a high mountain gully and feel the same urge to climb toward it.

—*Sir Edmund Hillary*

Home of James Osborne
Southern New Hampshire
Sunday, Feb. 10, 2008
5:30 a.m.

James Osborne is pulled from a deep sleep by the pulsing buzz of his alarm clock. The inky sky will not yield to the rising sun until 6:51 a.m. He lingers under his blankets in a pocket of warmth. Stop procrastinating, he tells himself. His first winter hike will begin in a few hours, and he welcomes the flutter of butterflies in his stomach that finally lift him out of bed.

Osborne moves slowly through the apartment where he's lived alone for three years. Still a bit lethargic and missing the warmth of his bed, he reminds himself that at this moment he would be pulling a bus away from the New Hampshire Welcome Center off Exit 6 in Nashua and heading to South Station and Logan Airport in Boston had the vacant driving shift not been filled.

After enjoying a bowl of cereal, Osborne starts preparing for his day outdoors. As he moves toward his gear room, he notes something strange. "My apartment has this hallway storage room where I store outdoor gear," says Osborne. "I remember walking out into that hallway and saying to myself, 'It's awfully cold today.' There's no heat in that part of the apartment, and I can remember thinking, 'This is the coldest I've ever been in this hallway.'"

The first thing Osborne grabs in the gear room is his large Kelty backpack, which is suitable for overnight camping. He sees his three-season sleeping bag in its compression sack lying on the floor. Not intending to bring it, but curious to see what it weighs, he picks up the sack and stuffs it down into the bottom of the pack. He then swings the pack around to his back and settles it on. "Oh, my God, this weighs way too much," he recalls saying out loud.

His curiosity quelled, Osborne takes the pack off and quickly extracts the sleeping bag. "It's always been a little torturous to think about how things might have been different for both of us had we had that sleeping bag," he says.

Osborne retrieves two 32-ounce Nalgene bottles and a water bladder and fills each with water. On one of their phone calls, Fredrickson has told him to put the bladder deep inside his pack so it won't freeze. He does not have insulated sleeves for the Nalgene bottles, so he packs clothing around them. Much of the clothing he's taking are items he'd typically wear skiing. He also packs a headlamp, a compass, a pair of multipurpose winter gloves with removable liners, a first-aid kit, a rescue whistle, a digital camera, a windproof jacket and pants, a spare fleece jacket, a balaclava, a neoprene face mask, an extra set of polypropylene long underwear, a pair of goggles, and trekking poles. For food, he'll pack a sandwich to eat when he and Fredrickson make their planned stop at Shining Rock Junction on Falling Waters Trail.

After preparing his pack, Osborne puts on a base layer of Under Armour tights and an undershirt, his new pair of hiking pants with a couple of Clif Bars stuffed into the cargo pockets, a wool shirt, and a pair of polypro liner socks under Smartwool socks. He plans to put on his boots and additional layers at the trailhead.

When Osborne emerges from his apartment, he steps out into a relatively mild winter morning. The sky is clear, the temperature is 32°F, and winds are minimal at 5 mph. He throws his pack into his blue Chevy Cavalier and pulls away.

At 6:37 a.m., the E-ZPass transponder on Osborne's windshield pings the sensor at the Hooksett tollbooth on Interstate 93. He's northbound and headed for Einstein Bros. Bagels in Concord to meet Fredrickson.

Shortly after 7:00 a.m., they convene inside the bagel shop. Perhaps looking ahead to the cold-weather hike and the need to get some protein and carbs on board, they both order bagel sandwiches to go.

While waiting for their order, the two discuss what they should do with the extra car. They agree to leave Osborne's at the Concord

Transportation Center (CTC) less than a mile away and take Fredrickson's car to Franconia Notch. The CTC is owned by the State of New Hampshire and operated by Concord Coach Lines. With breakfast in hand, they both make the three-minute drive to the center on Stickney Avenue.

It's around 7:30 a.m. when the two cars pull into the CTC parking area and still quiet on this Sunday morning. Osborne parks his car directly in front of the main entrance. They transfer Osborne's gear to Fredrickson's car and walk into the building so Fredrickson can use the restroom. There they encounter Christine Northrup, a customer service representative and ticket agent. Northrup works part time on weekends and has known Fredrickson and Osborne for years. "They were a couple of my favorite drivers," she says. "They were both always so happy. They would come in with a smile, and they would go out of their way to say, 'How's your day going? What have you been up to?' They were great to be around."

That day, Northrup, who's been on duty since 4:30 a.m., is surprised to see the pair, and asks what they're doing there. They tell her they're heading up to the White Mountains for a hike, and that it is Osborne's first time hiking in winter. Like most at the company, Northrup knows Fredrickson is an avid winter hiker and that he's been out many times. "I can remember thinking, 'Better you than me; that's not something I'd want to do,'" she says. "I think I was more nervous for them than James was. They seemed excited and ready to go. They seemed happy and prepared."

Just before Osborne and Fredrickson leave, Northrup asks them, "Hey, aren't we supposed to get snow?" She doesn't recall their exact response, only that it was brief.

The two men say goodbye and head out. Northrup's shift ends at noon, well before they're likely to return from their hike. She won't be working at the counter on Monday, because she'll be at her full-time job elsewhere.

VI
NORTHWARD

"It is in our nature to reach out into the unknown."

—Sir Ernest Shackleton

Interstate 93 North, near Exit 23
Sunday, Feb. 10, 2008
Shortly before 8:00 a.m.

Fredrickson and Osborne head toward Franconia Notch State Park in Fredrickson's bright yellow Saturn sedan. The story behind his acquisition of this car is a classic tale of buyer's remorse—and a glimpse into the lively personality for which Fredrickson is known and liked. According to son Trevor, his father originally purchased the same model car in red. At the time, the dealer didn't have many options to choose from. One day, Fredrickson was driving a bus on the interstate when he saw the yellow version of his car go by him. He was hooked. "He loved the color yellow," says Trevor. "Before the Saturn, he had a yellow Geo Tracker." Using the bus's cell phone, Fredrickson immediately called the dealership. "I really like that yellow," his father told his salesperson, and asked whether it was possible to exchange his red car for the yellow one. The salesperson did some checking and found what Fredrickson was looking for. "We'll have one shipped up from Pennsylvania," he told Fredrickson. "Just drive yours until the new one comes in, and we'll exchange it."

As Fredrickson drives north, he's encountering snow-covered pavement and the occasional state plow lumbering along, treating the roadway with a mixture of sand and salt. Overnight, a weak low-pressure system moved up from the mid-Atlantic Delmarva region to an area just south of the New England coast. Prior to its arrival off the coast, it connected with a much more powerful low-pressure system to the west, near Hudson Bay. The connection of these two systems formed a trough, an extended area of low pressure that dropped steady, light snow throughout the lowlands of the region overnight, with heavier accumulations in the higher elevations. The snow stopped around 7:00 a.m., and the trough has now settled over the Atlantic Ocean.

Plow operators from the New Hampshire Department of Transportation and municipal public works departments from Salem to Dixville Notch have been at work since 8:00 p.m. the previous night, and in some locales even earlier. Plows clearing I-93 in Franconia Notch are dealing with moderate winds, moderate drifting, and some icy spots, according to the New Hampshire Department of Transportation's "Road and Weather Conditions" log. A short distance to the east, on the Kancamagus Highway, operators are noting light winds, light fog, and some ice.

The pines and spruce lining the edges of the interstate are blanketed in layers of snow. So far, this has been a pretty benign weather event, resulting in a picturesque landscape that boosts Osborne's enthusiasm for his first winter hike in the mountains.

He and Fredrickson soon pass Exit 32 in Lincoln. As the Saturn rounds the bend to the right, the snowy tarmac starts its gradual rise toward the gateway to Franconia Notch. The Mount Washington Observatory records the skies as overcast, which limits the friends' ability to take in the full expanse of Cannon Cliff on the left and the high ridgeline of the Franconia Range on the right.

It's around 8:30 a.m. when Fredrickson takes the exit ramp for the Lafayette Place parking area and drives into the lot. Up ahead, standing prominently on a knoll, is the hiker information kiosk that marks the starting point for their day. The lot hasn't been plowed in a while because state highway crews are busy cleaning up the main thoroughfares, so snow reaches up to the bumper of Fredrickson's sedan. They glance to the right toward the larger parking lot and see that it's empty. The smaller, left lot seems like the better option, since other vehicles have already carved tracks with their tires, making it a bit easier for Fredrickson to navigate. He pulls into what is essentially an indiscernible parking spot, and the two prepare to collect their gear.

First, they turn off their cell phones and decide to leave them in the car. "There's probably no coverage up there anyway," Osborne tells himself. At that time, cell phones had yet to become what is now an extension of the human body. Today, their decision might have been different. Even if you have no intention of initiating contact with folks on flat ground, having a phone in your backpack allows authorities to ping the device in an effort to locate you if you get in trouble.

In addition to leaving a written itinerary with someone at home, some White Mountain hikers take the additional step of leaving one on the dashboard of their car. The information usually includes their intended route, the date and time of their departure, and their expected return time. Fredrickson and Osborne leave nothing with friends at home or on the car's dashboard.

Fredrickson does have a plan, however. The two will ascend Falling Waters Trail and hike the 3.2 miles to Little Haystack Mountain (4,760 ft.), a subpeak of Mount Lincoln. The 28th edition of the AMC's *White Mountain Guide* estimates it will take the average hiker, in normal conditions, three hours, five minutes to do this.

On their way up, at approximately 2.8 miles, they will stop at Shining Rock Junction (4,130 ft.) for lunch. The guidebook estimates it will take two hours, twenty-five minutes to reach this point. In addition to being a classic food stop, Shining Rock Junction is also a point where many winter hikers add layers of clothing, traction devices, balaclavas, and goggles, because treeline lies just up ahead. Fredrickson and Osborne don't plan to take the 100-yard spur path out to Shining Rock, a steep cliff-like feature that, on clear days, provides stunning views of Franconia Notch.

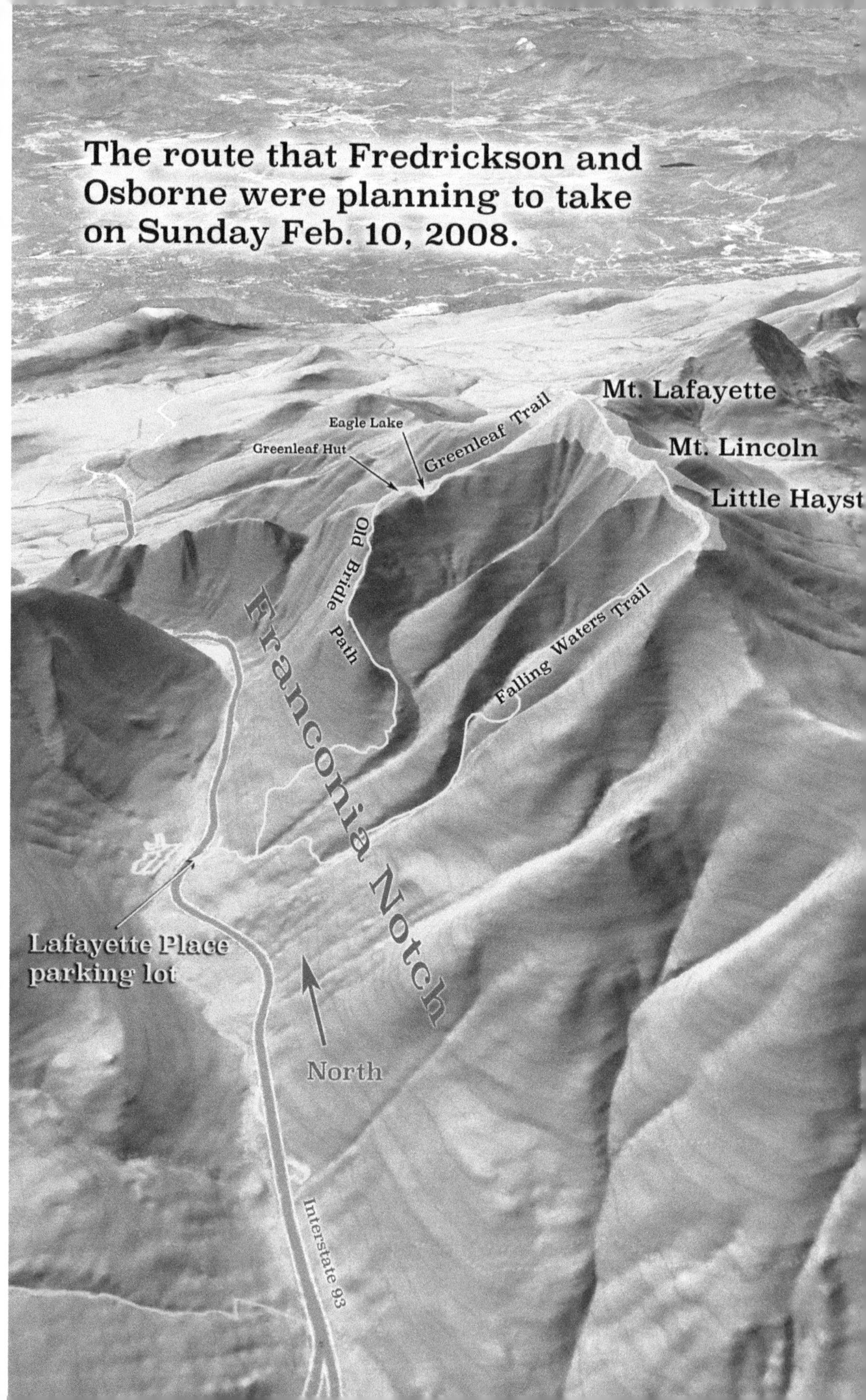

The route that Fredrickson and Osborne were planning to take on Sunday Feb. 10, 2008.

Mt. Lafayette

Mt. Lincoln

Little Hayst

Eagle Lake

Greenleaf Hut

Greenleaf Trail

Old Bridle Path

Falling Waters Trail

Franconia Notch

Lafayette Place parking lot

North

Interstate 93

After summiting Little Haystack, they plan to follow the trail as it bears left and link up with the Franconia Ridge Trail. From there, they will continue north along the sharp ridge for 0.7 miles to the summit of Mount Lincoln (5,089 ft.), which the guidebook estimates will take approximately thirty minutes.

From Lincoln, they will continue the ridge traverse for just under one mile to the summit of Mount Lafayette (5,260 ft.), an estimated forty-minute hike. They'll descend Lafayette via the Greenleaf Trail for 1.1 miles to Eagle Lake and Greenleaf Hut, then head down the Old Bridle Path for 2.9 miles to reach their car in the Lafayette Place parking area where they have started their morning.

The route that Fredrickson has planned is a powerful draw for hikers of every experience level. Franconia Notch and the surrounding White Mountains are no more than a day's drive for 70 million people. On any given day in the summer, 700 of those 70 million people might be found traversing the 1.6 miles of exposed ridgeline between Little Haystack Mountain and Mount Lafayette. This popular ridge hike generates a big-mountain feel, offering expansive views of the Presidential Range, the Pemigewasset Wilderness, and Kinsman and Cannon Mountains.

"The view once you reach the ridgeline is worth the trip," says Lt. James Kneeland, the current team leader of the New Hampshire Fish and Game Advanced Search and Rescue Team. "Other than the Presidential Range, there aren't many places in New Hampshire where one can hike almost two miles along the top of a ridge and get views along its entirety. The hike from Little Haystack to Mount Lafayette is spectacular."

The 9-mile loop requires a total of 3,860 feet of elevation gain. The AMC's *White Mountain Guide* allots seven and a half hours for this loop—more than what Fredrickson has planned—but Kneeland believes hikers should allow even more time:

> There have been a number of articles in various publications promoting this loop hike. The articles don't always talk about the conditions one might encounter, such as slippery rock and ledge along Falling Waters, the exposed ridge when the weather comes in, the terrain challenges on the ascent or descent of Old Bridle Path. This hike will take most hikers around eight hours to complete. A lot of people don't do the

math that gets them to start out at least eight hours prior to sunset. Hiking after dark is something a lot of day hikers aren't prepared for. When it comes to winter hiking, I often find that people have not planned accordingly by looking at a proper weather report—not the one you watch on the evening news the night before.

Many rescue personnel feel that the very accessibility of the Notch is a contributing factor in the number of accidents they see there. "It's so easy to get to it," says Sgt. Jeremy Hawkes, a veteran of New Hampshire Fish and Game's Advanced Search and Rescue Team. "You get on the highway and go straight up 93, and there's the Notch. It takes longer to get to Mount Washington. But the Notch itself is just straight up, steep, unlike other areas. That's what people don't realize."

Allan Clark, founder and president of the Pemigewasset Valley Search and Rescue Team (PVSART), echoes Hawkes's assessment: "I think people totally underestimate [this hike] because you've got an interstate highway that runs through the Notch. So you pull into what looks like a rest area, and you get out and take a little stroll, not realizing that what you're stepping into can lead to very severe conditions. If you actually had to travel ten miles down a dirt road to get to the trailhead, you might have second thoughts. But it's right there."

Mark Hensel, a former member of New Hampshire Fish and Game's Advanced Search and Rescue Team and currently a state trooper with the New Hampshire State Police, agrees with his former SAR teammate: "I think people look at that loop and think it's just a walk in the park. Then, routinely, something bad will happen and they get overcome by it. There's the weather that's always changing and then the daunting challenge of making the loop, which includes summiting three mountains."

Hawkes, who formerly did search and rescue work in the area that includes Franconia Notch, talks of the unusual demands the Notch puts on SAR crew members: "When you're assigned to this area, you can't go home and relax. I'd hold back on working out sometimes because I didn't want to be depleted when I got called out later that night. I'd even hesitate to go to dinner with my family. You work all day, and then you're going out for a five-mile hike. People we rescued doing that loop would say to me, 'We just didn't think it was like this.' A lot of people just don't do the research."

When hikers plan their route on the Franconia Notch loop, they may take wind direction into consideration. If the wind is coming into the Notch from a southerly direction, hikers ascending Falling Waters Trail will have it at their backs as they traverse the ridge northward. If winds are approaching from the north, hikers might choose to ascend Old Bridle Path and traverse the ridge southward, with the same result. Most often, though, seasoned ridge-loop hikers, particularly those who ascend there in winter months, prefer to go up Falling Waters Trail, because they know they will encounter more ice on the steep sections of that trail, and it is less risky to ascend in those areas than to descend in them.

That doesn't mean the risk on this trail is negligible, however, no matter what direction you're coming from. "Falling Waters, in particular, is a tough trail," says Clark. "When we have a carry-out there, we consistently set up ropes and anchors and belay the rescue litter on slides, because it's dangerous for us and dangerous for the patient."

None of this, of course, is on the minds of Fredrickson and Osborne as they prepare for their hike. While they certainly hope to take in the spectacular views, they are most excited about the milestone it represents for Osborne. Tim Peck and Doug Martland, in their blog, goeast.ems.com, include a post entitled "Alpha Guide: Franconia Ridge in Winter." They describe the ridge loop as "a fantastic winter test piece." It is a rewarding test, for sure, but one that the two friends will discover comes with hazards, some foreseeable, some not.

VII
LOADING OUT

"Prior to any outdoor activity, participants should consider the adage, 'Always prepare for the reasonable worst-case scenario.'"

—*Gordon Giesbrecht and James Wilkerson,*
cold-weather injury experts

Lafayette Place Parking Area
Falling Waters trailhead
Sunday, Feb. 10, 2008
8:30 a.m.

James Osborne opens the car door and steps out into light, fluffy snow that reaches just above his ankles. He finds it cold out, but not so cold as to spark the onset of chills. He checks his watch: 8:30 a.m.—right on time.

From the driver's side, Fred Fredrickson tosses him a pair of gaiters. Osborne sits on the edge of the passenger seat and puts on his uninsulated, three-season leather hiking boots and secures a gaiter around each leg. He has done most of his dressing for the hike at home, where he has also loaded his backpack.

Fredrickson laces on his double plastic mountaineering boots and adds gaiters as well. To start the hike, he decides to wear polypro underwear on his upper and lower torso; a pair of cold-weather tights; a full-zip, thin fleece jacket; a full-zip, softshell jacket; a winter hat,;and medium-weight insulated gloves. He affixes snowshoes to his boots and, like Osborne, will use trekking poles for balance.

Fredrickson then swings his red and gray 53-liter backpack over his shoulders. He'll be carrying a heavier load than his friend. His pack will hold his wallet and car keys, a soft glasses case, a pack towel, a first-aid kit, toilet paper, a mountaineering axe, extra straps, a pack rain cover, a candy bar, a plastic bag holding bread and cheese, insulated mittens, liner gloves, additional pairs of gloves, a gear bag, prescription glasses in a hard case, two thermoses (one with hot chocolate and one with tea), a headlamp, a water bladder, sunglasses in a hard case, two carabiners, a Franconia Notch State Park map, a compass, a whistle, five PowerBars and a Clif Bar, a knife, a pair of socks, a polypro shirt, a yellow hooded shell jacket, a neoprene face mask, a balaclava, goggles, shell pants, a pair of three-season hiking pants, two emergency Mylar space blankets, and crampons.

He has also attached two plastic "butt boards" to the bottom of the pack, planning to put these to use for the pair's final descent. "Fred had this notion we'd be able to coast down Old Bridle Path on them," says Osborne.

After pulling his new crampons onto his boots, Osborne dons his backpack. As he does, he notes a Subaru Outback parked nearby and three people walking from it to the trailhead. "They looked equipped," he recalls. "Everyone had snowshoes and a backpack. I think it was two women and a man."

It turns out the Subaru belongs to Jim Forrest and his wife, Catherine Miller, who are here to hike the same loop as Fredrickson and Osborne. Forrest and Miller have hiked together for over two decades and are getting an early morning start up Falling Waters Trail. They've hiked this ridge and the surrounding peaks numerous times in all four seasons.

In recalling that day eleven years later, Forrest, a founding member of the Pemigewasset Valley Search and Rescue Team, remembers that they brought their two standard poodles along to do the loop hike, as they usually did. He and his wife cannot recall the third person that Osborne believes he saw, but they acknowledge that it's possible a friend was along that day.

Forrest and Miller have packed for a "heavy and slow" hike. Though they're not planning to stay out overnight, they're bringing additional gear in case they get in trouble. The alternative, a "light and fast" approach, involves packing a minimal amount of gear to allow a faster pace. The strategy you choose is an individual decision that must be carefully considered based on your experience and fitness level, your itinerary, the terrain, and the weather forecast.

Forrest and his wife have decided that a light and fast strategy doesn't feel right for the traverse that day. They're bringing a sleeping bag, insulated jackets, energy bars, and extra clothing. Both wear winter hiking boots with crampons and carry snowshoes attached to their backpacks. Despite admitting that "my wife is disgusted by it,"

Forrest also carries his favorite staple for staying fueled during a hike: a peanut butter and mayonnaise sandwich.

The couple heads up the trail about ten minutes before Fredrickson and Osborne. They will meet the two friends higher up, though Osborne will not remember the encounter.

As Fredrickson and Osborne are making final preparations for their ascent, a Toyota Prius drives up and parks next to Fredrickson's car. It is owned by Dick Martel, a retired Manchester firefighter. Martel is planning a short hike that day—up and down Falling Waters Trail without traversing the ridge.

Martel's son, Tim, is a member of the North Conway-based Mountain Rescue Service (MRS). MRS is an elite group of climbers who are called upon to carry out the most complex and challenging rescues throughout the White Mountains, which often occur above treeline in winter. The elder Martel introduced Tim to climbing and hiking when he was a child, and his son has taken his passion for high places to the next level. At this point, Martel has no idea that Tim will become involved in the events that will begin to unfold later that day.

A trail runner who moves through the mountains quickly, Martel is generally able to ascend White Mountain 4,000-footers in about two hours. While the Franconia Ridge Traverse is one of his favorites, he has no intention of stepping onto the ridgeline that day, because he views it as a high-risk/low-reward endeavor. He knows bad weather is forecast for the afternoon, so he's here with two objectives: to summit Little Haystack and to improve his already high level of physical fitness in preparation for an April climbing trip to Ecuador with Tim. "That day was supposed to be nasty in the afternoon, and I knew there'd be possible whiteouts, so I was just doing Little Haystack," says Martel. "I checked the National Weather Service and the Observatory forecasts."

Martel has become an expert at reducing uncertainty. When he retired in 2006, he was deputy chief in charge of the Training Division of the Manchester Fire Department, the largest and busiest fire department in New Hampshire. As a firefighter and trainer, Martel spent over three decades managing risk, teaching his fellow firefighters how to do the same, and rescuing countless members of the public who were unable to manage it themselves.

He is also a highly experienced mountain hiker. By 2008, he had completed the New England Hundred Highest, and New Hampshire's forty-eight 4,000-footers, which he started one October and completed the following July while also working full time. In addition, he had summited Mount Rainer with Tim and a friend. "I really love being out in the wilderness," he says.

As Martel watches Fredrickson and Osborne walk across the parking lot to the trailhead, he puts on his insulated winter mountaineering boots and gaiters. In his pack, he carries a quilted puffy jacket stored in a stuff sack, a sleeping bag liner for emergencies, goggles, a balaclava, sunglasses, homemade gorp, energy bars, two insulated bottle parkas and two bottles of hot water mixed with powdered iced tea, crampons, a first-aid kit, a utility bag that houses a lighter, zip ties, a headlamp, gloves, mountaineering mittens, glove liners, hand warmers, a wind jacket, and a softshell jacket. He'll forgo snowshoes because he doesn't deem them necessary for the trail conditions on his planned hike. He'll wear softshell pants; polypro underwear; a medium-weight, hooded second layer; a winter hat; and liner gloves with a shell.

Fredrickson and Osborne hit the trail at 8:40 a.m. They will have ten minutes on Martel by the time he begins his hike.

VIII
WEATHER AND TERRAIN

"Outside in the cold distance.
A wildcat did growl.
Two riders were approaching.
And the wind began to howl."

—Bob Dylan, *"All Along the Watchtower"*

Falling Waters Trail
Sunday, Feb. 10, 2008
After 8:30 a.m.

As they take off from the Falling Waters trailhead, what Fredrickson and Osborne don't know is that the weather system moving east from Hudson Bay in northeastern Canada will complicate their lives over the course of the day and into Monday. The approaching system has an arctic cold front in its grip and is dragging it through the Midwest toward the northeast United States. Once a powerful area of low pressure, it is now in the process of weakening as it moves across the country. In doing so, it is transferring its energy over to the low-pressure system that's now off the coast of New England and moving northward into the Gulf of Maine. A complex set of circumstances has the two systems redeveloping into a strong winter storm. Unlike its predecessor, the new system will bring heavy snow, hurricane-force winds, and the type of cold that will make an outdoor adventurer feel as if he'd been dropped somewhere near the Arctic Circle.

At this hour, a steady band of snow is moving east through Albany, N.Y., and tracking toward Vermont's Green Mountains. It will slow considerably as it bumps up against the rising slopes of these mountains, but as it crawls up the steep terrain and breaches the ridgelines, it will continue its track east toward New Hampshire's White Mountains. To the west of this band of snow, more than 200 miles away and closing in at an average speed of 45 mph, is the arctic cold front. The front is in a dead sprint to catch up with the weakening second system and, when it does, all hell is going to break loose.

The storm's impending arrival is no secret. News and weather outlets have been sounding the alarm as the weekend approached. Based on Fredrickson's interpretation of the forecast and his optimistic assumption that it will take only four to five hours to complete the loop hike, he believes they will be down before the arrival of the storm. Osborne is relying on his friend's judgment, as he always has.

At the trailhead on Sunday morning, it's also pretty calm by Mount Washington Observatory standards, with a temperature on Mount Washington of 13°F, and southwest winds sustained at 30 mph. But those paying close attention to the forecast for the afternoon will be unlikely to head outdoors, especially not uphill. It looks as though the following day's weather will be tough as well.

As Fredrickson and Osborne head uphill, they are encircled by terrain fourteen to fifteen thousand years in the making. Sometime during the Upper Paleolithic period, the last ice sheet melted down to reveal this rugged notch. The geology of the area contributes to the severity of the weather systems that often converge there and will become a key factor in the ordeal that the two friends will experience in the hours ahead.

Thom Davis, professor of geology and paleoclimatology at Bentley University in Waltham, Mass., and a founding member of the Pemi Valley Search and Rescue Team (PVSART), has been hiking in the White Mountains for over four decades and has studied the geology of this area even longer. "Franconia Notch is a U-shaped valley carved out by glacier erosion," Davis explains. "The northeastern part of the United States was covered by the last ice sheet, and it's likely that, within the ice sheet, there were ice streams that could have carved out the valleys under the sheet itself. In the case of Franconia Notch, the ice stream was moving down through the Notch, while the ice sheet over Franconia Ridge and Cannon was moving much more slowly. We don't know for sure, but there's a lot of reason to believe the high peaks were covered by the ice sheet." That would mean the ice in Franconia Notch reached at least a mile high.

High up on the Franconia Ridge lies resilient, glacially molded bedrock, which has caused the ridge to maintain its sharp edge through thousands of years of exposure to extreme elements. "The ridge is made up of Lafayette granite porphyry, a course-ground granite that's very resistant to erosion," says Davis. "It has a topography to it because, as the ice sheet moved across the ridge, it created nooks and crannies."

Large boulders, also known as glacial erratics, were carried within the ice sheet and deposited on the ridge. Molded landforms across the ridgeline and slabs of granite stacked on top of one another with voids in between provide natural barriers for hikers seeking refuge from the strong winds that regularly sweep through the area.

Large glacial erratic on Mount Lafayette.

The uncommon terrain along the ridgeline is described as "a gothic masterpiece" in the AMC's *White Mountain Guide*, suggesting "the ruins of a gigantic medieval cathedral." The guide goes on to state that "the peaks along the high serrated ridge are like towers supported by soaring buttresses that rise from the floor of the Notch."

Like the Presidential Range to the east, the Franconia Ridge lies above treeline. According to Davis, treeline is determined by climate. Each kilometer of altitude gain is the equivalent of traveling 100 kilometers north in the direction of the Canadian tundra. In the White Mountains, treeline is lower on the western side than on the eastern. On the eastern side of Franconia Ridge, vegetation reaches up to the ridgeline in several locations. Davis believes that treeline is lower on the western slopes because that side bears the brunt of systems coming from the north and west. "We think this is because of high winds," he explains. "In the wintertime, the winds are laced with ice crystals, which are bad news for scrubby vegetation. You see [the vegetation] hanging in there with rime ice, but it gets hit pretty hard by the prevailing winds. It is temperature, ice crystals, high winds, the amount of precipitation, and late-lying snow in the spring that keep the vegetation low."

Because of the north-to-south positioning of Franconia Notch and its mix of high walls and undulating slopes, weather here closely mirrors that of its iconic neighbor to the east, Mount Washington. The primary weather factor is the way the wind behaves as it interacts with the topography. "There's open terrain just to the north of the Cannon and Lafayette ridgelines, so as the wind approaches, it squeezes together when it comes through the I-93 corridor in the Notch," says Tom Padham of the Mount Washington Observatory. "It's a pretty well-known area for a funneling of the winds and severe windstorms. Sometimes winds are well over a hundred miles per hour here, which you wouldn't expect to see on other peaks in the Whites at the same elevation."

Brian Fitzgerald, also from the Observatory, says it's smart to develop a healthy respect for the wind's power in this region: "We tell

Looking east, with Franconia Ridge in the foreground and the Presidential Range in the background.

people that Mount Washington is the tallest thing around for thousands of miles, but on Mount Lafayette, if winds are coming from due west, it's the tallest thing around for miles and miles, and winds hit there first."

Padham believes that because of the rapid change from flat open space to high ridgelines, Franconia Notch will "also experience localized, heavy snow showers and winter conditions similar to those on Mount Washington. The Notch is basically wringing out moisture because you have air that's being forced to rise at least three thousand feet or so up and over the ridgeline. So you'll see wind-speed maximums that can actually enhance some of that precipitation as the air is just funneling through."

While Mount Lafayette experiences high wind speeds because of its height, the lower peaks lying southward on the Franconia ridgeline are subject to what is known as downslope winds. "If there are steady and fairly strong winds coming from the west and traveling down the eastern side of the ridgeline, those winds can be enhanced as they travel downslope and be further amplified through squeezing," says Padham. He explains that north/northwest winds entering Franconia Notch at Cannon and Mount Lafayette can produce higher winds on the southern end of the ridgeline, at Mount Lincoln and Little Haystack. "A twenty-mile-per-hour wind at the top of the Notch could increase to sixty miles per hour by the time it reaches the other end."

Residents who live and operate in and around Franconia Notch—and who've studied topics other than meteorology—have their own take on the weather here. "I think people underestimate the weather in the Notch," says Gordie Johnk, a founding member of the PVSART. "People don't understand how rugged it is. Mount Washington has 'the worst weather on Earth' reputation, but it gets [to the Notch] first. When the weather hits, many people are just not ready for it."

PVSART's Allan Clark shares a similar perspective. "Franconia Notch creates its own weather pattern, because it serves as a barrier: the weather to the north and south of it can be totally different."

Clark has seen countless instances of hikers struggling with the area's weather. "I think people get themselves into a lot of trouble by two things," he says. "The weather tends to come from the west, so it can go undetected behind Cannon Mountain. Unless you're higher up on the ridge and looking west, you're not going to see approaching weather, especially early in the day. The same thing happens at the end of the day, because the sun goes down behind Cannon and, when it does, all of the sudden it's dark; there's nothing in between. When the sun drops behind Cannon, you really lose a lot of light, especially in the winter, because the sun is already low on the horizon. The ridge is usually windy, and you're totally exposed to it. I don't think people realize what they're getting themselves into."

Mark Hensel, then a member of New Hapmshire Fish and Game's Search and Rescue Team, has experienced these winds firsthand:

> You can hear the wind before you get up there. Every step you take, it's a little bit louder and stronger. When you break out above treeline, you're just bombarded with it, and on the ridge, you're totally exposed—it just hits you. There's no shelter; there's no break from it. If it hits you head-on like a wall, you have to turn away from it. Survival up there is limited to minutes. You have to get off the ridge and down out of it and be well equipped. Nobody can survive it forever. You need to shelter for a short period of time until you can get to a different location. People think, 'Oh, I know what wind is.' They've been to the ocean or wherever. But when you're at four thousand feet and it hits you, that's a totally different story. It gets everybody.

In their seminal book, *Forest and Crag*, Laura and Guy Waterman capture the essence of the winds in the Whites: "In the northeastern United States, the weather's fickleness is notorious, and with the relative safety of the trees nearby, climbers may find themselves trying to move in driving winds, low visibility, and extreme cold, where elsewhere no one would move" (p.134).

Given the projected forecast and Fredrickson's ambitious timeline, which he has based on the pace he's managed before on the same loop, it would not have been out of place for Osborne to feel some concern as the two head up the trail. Yet, he's still feeling pretty relaxed and exhilarated. But when he thinks back on that day with the perspective of time, he acknowledges that he was "classically unprepared for what we were about to do."

Franconia Notch, Franconia Ridge, and the Cannon Mountain ski resort from the northwest. Arrows indicate relative wind direction Feb. 9-10, with green signaling lighter winds and red signaling stronger blasts. Localized funneling and enhancement of the wind are likely occcurring in the lower elevations and along the exposed portion of the ridgeline.

IX
MESSENGERS

*"It's always a little twist here or a little something there that don't
seem like big problems until they accumulate. At some point, you've
got to say to yourself, 'It's not going to happen today.'"*

—*Alain Comeau, Mountain Rescue Service*

Falling Waters Trailhead
Sunday, Feb. 10, 2008
8:45 a.m.

Fredrickson and Osborne are on the trail and moving quickly at
this early stage. As usual, Fredrickson is in front, while Osborne
follows, immersing himself in his wintry surroundings. The air is
crisp and cool. Aromas are pronounced, particularly the pines, and
muted sounds emerge from a forest cloaked in snow. This section of
Falling Waters Trail is flat as it weaves its way through the woods.
Still, excitement at the day ahead is causing Osborne's adrenaline to
flow not long after he steps from the parking lot onto the trail.

Although snow fell here overnight, Osborne finds that the trail is
fairly packed down. That is understandable, given the heavy activity
reported here on the previous day. In a blog post on the *Views From
The Top* website, "Big Earl" has written:

> We encountered four large groups and four pairs totaling
> close to forty hikers on the trail Saturday. All of them were
> hiking the same route as us (Falling Waters Trail, Franconia
> Ridge Trail, Greenleaf Trail, and the Old Bridle Path).
> Roughly half were hiking clockwise and the other half
> counterclockwise. We were hiking clockwise. Nearly all were
> wearing snowshoes. I believe there were ten that were bare-
> booting or using crampons. Two were on skis. Additionally,
> there were two more groups hiking the area below the final
> crossing of Dry Brook on the Falling Waters Trail. I'm sure
> they did not continue to the ridge. Bottom line: the Falling

Waters Trail was really well packed by the end of the day on Saturday. We were probably the last group to hike it from the ridge that day.

Buried deep beneath the snowpack are the root loops and boulders that occupy this and virtually all trails in the Whites. Fredrickson is making good progress in snowshoes, while Osborne is still adjusting to his new crampons. Twice, he plants his foot just outside the packed-down trough and post-holes up to his hip in deep snow. It's not an easy extraction, by any means. Later, the pair will stop briefly when the front prongs from a crampon puncture his leg, causing him to bleed and ripping a hole in his new pants. The first-aid kits they've brought come in handy.

Within fifteen minutes of starting out, Fredrickson and Osborne reach the first bridge crossing at Walker Brook. The narrow bridge can be challenging to cross when the snowpack domes on its planks. But they manage to cross it without incident.

Soon after, they determine that they've started out wearing more layers than they need. Osborne is wearing his Columbia jacket and zip-out fleece and has overheated quickly. "We were pouring sweat and decided we had to make some adjustments," he recalls. "I took my balaclava and outer jacket off."

Fred Fredrickson heading up Falling Waters Trail on Sunday, Feb. 10.

At approximately 9:00 a.m., Osborne removes his digital camera from his pack and snaps two photographs of Fredrickson. They are quintessential images of a veteran winter hiker. The trees surrounding Fredrickson are blanketed in thick snow, which shrouds the forest expanse behind him. He projects discipline and experience. His gear is crisp and clean, well cared for, and orderly—not a lace undone, not one strap on his pack longer than the other. His blaze-red jacket draws one's eyes away from the white landscape around him and directly to his upper torso. A red winter hat adds flair to his kit.

Fredrickson is considered a perfectionist by those closest to him. He is continuously researching outdoor gear and upgrading it to improve his performance. In these photos, his smile is genuine, portraying a man who's happy where he is and looking forward to reaching higher places.

Osborne hands the camera to his friend, walks back to the trekking poles he's jammed into the snow, turns toward Fredrickson, and poses to memorialize the milestone hike. His cheeks are flushed from a combination of exertion and crisp air. He seems to be mid-sentence when Fredrickson depresses the button on the camera, and

James Osborne pauses for a photo on Falling Waters Trail.

he gives every indication of being committed and determined. He, too, is where he wants to be and happy to be there with his good friend.

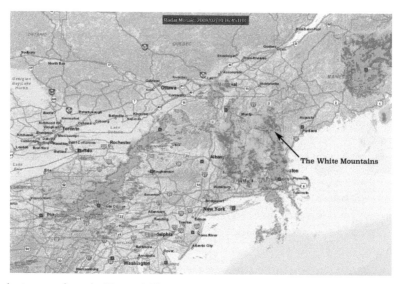

Radar imagery from the National Climate Center showing a heavy band of snow arriving in the White Mountains at 11:30 a.m., Feb. 10. Snow will continue through the evening, with heavy snow showers and squalls occurring over Franconia Ridge and to the east on Mount Washington.

Light snow flurries appear in all the photos, a subtle precursor of things to come. At this hour on the summit of Mount Washington, the Observatory notes a temperature of 13°F, with winds out of the southwest at 24 mph, and visibility at 1/8th of a mile with heavy fog.

Farther ahead on Falling Waters Trail, Jim Forrest and Catherine Miller continue their trek upward. Their dogs run freely, sometimes out ahead and other times on their owners' heels to make for easier going. Behind Fredrickson and Osborne, Dick Martel is making good time on the packed-out trail.

After crossing over the first bridge, Martel comes upon Fredrickson and Osborne while they're still removing layers by the side of the trail. Martel pauses briefly to chat with the pair. "I talked to them for a little while," he recalls. "They were taking gear off. One was wearing snowshoes and one wasn't."

Osborne recalls that he and Fredrickson lost the trail once or twice on their way up. One of these instances may have occurred at Dry Brook, a river crossing approximately 25 yards across that can be a challenge in winter. Hikers can punch through and soak their socks and boots, ending a day out way too prematurely. To avoid that risk, hikers sometimes walk up and down the brook looking for the easiest crossing. It's possible the two friends did this and lost the trail as a result. They never veered significantly off course, says Osborne. "But we had to recorrect a couple of times."

Meanwhile, the band of snow that was over Albany, 150 miles to the southwest, at 8:00 a.m. has slowed considerably after running into the high walls of the Green Mountains of Vermont. This delay allows the cold front, still on its tear eastward and working its way into Pennsylvania and New York, to further close the gap with the trough that's out ahead if it.

The deeper into the woods Fredrickson and Osborne go, the steeper the grade. The two eventually arrive at the slabs below Stairs Falls. There's not a lot to grab on to as you ascend the slabs. Beyond are Swiftwater and Cloudland Falls. The presence of so much water causes much of this portion of the route to accumulate a lot of ice, and it is often hazardous in winter. Some hikers choose to rope up and rappel down these icy inclines. It is actually risky terrain in all

Cloudland Falls

four seasons and a hot spot for injuries and rescues. Many an ankle has been sprained or broken here.

In spite of the hazards, it is still a rare gift to be surrounded by these sparkling waterfalls and cascades. On one of the slabs here, Fredrickson decides to test out his gear. "There was a snow-covered rock to scramble up," says Osborne. "It was very important for Fred to show off his snowshoes. The back of each snowshoe had this piece of metal you could flip up to aid you in ascending. But it just wasn't working. 'It's supposed to work this way!' Fred said. He was so exasperated, but I was laughing. 'Well, it's not working that way,' I yelled up at him."

After more tricky ascents and water crossings, the trail steepens and transitions to a series of switchbacks. Osborne is perspiring heavily and takes periodic breaks to hydrate and snack on one of his Clif Bars. It won't be long before they reach Shining Rock Junction for lunch and some rest.

❆ ❆ ❆ ❆ ❆ ❆

Dick Martel can hear the squeak and crunch of the fresh snowfall as it collapses under the weight of his body and well-stocked alpine pack. Thus far, it's been a good morning in the mountains. Ascending one of his favorite trails in the Whites, he embraces the solitude as he leaves treeline behind. He's in the zone.

It is snowing now, and the winds are steady. During this morning's ascent, he's encountered a handful of other hikers. Besides Fredrickson and Osborne, whom he passed much lower on the trail, he's met Forrest and Miller, who "looked well equipped." Since overtaking them at treeline, he has followed a single set of footprints in the snow ahead that continue toward the summit of Little Haystack, hidden in the clouds. He relishes this brief moment of isolation between human contacts. "I love the solitude of winter hiking," he says. "It drives me crazy when there's a lot of people."

Only a handful of hikers on a weekend day on this popular winter route: that's a strong indication to Martel that the greater hiking community is taking heed of the forecasted bad weather making its way east toward the Notch. Had Martel been here yesterday he probably would not have enjoyed the presence of the more than forty hikers traversing the Franconia Ridge. While forty hikers seems like a lot for a winter traverse, it's a far cry from the 450 people Martel says he once encountered on the ridge in the summertime.

Martel is 100 feet below the summit of Little Haystack when his solace is interrupted. There on top, partially submerged in a blend of thick clouds and lightly falling snow, is the silhouette of the solo hiker whose footprints he's been following.

At 11:18 a.m., Martel reaches the summit, and greets the other hiker. His body temperature starts to cool when he stops moving, but he's properly layered and comfortable, and the steady winds and light snowfall are of no concern to him. He's seen much worse weather in these winter Whites.

On the summit of Mount Washington, the temperature remains at 13°F, winds have decreased ever so slightly, and visibility is 1/16th of a mile because of fog and snowfall.

The visibility on Little Haystack is low as well. Martel can see only 100 feet in front of him. Hidden behind the 360-degree amalgam of frozen fog and snowfall lie some of the most familiar features of the White Mountains. On this day, the images of these peaks and valleys can only be accessed from memory. There's nothing to see but ice-covered boulders, krummholz, and the imprints made by their heavy mountaineering boots. But it's still damn good to be up here.

Standing shoulder to shoulder in silence, as if on watch at a high outpost, Martel and his fellow hiker look northward from Haystack in the direction of the ridgeline neither one of them can see. "You know, they couldn't pay me enough to go across the ridge today," says Martel. His companion stares northward, likely contemplating the thought of being out there alone on the ridge. "Yeah, the weather's supposed to be turning really bad later on," he agrees.

A short distance below, Jim Forrest, his wife, and their dogs break treeline. They are 50 feet beyond the trees when Forrest stops suddenly and turns to his wife. "Screw this," he says. Recalling that moment today, Forrest says, "We were going right into the wind. It was cold. I felt my eyelids starting to freeze. We didn't have goggles. We now carry goggles."

Husband and wife, with dogs in tow, immediately abandon any thought of summiting Little Haystack, let alone crossing the ridge. They waste no time heading back down Falling Waters Trail. "We've crossed that ridge many, many times in summer and winter," says Forrest. "It didn't take very long at all to decide to turn around."

Martel and his companion pull their gaze away from the invisible ridgeline and reorient themselves to the terrain around them. Martel turns toward the west and Falling Waters Trail. He's logged approximately five minutes of summit time, and he's good with that. He bids farewell to the other man and drops down quickly off the barren summit. As he approaches treeline, he's careful to ensure that he finds his way back onto Falling Waters Trail. With no cairn to mark the entrance, it's a tricky spot, especially in low visibility.

Still making their way upward, Fredrickson and Osborne approach Shining Rock Junction. The tree canopy overhead thins. The trail is steep here and tends to accumulate heavy snowpack because it's shielded from high winds. Descending the trail, Forrest and his wife encounter the pair. He doesn't express it, but Forrest is surprised to see anyone still ascending at this hour, given the afternoon forecast and how poor the weather already is up top. They continue back down, and Fredrickson and Osborne continue toward treeline.

Martel also encounters Fredrickson and Osborne on his way back down, 200 yards below Shining Rock Junction. "They were moving pretty slowly," he recalls. "The other couple had obviously turned around before me, because I didn't see them again."

"How far is it to Shining Rock Spur Trail?" Fredrickson asks Martel. "We plan on having lunch there." Martel responds, "It's just up there a few hundred feet."

Seeing the heavy load Fredrickson appears to be carrying, Martel asks if they are planning an overnight, but they tell him they're just day-tripping. He notices the butt boards secured to Fredrickson's pack. "Oh, you're taking the express way down," he says.

Martel now regrets he didn't bring up the subject of weather. "The weather was nasty," he says. "I should have been more nosy and asked them where they were headed, because if they'd said, 'across the ridge,' I would have told them that the weather was going to be really bad. I kick myself for that."

Shortly after their brief exchange with Martel, Fredrickson and Osborne arrive at Shining Rock Junction. At that moment, the band of snow that was jammed up in the Green Mountains has arrived in the Whites. Light snowfall has turned steady and will continue throughout the afternoon. Much heavier bands of snow associated with the cold front, now in the vicinity of Buffalo, N.Y., are on track to arrive here later.

Osborne notes that the Spur Trail out to Shining Rock has remained untrodden—another sign that today's visitors to Falling Waters aren't here for the scenic views often found at this popular lookout. The two friends remove their packs and retrieve their lunches. Osborne takes out his camera and snaps another photo of his friend. Fredrickson is removing his shell and looks back at Osborne with a wide smile on his face. At the speed they're going, they're now

Fred Fredrickson at Shining Rock Junction, on the way up to Little Haystack Mountain on Feb. 10.

about forty minutes from the summit of Little Haystack, and it looks as though Fredrickson can feel it.

Not long after they arrive at the junction, the hiker who stood on the summit with Martel emerges on his way down. Osborne describes the man as being between 50 and 60 years old and "a Grizzly Adams kind of guy." He has a big beard and is using a wooden walking stick. To Osborne, he looks like a "kind of a no-nonsense New Englander."

"If you're looking to see things, the summit is socked in," the hiker informs them.

"We're going over to Old Bridle Path and coming down there," Fredrickson replies.

"You guys ought to just go to the top and come down," the man tells him. "There's no view; it's all socked in at the top."

"He brought up the weather," Osborne recalls today. "He was probably saying, without being direct, that the weather wasn't going to be good and to rethink this."

But the conversation with the lone hiker doesn't alter their plan. Osborne sits on a big rock and eats the sandwich he brought and drinks water from his Nalgene bottle. During this pause, he begins to feel the chill. "I went from cold to really cold," he recalls. He has always believed this was the moment the weather began to worsen.

In fact, the cold front is still a significant distance to the west of them, and the temperature in the region remains stable during this timeframe. Still, Osborne tells Fredrickson that it's gotten colder. Fredrickson is cold as well, but he's used to it because of his lean build. But Osborne is so cold that he decides to run up and down the trail "to get my blood going." He doesn't add any layers at this point, and neither man has brought along a quilted puffy jacket for extra warmth.

Rather than feeling a sharp temperature drop, Osborne is likely experiencing his body's cooling off through evaporation while he remains static. He's been perspiring heavily for hours and has come to a sudden stop. Any heat he's generated is evaporating from the sweat on the surface of his skin. In their book, *Hypothermia, Frostbite, and other Cold Injuries,* Gordon Giesbrecht and James Wilkerson explain the dynamic:

> Heat loss through evaporation is obviously greatly increased
> by the heavy sweating associated with the high heat production

of vigorous exercise or a hot environment. Evaporative heat loss may increase in a cold environment also. Evaporation of water from wet clothing causes great heat loss, particularly in wind. Wet clothing is also a threat because it loses its insulating ability, leading to greatly increased convective cooling. Winter outdoor enthusiasts must be aware that heat and water loss is occurring, must eat enough food to regenerate heat, and must drink enough liquids to replace the water (p.36).

Osborne is right to generate heat through more exercise. He also needs to thermoregulate to stop the heat loss by adding layers of clothing while sitting or standing. Extra exercise will burn calories, so it will mean he'll need to take in more food and water to stay fueled and hydrated. "You have to anticipate sweat production and you have to control your work rate," says Dr. Murray Hamlet, a renowned expert on cold-weather injuries.

Dr. Frank Hubbell, founder of Stonehearth Open Learning Opportunities (SOLO) in Conway, N.H., and a wilderness medicine expert, explains what he calls our "perception of cold":

People always comment on being hot or cold. It could be seventy-two degrees inside, and someone says it feels really cold or someone says they're hot. That's their perception. Some people are temperature sensitive, and part of that is your perception of what [temperature] means. Cold might mean death to someone if they haven't had a lot of exposure to it. It's their perception of cold that can lead to fear.

Hamlet adds this comment: "The perception that the temperature has gotten colder is likely due to the increased cooling of the body. Increased heat loss can create the perception of a change in ambient temperature."

"It could have been that I was cooling off because I was sitting there eating," acknowledges Osborne. "It was probably more of a body issue. I do perspire a lot when I exercise. I don't think I had enough knowledge as a winter hiker to be alarmed by that, though."

❋ ❋ ❋ ❋ ❋ ❋

At around 12:15 p.m., Fredrickson and Osborne wrap up and resume their way toward the summit of Little Haystack. In anticipation of reaching treeline soon, Fredrickson has put on his Moonstone shell pants and shell jacket, and Osborne has added his outer jacket and balaclava.

Two thousand or so feet below them, in Franconia Notch, the band of snow that arrived here forty-five minutes earlier is settling in and causing a host of problems for local first responders and highway crews. Two motor vehicle rollovers on the parkway within minutes of each other have Lincoln Police, Lincoln Fire Engine 2, Rescue 4, and a Linwood ambulance responding. Fortunately, no one is injured in either crash, but emergency crews are having difficulty accessing the southbound lane because of the traffic backup. Three hundred miles to the west, near Rochester, N.Y., the cold front is in the early stages of inflicting damage. At 12:30 p.m., winds are close to 40 mph, and in combination with the cold temperatures and heavy snowfall, are causing whiteout conditions. According to a report published in Rochester's *Democrat & Chronicle*, on Interstate 390, "drivers who just moments before had no problems with visibility suddenly couldn't see more than a foot ahead of their vehicles." This results in a thirty-six-vehicle pileup that injures twenty-four and tragically takes the life of a seventeen-year-old.

Fredrickson and Osborne are now just below treeline and continue working their way up toward the summit. Fredrickson is still in the lead. Osborne notes nothing out of the ordinary during this phase of the hike. He recalls only "fog and clouds and a little bit of snow, and no rime ice."

But when they break treeline and move closer to Little Haystack, Osborne senses a change in the conditions. "I looked back over my shoulder and couldn't see twenty feet. I could see the trail going into the fog behind me, but no view and no trees." He also notes how different things appear in winter. "All of a sudden, you're in it. You've gotten up through the trees and the scrub, and the air feels completely different."

As they move up toward the summit, Osborne begins to worry. "The concerning moment for me was the moment when we hiked through the little alpine section and then came up, cut around to the right, and reached the final summit approach to Haystack," he recalls. "When we made that right turn, the path was marked with small boulders. That section ended, and we were following cairns to get to the summit. I looked back and thought, 'Geez, I can't even see where I just was because now it's socked in with clouds.'"

Arriving at the summit at approximately 1:00 p.m., Osborne keeps thinking about the conditions and asks his friend, "How are we going to find the Old Bridle Path to get down?"

"We'll be okay," Fredrickson assures him.

Twenty miles to the east, at the Mount Washington Observatory, the temperature is still hovering between 12° and 13°F, southwest winds are sustained at 26 mph, and visibility is still 1/16th of a mile. Should Fredrickson and Osborne choose to traverse northward across the ridge, the southwest wind will be at their backs.

Down on the Franconia Notch Parkway, another motor vehicle rolls over, this time near Cannon Mountain. There are again no injuries, but first responders are still at the mercy of stopped traffic on this narrow, two-lane parkway. Conditions are continuing to deteriorate, with snow falling at a steady clip.

James Osborne on the summit of Little Haystack Mountain at approximately 1:00 p.m., Feb. 10.

Up on Haystack, Fredrickson and Osborne make final gear adjustments. Osborne again takes out his camera to capture their moment on the summit, and each takes two photographs of the other. Osborne will later put on goggles, which is a good call. It's snowing in earnest now, and behind him there is thick fog pervading the atmosphere. One summit photo shows Osborne in a moment of levity, his eyes jammed shut and his teeth clenched, indicating his delight and excitement to be there amid the falling flakes. Photos of

Fred Fredrickson on the summit of Little Haystack Mountain
adding layers against the blowing snow.

Fredrickson show him in his bright yellow shell jacket and yellow-lensed sport glasses. His hood is up to prevent heat loss from his head and neck and to block the falling snow from finding its way down his back.

❄ ❄ ❄ ❄ ❄ ❄

At around this time, after a rapid descent, Dick Martel emerges from Falling Waters Trail and walks into the parking lot. "By the time I got back to the car, the weather had turned," he says. "There weren't high winds, but it was snowing like crazy. That was around one o'clock p.m."

Martel walks through the shin-high snow to his Toyota Prius, which is now blanketed in white. While the car warms up, he removes any snow that might obstruct his view on the drive home. It could be a long commute.

Martel leaves the parking lot and cautiously begins the drive toward home. He tightens his grip on the steering wheel and leans in toward the windshield in the hope that it will improve his ability to see through the onslaught of snowfall. He may be wondering what's happening with the two guys he saw on the trail, the two who were still climbing up. Did they reach treeline, find the deteriorating weather, and turn around? But he can't manage to worry about the other hikers right now. He's passed emergency vehicles tending to an accident and is finding the drive rough going. He has enough of his own risk to manage right now.

X
HUMAN FACTORS

"The question is not what you look at, but what you see."
—Henry David Thoreau

Little Haystack Summit
Sunday, Feb. 10, 2008
Shortly after 1:00 p.m.

Traverse or turn back? It's an easy decision for some and a complex one for others.

Fredrickson and Osborne don't realize it, but they're about to spring a series of traps that were set over the course of their months and years of visiting high places. Despite his concerns about the changing weather conditions, Osborne says today, "At this point, there was nothing uncomfortable about what we were doing. It still felt like a regular hike. It was cold, but it was February."

The traps Fredrickson and Osborne have set involve cognitive biases known as heuristics. These biases, also known as "rules of thumb" or "mental shortcuts," provide us with a streamlined way to make decisions and solve problems based on our past practice and experiences. The effects of these biases occur at the unconscious level and work automatically, so they are difficult to detect and manage. Most often, these shortcuts benefit our decision-making. But if the new event we're encountering involves different information or important variables, our reliance on past experience can lead to error.

According to Ian McCammon, a renowned expert in avalanche research and safety, "In order for heuristic decision-making to work in high-risk situations, the cues we rely on must be relevant to the actual hazard [we're facing]. If, out of unconscious habit, we choose wrong cues, our decisions can be catastrophically wrong. This mismatch, where we base decisions on familiar but inappropriate cues, is known as a heuristic trap."

In two papers, titled "Heuristic Traps in Recreational Avalanche Accidents: Evidence and Implications" (*Avalanche News*, No. 68, Spring 2004) and "Evidence of heuristic traps in recreational avalanche accidents" (*International Snow Science Workshop*, 2002), McCammon identifies a number of heuristics that he says we use regularly when making even everyday decisions. "Because these heuristics work so well and because we've used them for much of our lives, we are largely unaware of using them, even when we are making critical decisions," McCammon writes. "Such conditions are fertile ground for heuristic traps."

McCammon himself is an avid backcountry skier and mindful of his own susceptibility to the heuristics he's so closely studied. In an interview for a Utah Avalanche Center podcast on Feb. 27, 2019, he said, "The terrain may be just fine, but the psychological terrain for me is dangerous. Understanding the difference between physical terrain and psychological terrain is really the first step to seeing the reflection of yourself.... It's our own fears or weaknesses that are going to lead us to those mistakes."

There's no way of knowing to what extent heuristics are at play on the summit of Little Haystack. But four of the biases McCammon cites may offer some insight into what could be influencing the friends' decisions about their next movements: the Familiarity Heuristic; the Commitment or Consistency Heuristic; the Acceptance Heuristic; and the Expert Halo Heuristic.

According to McCammon, the Familiarity Heuristic "relies on our past actions to guide our behavior in familiar settings." He explains that instead of taking the time to determine the best course of action in a new situation, we'll do what we've always done before in a similar setting with similar circumstances. Most often, he says, this process is reliable. The trap is sprung, however, "when the hazard changes, but the setting remains familiar." When we're on a mountain that feels familiar to us, for example, we may not pay attention to variables that are different from what we have seen in our past experiences in this place.

Fredrickson is on his fourth winter hike of the season and is a veteran, four-season White Mountain visitor. Only a week before, he was here and successfully completed the same traverse on a day when the weather was very similar to what he's experiencing now. In fact, up to this point, it has been warmer and less windy than it was a week ago. Might this be translated by Fredrickson into confirmation that the weather will remain the same today as it did last week? And because the 1.6-mile traverse over to Mount Lafayette is so familiar to him, does he conclude that he can navigate it without problems even in poor visibility?

One of the critical variables for Fredrickson and Osborne is the location and timing of the incoming cold front. But they don't have a grasp of it. These are the moments when taking an inventory of the situation is so important. Ideally, they would be doing the math and making projections based on the remaining terrain, the current and forecasted weather, their available gear, the viability of their planned timing, and their sense of their own physical status. Including their forty-five-minute stop at Shining Rock Junction, it has taken Fredrickson and Osborne nearly four and a half hours to reach this point, compared to the two and a half for Martel and the two hours, forty-five minutes for Forrest and Merrill, none of whom stopped along the way. While the ridgeline is less steep than Falling Waters Trail, it is still undulating terrain and has not been traveled since the snow fell overnight. It will likely take them more than an hour to reach Mount Lafayette, bringing them deeper into the afternoon.

The Commitment or Consistency Heuristic, according to McCammon, can occur after "we have made an initial decision about something." Once we've committed to that choice, "subsequent decisions are much easier if we simply maintain consistency with that first decision." He explains that it's easy for us to do this "because we don't need to sift through all relevant information with each new development." Like the Familiarity Heuristic, this consistency usually guides us well, but the trap catches us "when our desire to be consistent overrules critical new information about an impending hazard."

Is Fredrickson so locked into completing his full itinerary that he is not considering their slow pace thus far and the weather forecast? "Fred might have been basing his decision to continue on his usual fast pace," says Osborne. "I slowed him down."

At present, the wind is at their backs from the southwest and will provide some welcome assistance as they progress northward. Is Fredrickson considering the forecasted shift in the winds that will create a strong headwind for them and one that carries with it much colder air? Or is he simply intent on staying with the plan?

The Acceptance Heuristic occurs because, according to McCammon, we "have a tendency to engage in activities that we think will get us noticed or accepted by people we like or respect, or by people we want to like or respect us." Osborne is on his first winter hike. He views this as a natural progression in his passion for hiking. A successful winter hike today will likely lead to others with Fredrickson, whom he admires. For his part, Fredrickson knows how much this new experience means to Osborne and would be reluctant to disappoint him. For both of them, the fact that their families and coworkers know they're doing a winter hike, which they all perceive as a daring outdoor pursuit, may provide an added incentive to succeed at it.

The Expert Halo Heuristic is perhaps the biggest trap Fredrickson and Osborne are caught in at the moment. It happens when there is "an informal leader who, for various reasons, ends up making critical decisions for the party." Fredrickson has extensive experience in the mountains, and Osborne has deferred to him on every outing they've done together. He has yielded all planning and decision-making to Fredrickson and the other people he's hiked with. "To a certain extent, that was me back then," he admits ruefully.

This is not uncommon. We tend to shrink from raising concerns in a group setting when we perceive that there's a higher level of experience or expertise within the group or if there is an authority figure present. We fear being criticized, marginalized, or isolated, so we cross our fingers and follow, even when we see potential complications ahead. It is possible Osborne is putting aside any misgivings he may be having because he has always put full trust in Fredrickson's expertise and opinion, and Fredrickson is still saying everything will be okay.

Throughout the morning's hike and now as they stand on top of Little Haystack, Fredrickson and Osborne have been offered crucial information—in subtle and not-so-subtle ways. They've heard warnings from the hikers who've turned back and are aware that they are moving more slowly than they had anticipated. Their planned early afternoon descent has already been compromised, making them vulnerable to the storm forecasted for later in the day. Unfortunately, they are not taking inventory of all this data. They're not processing it. They aren't even talking about it.

At approximately 1:15 p.m., they make the call to go on. Fredrickson steps onto the Franconia Ridge Trail, and Osborne follows.

XI
TROUGHS

*"I don't like surprises. When I'm planning my route, looking at maps,
I always identify lots of ways to abandon my climb and escape to safety.
This includes knowing alternative trails, safe ways to get back below
treeline, or locations to find shelter."*

—Jeff Fongemie, Mountain Rescue Service

Franconia Ridge Trail
Sunday, Feb. 10, 2008
After 1:00 p.m.

Nothing about walking into frozen fog in the alpine zone in winter feels even remotely three-dimensional. Sometimes, the only thing that distinguishes sky from ground in these conditions is the occasional sliver of granite or weathered vegetation poking out of the snow. On the Franconia Ridge Trail, two borders of stacked stones line much of the traverse from treeline on Little Haystack to Mount Lincoln. In winter conditions, the stones are either completely hidden under deep snow or stripped bare by high winds that send whatever

The "trough" leading to Mount Lincoln in better weather conditions.

precipitation that hasn't frozen solid over the edge into Walker Ravine or the Pemigewasset Wilderness below. Each stone was meticulously placed there by famed stewards of this ridge, Laura and Guy Waterman, after their careful observation of hiker behavior. Between the stone borders lies the well-worn hiker's trough, the path that guides you across the traverse.

As Fredrickson and Osborne follow this trough northward toward Mount Lincoln, there's another kind of trough hovering overhead. The low-pressure weather trough that arrived here from the west a little over ninety minutes ago has stalled on the Franconia Range, its presence signaled by the steadily falling snow that's accumulating on the ridge's crown. But snowfall in February is common in the Granite State, and Fredrickson and Osborne push on.

Meanwhile, the arctic cold front to the west, with its elongated north/south orientation, high winds, and menacing snow squalls, is moving quickly eastward through Pennsylvania and New York and will soon reach Vermont. When that front collides with the trough overhead, which is certain to happen soon, the snow that's falling and already on the ground will be whipped around by the front's powerful winds.

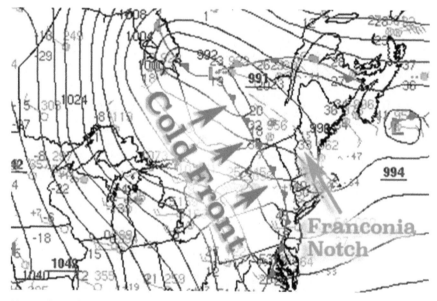

National Weather Service surface analysis map showing the location of the fast-moving cold front to the west of Franconia Notch at 2:00 p.m., Feb. 10.

Fredrickson remains in the lead, laying down first tracks in the untouched snow. When his snowshoes penetrate the powder, a whoomp announces that the built-in crampons are biting into the icy layer of crust underneath. Osborne follows about 20 feet behind. It's a good thing his friend is wearing his bright-yellow jacket, because otherwise Osborne would lose sight of him.

Their pace is moderate and steady. Fredrickson is aware that he must not get too far ahead of Osborne in order to remain visible. As usual, the friends keep the mood light, exchanging sporadic banter as they go. But this exposed portion of the itinerary is probably all business for Fredrickson. There's no view for them to take in, and the menacing afternoon forecast has got to be drifting somewhere in his psyche. Osborne, on the other hand, is feeling happy. He's above treeline in winter on a legendry ridgeline. This is big.

While the AMC's *White Mountain Guide* describes the terrain here as a "nearly level ridge crest in the open to the foot of Mount Lincoln," there are subtle drops and rises along this leg. Fredrickson and Osborne descend a gradual slope that takes a hard turn to the left before resuming a direct approach to the foot of Mount Lincoln. The mountain is completely smothered in fog, and they're robbed of the opportunity to take in the "gothic" rock structures that line the western side of the trail. In warmer months, when rainstorms pass over, hikers seek shelter behind these formations. This flat section offers a brief respite before the trail turns upward again. When it does, the friends' pace will slow even further.

Things are not so serene down on the Franconia Notch Parkway. Authorities continue to respond to motorists in distress. Near The Basin Trail off Interstate 93, a large wrecker is on its way to extract a tractor-trailer unit that's stuck on the roadway. A state highway plow has been redirected to drop sand and salt on Basin Hill because two other tractor-trailer units can't get up the slippery incline. The storm is already wreaking havoc with public service operations, and the worst hasn't even arrived yet.

Three hundred miles southwest of Franconia Notch, the arctic cold front continues to do damage, with heavy snow squalls causing multiple breakdowns and accidents. At about 2:15 p.m., the front arrives in Albany, where squalls and wind gusts exceeding 40 mph create whiteout conditions and cause power losses and property damage. Nearly all of the Green Mountain State is affected now as well. The scope and power of this cold front is clearly significant.

Cannon Mountain Ski Area
Franconia Notch Parkway
White Mountain National Forest

Darlene Deschambeault is skiing with a friend. The day before, she hiked on Kinsman Mountain with a small group, and today she's right back outside. It's been cloudy for most of the day, and Deschambeault misses the striking view of the Franconia Ridge, which is completely socked in. The Cannon tram has been down all day, but there's nothing to see anyway. As the two friends are making one of their runs, things suddenly change. In her post on the *Views From The Top* website, Deschambeault describes the moment: "That wind and whiteout conditions came really fast. [On] one run we could see from the top, and after that the wind picked up so bad you couldn't see to ski. We were feeling our way down the mountain."

As Deschambeault and her friend are descending, Allan Clark, who in addition to his duties with Pemi Valley Search and Rescue, is also the fire chief in the town of Sugar Hill and a member of the Cannon Ski Patrol, is on a snow machine. He's making his way from Peabody Slopes to the tram when the squall hits. "It was all I could do to get there," he says. "It was unbelievably bad. You couldn't see. It was socked in."

Deschambeault and her companion inch their way down the slope and call it a day. They are forced to wait in the lodge and then again in their car for quite some time until Route 3, which has been closed by state troopers, is reopened and the ramp onto I-93 is cleared of cars. On her drive out of the Notch, she finds the roadway covered in a sheet of ice and cars off the road everywhere.

Exit 23
Interstate 93 South
New Hampton, N.H.

Having successfully navigated his Toyota Prius out of Franconia Notch an hour before, Dick Martel finds himself back in a risky situation as the squalls overtake the central part of the state. "It really turned bad, and by then there was a lot of snow in the trees," he recalls. "All of a sudden the wind picked up, and it blew all of that snow out of the trees. I was in a whiteout for ten seconds."

Fortunately. Martel's many years of emergency driving experience kick in. He stays calm, and rather than coming to a dead stop in the middle of the highway, eases the car forward until the swirling air around him settles enough for him to see. He'll arrive home safely.

Waterville Valley Ski Area
Mount Tecumseh
Waterville Valley, N.H.

North of Martel's location, skiers in Waterville Valley are experiencing their own encounter with the weather. John Hansen, an elementary school principal and member of the Pemi Valley Search and Rescue Team, is skiing the Funny Hat Trail with a group of kids at approximately 2,800 feet when things go bad. "It was moderately windy and snowing, and then all of a sudden, it was a total whiteout with an instantaneous increase in the wind," he recalls. "At about 2:00 p.m., this weather front came right over the mountain, and it was pretty awesome in its power."

Being responsible for a group of children made the moment especially frightening for Hansen. "You literally could no longer see at all," he says. "You were completely without reference to place. I was afraid I was going to be hit by someone going down the trail. None of us could see anyone or anything, but we knew that downhill was the right way to go. It normally takes us two minutes to descend the trail, but we were snowplowing all the way, and this one took four to five minutes."

Years later, Hansen still feels the effect of the event. "I've been a snowboarder and skier for years, and it was one of the most awesome displays of weather I've ever seen, probably the most awesome," he says. "It was all-enveloping. I can't even imagine what it was like up on Franconia Ridge. I remember thinking at the time, 'Wow, they really forecasted this right.'"

Drew Knight, who was skiing Upper Bobby's Trail at Waterville

Valley with his 10-year-old son that afternoon, describes a similar experience. "I didn't want to lose my son in the whiteout," he recalls. "He thought it was fun because we were making a game out of trying to get down. If he got more than fifteen to twenty feet away, I couldn't see him. Years later, Knight can still feel the moment. "I remember saying to myself, 'Geez, I hope there's no one out on the high peaks today.' It all happened so quickly. It was like a switch had been thrown."

XII
THE SWITCH

"Everyone has a plan, until he gets punched in the mouth."
—Mike Tyson, *heavyweight boxer*

Franconia Ridge
Sunday, Feb. 10, 2008
Between 2:00 and 2:15 p.m.

Through the frozen fog and falling snow, Fredrickson and Osborne can just barely make out the portion of the ridge trail that starts upward. They're just feet away from the main climb up to Mount Lincoln, the second summit of the three they plan to make today. Large boulders come into the frame as they near the slope, with Fredrickson leading the way onto the incline. Surrounded by quiet, the friends are feeling calm. "We had dropped down into a col-like feature just before the climb up to Lincoln," recalls Osborne. "It just seemed like a normal hike. I could see Fred within twenty feet. I could see the edges of the trail. I thought everything was functioning as it should at that point."

Until it wasn't.

The arrival of the squall is instantaneous and violent. Without a single preemptive indicator, the storm collides with the ridge—and with Fredrickson and Osborne, who are totally exposed and vulnerable. The ridgeline is buffeted by winds coming directly from the west. Within seconds, the winds that were at their back and aiding their forward progress are now hitting them hard from the side and front, and they're being struck by a churning wall of white that overtakes them like a big-breaking wave in wild surf.

"I had never experienced anything like that," says Osborne. "It was like somebody flipped a switch. All of a sudden, there was all this sensory input. The wind was absolutely howling. It was like a freight train, a jet engine, like jumping into icy water."

Osborne is frozen in place, pinned upright by the blowing wind. He instinctively drives his left shoulder into the wind, tucks his chin into his right collarbone, and leans into it. Gingerly, he glances ahead. He can see Fredrickson but only a limited amount of terrain in front of him and nothing to the side. He worries that if he moves even slightly, he'll lose his fragile footing, so he braces himself. "My immediate thought was 'I wish I was home right now,'" he recalls. "I felt incredibly alone at that moment."

The loose snow that was on the ground is now airborne, swirling in every direction with the falling flakes. Fredrickson and Osborne are standing in a ground blizzard being continuously fed by the heavy bands of snow that have moved in with the wind. They don't know it, but these heavy bands also signal the imminent arrival of the arctic cold front, which will make its presence known shortly.

The shift in the winds from southwesterly to westerly contributes to the existing crisis. As warmer air coming from the south is cut off, the floodgates open, allowing dangerous arctic air to pour into the region. The temperature is already sliding downward. According to the thermograph on the summit of Mount Washington, the ambient air temperature has dropped from 14°F to 8°F over the course of fifteen minutes. The windchill follows suit, dropping sharply from -6°F to -20°F. The Observatory's Tom Padham describes the impact of this rapid change: "The temperature drop of six degrees in the middle of the day eliminates any further daytime heating. That is a significant drop."

The high winds and whiteout are making it difficult for Fredrickson and Osborne to orient themselves. Although they know where they are on the ridge, they have lost much of the spatial awareness that would allow them to use the terrain's landmarks for navigation. If they remain in the open, they'll develop frostbite on any exposed skin within thirty minutes.

"There are three things that tell us where we are," says Dr. Frank Hubbell of SOLO Wilderness Medicine. "First, our eyes. They have a great deal to do with balance and knowing where we are in space. Next, our ears and the three ear canals that run perpendicular to one another. There's fluid in the canals that moves and provides us with spatial awareness. Lastly, the big joints of our knees tell us we're upright."

When one of these indicators is absent, we lose a sense of where we are and become fearful. "If you eliminate two of the three, you're completely disoriented," says Hubbell. "You cannot tell the horizon from the sky, and you lose the sense of up and down. When you remove their ability to know where they are in space, people panic."

Fortunately, Fredrickson and Osborne are close enough together to see each other. Fredrickson takes a few steps back to where Osborne is standing, and they huddle against the maelstrom. But communication is difficult. "It was so loud that we had to shout in each other's ear up close," recalls Osborne.

Fredrickson is clear and decisive about their next move. Yelling into his friend's ear, he tells Osborne they're going to turn around and go back the way they came. Fredrickson says he will look for an exit point on the leeward side of the ridge where they can drop down just enough to avoid taking the brunt of the wind. They'll follow the ridge to Little Haystack, which is only about a half-mile back, and head for the security of Falling Waters Trail. Fredrickson is adamant that they will not bail out down into the Pemigewasset Wilderness. They agree that bailing off either side of the ridge and down the steep slopes and drainages carries too much risk of avalanche. In addition, Fredrickson thinks that route would be very slow going. As long as they're able to stay close to the ridgeline, they'll be able to get back, he says. With this plan set, Fredrickson takes the lead again and retraces their steps. He moves quickly, clearly aware of the urgency to get back to a safe place.

"When we decided to turn around, facing in the direction of Little Haystack, the trail was flat with a right-hand bend," says Osborne. "In the moments after we turned around, Fred got way out in front of me. I was always the slower hiker, and I was quickly falling behind. Fred probably could have run back and down, if he'd been alone."

Although they're heading toward what they both understand as safety, Osborne can't shake the anxiety that has overtaken him. The full conditions are having their impact. "On the way back, we really started to get blown around," he says. "We didn't travel far."

Seven months after the accident, in a September 2008 interview with Patrick Meighan of the *Nashua Telegraph*, Osborne said it wasn't just the cold or even the wind that kept them from getting back down.

"Visibility is really what got us. We had all this blowing snow."

Still, it's impossible to discount the probable effect of the wind on that high, exposed ridge. In the hours leading up to the squall, winds averaged 28 mph on Mount Washington, and likely were slightly lower on Franconia Ridge. When the squall hit, the wind shifted direction, and its speed rapidly increased to an average of 52 mph, with some stronger gusts reaching a peak of 79 mph. "The wind in this case is right on that edge of most people's comfort level," says Tom Padham. "You might think you can still manage it because even though it's knocking you around, you're not crawling on your hands and knees. But when combined with a prolonged exposure to the cold, it's a major concern."

An instantaneous and significant change in wind strength and direction, combined with almost total sensory deprivation, is difficult for even an experienced winter hiker to handle. Having never experienced winds this high, Osborne has no frame of reference to help him process the situation he's in. Hiking up into high winds above treeline allows you to ease into the change in conditions and decide whether or not to continue. But when you're already above treeline and things suddenly go bad, it can be overwhelming. Your fear of the wind becomes even more pronounced when you can no longer see, as Osborne says. You might tell yourself you have only two options: stand there paralyzed by fear and wait for the potentially deadly force to overcome you, or try to get as far away from the danger as you can. If you choose the flight response, you may not even have a sense of what direction to follow because you can't see what's around you.

Fredrickson looks back and notices the gap that's formed between them. When Osborne sees him turn, he stops and motions for Fred to come back to him. "I thought we needed to figure out something different to do," says Osborne, who is fearful at this point and convinced they're not going to survive if they keep going. "At the time, I thought the wind was going to spell our doom, that we were not going to survive it. In my mind the immediate need was to get out of the wind and find a place to hunker down."

They reconvene. Though Fredrickson has clearly responded with urgency, Osborne is struck by his friend's calm demeanor. "I didn't sense any panic in Fred," he says.

Yelling into Fred's ear to be heard, Osborne makes an impassioned plea: "We're not going to make it if we do this! This isn't going to work! We need to seek shelter; we need to get out of this wind!"

"That's not possible up here!" Fredrickson yells back.

And that's the moment another switch is flipped: Osborne begins to exert his influence in planning what they should do next. He can't break free of the fear that's gripping him and is demanding immediate relief from the raging wind. He's telling Fredrickson that he must find a way to bring him that relief—now.

This is new territory for Fredrickson, since the less-experienced Osborne has always accepted his judgment and gone along with his planning. Up to this point, he's led all aspects of the hike, and he's focused on a clear contingency plan he believes will work. He must now decide if he should take an autocratic approach and demand that they retrace their steps back to Falling Waters Trail or acquiesce to Osborne's need to escape the wind. He's trying to calculate the pros and cons of each strategy, and he's doing it under extreme duress.

Alain Comeau, a veteran member of Mountain Rescue Service, believes that decisions around bailing out or seeking shelter nearby represent a significant challenge. "I don't think there's a right answer to that because it depends on the conditions: the forecast, the people, the equipment," he says. "Every individual, pair, or group may do something different in a similar situation. Not everybody's prepared to hunker down if they don't have the clothing or gear."

Comeau goes on to explain the difficulty of mitigating risk even when you're not under duress: "In risk management, it's about being aware of the hazard, then assessing the hazard," he says. "How severe could it become?" Comeau stresses that you have to be brutally honest with yourself and avoid rationalizing that things are better than they appear. "Then you have to develop a plan to eliminate or mitigate the hazard. You're always trying to tip it in your favor. But if you can't, you've got to do something about it."

Fredrickson is in a quandary. Are the full conditions and Osborne's growing concern affecting his ability to take a careful, objective inventory of the critical factors of terrain, weather, gear, and their physical condition? Is it better to shelter in place somewhere or head back the way they came? How will time affect all of this? How long is the storm forecasted to last, and is their gear better aligned for a bivouac or a bailout? Does he have the time to pause, properly assess, and either alter the existing plan or develop a new one?

A major concern for Fredrickson is determining what Osborne can tolerate. Seeing his friend in such distress, the decision he makes in that moment is likely driven more by emotion than by reason. He accedes to Osborne's wishes and tells him they'll stop their retreat and return to the base of Mount Lincoln in search of shelter. They're approximately 100 feet away from where they were when the squall hit.

With a new plan in place, Fredrickson moves quickly toward Lincoln, creating another gap between him and Osborne. Though this is what Osborne wants, he will not get rapid relief unless Fredrickson finds adequate shelter from the wind. "When we turned again to the north, I had this moment of despair and thought, 'Oh, my God, how did I get into this situation?'" he says.

As Osborne reaches the base of the slope, Fredrickson points one of his trekking poles downward toward the east. He drops down over the ridgeline, his lean silhouette disappearing into the whiteout. Osborne can no longer see his friend but follows his tracks. A few minutes later, Fredrickson pops back up onto the trail and waves Osborne over to him. "There's a rock outcropping down there where we can get out of the wind," he tells him.

The two drop approximately 15 feet down off the Franconia Ridge Trail and walk the slope in a horizontal line for about 50 yards. Between 2:30 and 3:00 p.m., the battered friends arrive at the rock outcropping they hope will shelter them from the raging storm.

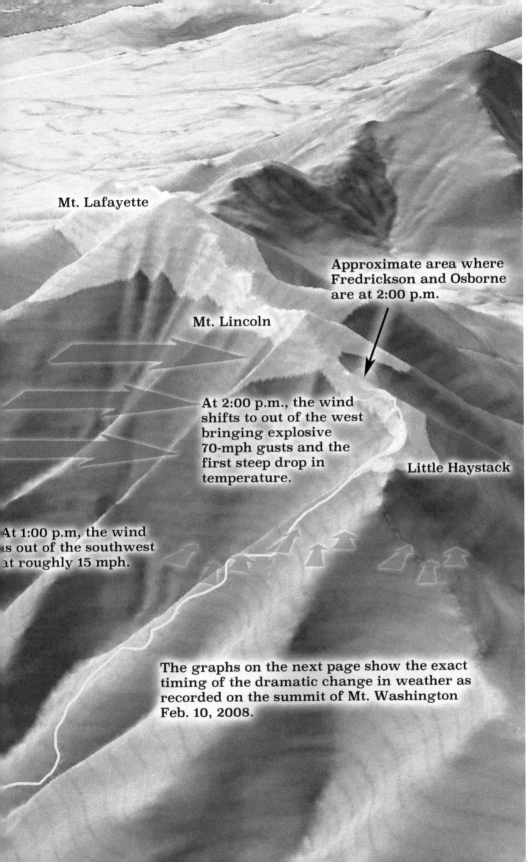

Mt. Lafayette

Approximate area where
Fredrickson and Osborne
are at 2:00 p.m.

Mt. Lincoln

At 2:00 p.m., the wind
shifts to out of the west
bringing explosive
70-mph gusts and the
first steep drop in
temperature.

Little Haystack

At 1:00 p.m, the wind
is out of the southwest
at roughly 15 mph.

The graphs on the next page show the exact
timing of the dramatic change in weather as
recorded on the summit of Mt. Washington
Feb. 10, 2008.

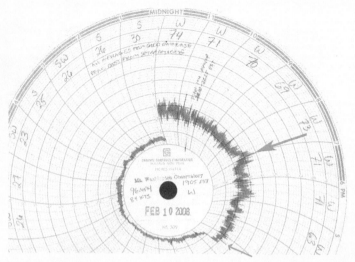

The image (top) is of the chart from the Hays Recorder at the Mount Washington Observatory on Feb. 10, 2008. The red pen lines represent wind speeds measured with a complex system of gauges by a pitot static tube anemometer. When the wind speed increases, the red pen is pushed farther away from the center. If the winds are gusty, the pen responds by recording peaks and valleys. In especially gusty weather, the red line grows thicker over time. The Hays is calibrated to record speeds up to 140 mph. The numbers at the outer rim represent time of day, the average hourly wind direction, and the hourly average wind speed. You'll note the sharp increase in wind speed from 28 to 52 mph at approximately 2:15 p.m., indicated by the red arrow at the bottom right. The arrow just above that at 7:00 p.m. indicates the peak wind gust of the day at 96 mph.

The image (bottom right) is a chart from the thermograph at the Mount Washington Observatory. The numbers at the outer rim indicate time of day, while the numbers on the inner rim represent the average hourly temperature. The red arrow at approximately 2:15 p.m. shows the drop in temperature from 14°F to 8°F over the course of 15 minutes. Windchill values, not measured by the thermograph, dropped rapidly from -6°F to -20°F, and winds shifted from out of the southwest to out of the west.

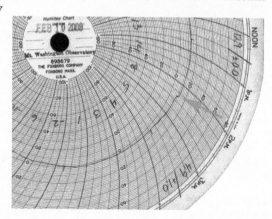

XIII
SHELTER FROM THE STORM

*"Take long walks in stormy weather or through deep snows
in the fields and woods, if you would keep your spirits up.
Deal with brute nature. Be cold and hungry and weary."*

—Henry David Thoreau

**Mount Lincoln/Franconia Ridge
Between 4,800 and 4,900 feet
Sunday, Feb. 10, 2008
Around 3:00 p.m.**

*Mount Washington Observatory Surface Weather Observations (3:00 to 4:00
p.m.): Temperature 5°F; winds out of the west averaging 64 mph; visibility 0
miles, snow/fog/blowing snow; windchill -27°F. Peak wind gust: 77 mph.*

James Osborne is somewhat relieved after an unnerving traverse
of the slope leading to the bivouac site Fred Fredrickson has found
for them. When winter's strong northwesterly winds arrive above
treeline, they generate a continuous spin cycle of snow along slopes
and ridges. This can result in waist-high drifts that stop a hiker's
forward progress. Much of the fresh snow that fell here overnight has
been sheared off by the strong westerly winds, exposing a layer of icy
crust.

Osborne is thankful he's wearing crampons, especially since the
westerly gusts are making every effort to send him sliding downslope
with no tools in hand to arrest a fall. He uses great care with his
footing, ensuring with each step that the sharp points of his crampons
drive deeply into the crust. Standing before the rock outcropping, he
ponders the shelter Fredrickson has selected. It doesn't look optimal
to him, but it seems much better than the alternative. Both friends
sense the wind ramping up and the temperature biting down harder
on them. They'll need to hunker down quickly to stem heat loss.

Their closeness to the ridge trail preserves a deceptive connection
to "the outside world." But having turned their backs on Falling

Waters Trail, just a half-mile away, they're now essentially isolated. No one is nearby; no one knows what they're enduring. The hikers they met earlier are likely somewhere safe and warm.

Fredrickson removes his snowshoes and instructs Osborne to take off his crampons. Sharp objects will not be welcome in a small space occupied by polyester, fleece, and shins. The risk of a rip or puncture is too high. They step onto a large, weathered, granite boulder that Osborne describes as a "landing." There's approximately 3½ feet of surface area on which to stand. According to Osborne, it would have been quite easy to fall off.

The landing faces due east toward the Pemigewasset Wilderness. Resting at an angle on the left side of the boulder, and partially embedded in the slope among other boulders and heavy scree, is an elongated piece of granite. All of this was deposited here thousands of years earlier by the melting ice sheet. In between the landing and the elongated rock is a horizontal chamber that, to Osborne, resembles "a long narrow hole." The entrance to the chamber is just high enough and long enough for a person to slide into it lying down.

The right side of the structure is slightly elevated and points northwesterly in the direction of the ridgeline. It has an opening at that end, but not wide enough for either Fredrickson or Osborne to crawl through. Both remove their packs, and Fredrickson pushes them into a narrow part of the chamber. There's not enough room in the larger area of the chamber where they will shelter to keep their packs next to them.

Though the front has moved past the Franconia Ridge and is now assaulting the Presidential Range to the east, heavy snow continues to fall here and, because of the high winds, visibility is still mere feet. The front will clear the White Mountains entirely by 3:45 p.m., but this does not mean the weather will improve. In fact, it will get much worse. The low-pressure area that's positioned along the coast of Maine has spent its afternoon strengthening rapidly. It is pulling dangerously cold arctic air into the region. It's time for the two friends to hunker down in their rudimentary bivouac.

Fredrickson tells Osborne to get into the chamber. Osborne pauses for a moment to work through the mild anxiety he's feeling over what he's about to do. He mentally rehearses the moves it will require to get inside. Then he turns his back to the northwest, drops to his knees, lowers his torso to the landing, and rolls onto his back. With his head pointed to the northwest, he lies supine on the cold granite. Blowing snow skids across his goggles and balaclava. Using his elbows, shoulder blades, buttocks, and heels, he inches his body to his right, crosses the short gap between him and the narrow space, and disappears into it. When he reaches the inside wall, his right side pressing against the granite, he yells to Fredrickson that he's in.

Osborne cants his head to his left and watches as Fredrickson drops into view and goes through the same series of maneuvers. With no other option, Fredrickson positions himself alongside Osborne. They lie shoulder to shoulder, with their upper torsos on a slight incline. In an instant, they both realize an immediate adjustment must be made. The opening at the end of the formation is near their heads and is allowing cold air and heavy spindrift to pour into the space and wash over them. They quickly shuffle out of the shelter. Fredrickson pulls his pack from its narrow resting place and detaches the two butt boards. He hands them to Osborne, who bear-hugs them against the winds. Fredrickson also retrieves two Mylar space blankets from inside his pack, stuffs them into his jacket pocket, and jams the pack back into its hold.

Fighting the headwind, the two move over to the opening that's allowing the elements to violate their granite sanctuary. They yell at each other over the howling winds to find the best way to seal off the hole with the boards. They also want to make sure the wind doesn't jettison the boards and send them toward the Pemigewasset Wilderness. Each places a board over the opening and packs it in snow. Side by side, the boards hold nicely and bring an end to the onslaught of wind and spindrift into the shelter.

With the opening sealed, they retrieve their packs, rummaging through them to assess their gear. They remove their headlamps, knowing that sunset will arrive soon. Fredrickson also retrieves the two thermoses, one with hot chocolate and the other with chai tea, though the beverages are lukewarm at best. With their backs to the wind, they stand on the landing and share what's left of the tea, saving the hot chocolate for later. They're discouraged to learn that they've already consumed most of the water they brought with them and what remains is frozen.

In their book *Hypothermia, Frostbite, and other Cold Injuries,* Gordon Giesbrecht and James Wilkerson discuss the importance of maintaining hydration. "Water and food support and fuel physiologic functions, maintain physical condition and mental acuity, and help prevent cold injury and hypothermia," they write. It is therefore dangerous to forgo a brief stop to take in fluids or fail to protect your water source in a cold environment. "Failure to replace normal water losses through the kidneys, skin, and lungs, or abnormal losses by other routes, result in dehydration, decreased blood volume, and in a cold environment, impaired heat production by exercise," they write. "Dehydration is typically accompanied by weakness, fatigue, dizziness, and even a tendency to faint when standing, all of which impede efforts to deal rationally with a threatening environment" (p.120). In a nutshell, dehydration opens the door for hypothermia and frostbite to walk in.

Before reentering the shelter, Fredrickson grabs the snowshoes he jammed in the snow next to Osborne's crampons. Having learned a valuable lesson with the butt boards, he'll use snowshoes to seal off the entrance to the shelter as best he can. The windchill is brutal on the landing, so they store their packs again, reenact the earlier ritual, and enter the chamber. Once inside Fredrickson positions the snowshoes, end to end, along the horizontal entrance. The snowshoes do counter some of the wind and snow that is buffeting Fredrickson on his fully exposed left side, but it's by no means providing him with complete coverage. Mere inches separate his left side from having no protection at all. He is pressed right up against his snowshoes at the leading edge of the overhanging stone. Years later, Osborne remains deeply moved by Fredrickson's decision to position himself there. "I really believe Fred took the outside to be the protector," he says.

The space is definitely confining, especially for Osborne on the inside, and he is battling claustrophobia. The coarse ceiling looms just six inches above their faces. Fredrickson retrieves the Mylar blankets from his pocket and gives one to Osborne. They take turns rolling side to side as they clumsily slide the blankets under and around their torsos. Both men can raise their legs a bit higher than their heads because the ceiling is higher at that end. Beyond their feet and their stored packs, it is pitch black. "The cave wasn't awful, but I can't say it was comfortable either," says Osborne.

The two men stare at the ceiling and watch as their frozen exhalations collide with the stone and burst open like white, opaque flowers. It's a simple but welcome distraction that will eventually subside as the ambient temperature of the chamber rises from their body heat.

Giesbrecht and Wilkerson validate the importance of Fredrickson's decision to cover the small opening and preserve heat: "In a cold climate, temporary shelter must provide protection from convective cooling of wind. Since the air inside is relatively stationary, it can be warmed by heat from the body and provide a much more comfortable environment" (pp.117-118).

Dr. Murray Hamlet adds this caveat: "Their body heat will add warmth to the chamber, but it won't heat the rock they're lying on. The portion of their body touching the rock is going to lose heat through conduction. They'll lose heat that way all night, and as they cool, their ability to warm the chamber above them will be compromised." In a situation like this, Hamlet recommends putting as much insulation between your body and the ground or rock you're lying on. "The more insulation you put under you, the less you need above you," he says. "It doesn't matter what it is as long as it has a nonconductive surface: a sleeping pad, leaves, bark from a tree. Get yourself off direct contact with the ground and you'll lose less heat."

Fredrickson retrieves a single Hershey's Bar from his pocket and breaks it in half, handing a piece to Osborne. They consume the sugary treat quickly and enjoy a brief but welcome emotional boost. Having taken in a negligible amount of food and drink, and with the accommodations as comfortable as they're going to get, it's time for them to formulate plans.

"We decided that one of us would always be awake," says Osborne. "Every four hours, we were going to get up and get out of the cave in order to keep moving and to assess the weather." They are keenly focused on getting out of this situation as soon as a window of opportunity presents itself. "We felt if there was a break in the weather, we'd be able to hike out," Osborne says. "We were having ongoing discussions throughout the night about what we were going to do."

Although they have a pretty straightforward plan that includes periodic assessment, Osborne is feeling anxious. "I was thinking to myself, 'What if we both fall asleep and never wake up?'" he recalls.

They decide that if they're unlucky and an opportunity to bail out doesn't present itself during the night, they'll get up at 6:00 a.m. and depart at sunrise, which will occur at 6:53 a.m. At this point, they both know they are not prepared for the situation they find themselves in. "We specifically talked about not having any way to start a fire," says Osborne.

Todd Bogardus, now retired as a lieutenant with New Hampshire Fish and Game and a former team leader of the department's Advanced Search and Rescue Team, explains the importance of always packing survival tools, particularly those that can start a fire:

> Not only are fire tools small and light, but they can play a major role in one's survival and comfort should a situation occur where one is stranded. Fire can provide many aspects of relief. It will, of course, aid you in staying warm. But tending a fire also keeps you occupied, thus keeping you alert and active. It also provides psychological comfort to a person who is lost, stranded, or injured and unable to get out of the situation. A fire can serve as a signaling device for searchers who are looking for you, especially from aircraft. The smoke and light can be seen from the aircraft, and the smoke can be smelled and detected by searchers on the ground. Finally, fire can be

used to provide nourishment and energy. You could use it to melt snow into drinking water, boil water to make it safe for consumption, or even cook food, for example a fish you caught in a backcountry stream while trying to survive.

While the intrinsic value of fire tools is clear, it is also true that if Fredrickson and Osborne did have them, their position near the ridgeline in extreme conditions would make starting and maintaining a fire nearly impossible. When selecting a bivouac site, the book *Wildcare: Working in Less than Desirable Conditions and Remote Environments*, published by SOLO (Stonehearth Open Learning Opportunities), identifies four important basics to consider: protection from water danger, protection from wind, the availability of fire/heat/warmth, and the availability of food and drinking water. The book also cites three important considerations regarding terrain selection: avoid high-exposed places; seek natural shelter, e.g., caves, big boulders, cliff overhangs, depressions, and talus fields; and enhance your sightline by building a windbreak (p.303).

Fredrickson has done well, in adverse conditions, to find a substantial rock outcropping that has gotten his anxiety-ridden friend out of the wind as quickly as possible. The shelter he selects offers good protection from the arctic winds, especially after he enhances it by improvising with his available gear. Unfortunately, without a fire, they'll need to focus on consistent hydration and fuel intake if they hope to maintain body heat. Most of their fluids are already gone or have been compromised by the cold, and their limited food supply is at risk of a similar fate. They've been reacting to an accumulation of unexpected variables for hours now, and they'll be forced to continue doing so as more are introduced over the next several hours.

Mount Washington Observatory Surface Weather Observations (4:00 to 5:00 p.m.): Temperature 4°F; winds out of the west averaging 63 mph; visibility 0 miles, snow/fog/blowing snow; windchill -28°F. Peak wind gust: 80 mph.

Conservation Officer Mark Ober Jr., a three-year veteran of New Hampshire Fish and Game's Law Enforcement Division and for the past year a member of its Advanced Search and Rescue Team, drives into Franconia Notch on I-93 North in his 2003 Chevy Silverado 1500 cruiser. Ober is headed for home after starting his shift at 7:00 a.m. Today he was assigned to patrol the 29th Annual Great Rotary Fishing Derby on New Hampshire's Lake Winnipesaukee, and it was an active one. Between 7:00 a.m. and 3:00 p.m., he logged 29 miles on his department-issued snow machine and conducted checks on fifty off-highway recreational vehicles and thirty fishing licenses. As he drives, Ober reflects on how lucky the derby winner must feel, having landed a 3.06-pound rainbow trout and the grand prize of a new fishing boat and trailer.

It's a slow commute home for Ober. He records "snow and icy conditions" in his daily log and recalls that "the weather was really bad in the Notch." Department of Transportation plow operators working the Notch are keeping their own notes: "snowing, drifting, wind, poor visibility." Fortunately, the wave of accidents that clogged this narrow highway earlier in the day has ceased, with many people heeding the warnings to stay off the roads. Ober approaches the Lafayette Place exit, the trailhead for Old Bridle Path and Falling Waters, and he's happy to see that the ramp has yet to be plowed. There are no parallel indentations in the deep snow, which tells him that no one has driven into the parking lot recently. "I'm always checking trailheads," he says. "It looked like no one was out, so I was relieved at the thought that no one was up there."

Unfortunately, on this day Ober's perception doesn't match the reality, because he can't see the car Fredrickson and Osborne have left in the inner parking lot. At 5:00 p.m., following a slow, two-hour commute, Ober pulls into his driveway and signs off for the night with dispatch. He'll be back on patrol tomorrow morning.

Mount Washington Observatory Surface Weather Observations (5:00 to 6:00 p.m.): Temperature 3°F; winds out of the west averaging 71 mph; visibility 0 miles, snow/fog/blowing snow; windchill -31°F. Peak wind gust: 88 mph.

The sun, hidden all day, sets at 5:08 p.m. Because Fredrickson and Osborne are on the eastern side of the ridge, dusk turns quickly to darkness for them. The sun dipped below Cannon Mountain to the west a while ago, so the friends are not blessed with any ambient light. They are wearing their headlamps but use them infrequently to save batteries.

Heavy snow showers and squalls continue blanketing the range. There's no sign of an escape window opening anytime soon. Time passes slowly in the shelter, which gives the two friends a chance to reflect on what they don't have with them. "We talked about not having a cell phone," recalls Osborne. "In 2008, we weren't such a 'bring your phone' culture as we are now." Weather conditions are clearly worsening, and they discuss the likelihood that they won't be able to get out of this situation on their own. "We did talk about rescue and what that might look like," says Osborne. "Fred would be overdue for work very early in the morning, and I'd be overdue by 7:00 or 7:30 a.m. We understood the seriousness of that, but we weren't overly anxious about it at the time."

As Osborne lies there facing the reality of a long night's stay, his decision to leave behind the three-season sleeping bag that morning is weighing heavily on him. He doesn't share this with Fredrickson because it's one of those things in life he knows can't be changed.

In giving advice about hiking safely, Todd Bogardus stresses the importance of including a sleeping bag in your kit, regardless of the added weight or expected duration of the hike:

> During the winter months with any plan of going above treeline, a day hiker should most certainly carry a sleeping bag. Even if it's not a three-season or winter bag, some type of bag would still be beneficial should an emergency arise. Today's fabrics and materials are generally very lightweight and compact. It is better to be prepared with a little extra weight and not need it than to get stuck and not have it. One needs to be prepared for the 'What if?' You don't plan on getting yourself into an emergency situation, but you must plan to get yourself out of one. If you need that sleeping bag, you'll be very happy you carried it. It may not be you who needs the bag, but an unprepared hiker you may come upon. An alternative to carrying a sleeping bag would be to at least carry a bivy bag. There are many lightweight varieties. The emergency shelter it provides will get you out of the elements and aid in conserving heat.

Osborne has been considering the "What ifs" for years now. "I've often thought that with a bivouac sack and sleeping bag, we could have easily waited out the storm in relative comfort," he acknowledges.

Mount Washington Observatory Surface Weather Observations (6:00 to 7:00 p.m.): Temperature 1°F; winds out of the west averaging 71 mph; visibility 0 miles, snow/fog/blowing snow; windchill -34°F. Peak wind gust: 92 mph.

National Weather Service radar notes two separate heavy bands of snow over Franconia Ridge and Mount Washington at 6:30 p.m. With wind speeds now near hurricane force, snow on the windward slopes and ridgeline continues to move through violently. Fredrickson and Osborne chat back and forth about the scope of their isolation. "We talked about no one knowing where we were, that we were both single at the time, and that there was no one at home to know we were overdue," recalls Osborne. Their decision to bivouac rather than bail out doesn't come up in their conversations. Perhaps it's being avoided or just accepted.

Steve Larson, a veteran of Mountain Rescue Service, believes they made the right call in the circumstances. "Experience tells you that the last thing you want to do in a situation above treeline is stop," says Larson. "I don't care where you are, get out of the teeth of it. If you can just get down out of the wind, you'll be able to survive the night a lot better."

Todd Bogardus has a similar reading of their decision. "They were getting blown over, and they made a decision to hunker down. I'm not going to second-guess them; that's the decision they made. In fact, we would recommend people do that if you don't want to get yourself in worse than you already are. Should they have gone down on the Pemi side? It would have been hard to judge at that point. They might have thought that it was just going to blow through. Unfortunately for them it was there to stay."

What's really gnawing at Fredrickson and Osborne during that night is their failure to leave a clear itinerary with someone. It's one more "What if?" to add to the stack that neither of them can do anything about.

Again, Bogardus offers great advice:

It is extremely important from a rescue standpoint for folks to leave their planned itinerary with someone at home. This is important from a response perspective, because it eliminates unnecessary delay in searching for the starting point of someone's trip. Numerous times, we've been told that so-and-so went hiking in the White Mountains. That tells us nothing except that they are in either New Hampshire or Maine. Specificity is essential, and though situations may alter, the starting point is key.

Mount Washington Observatory Surface Weather Observations (7:00 to 8:00 p.m.): Temperature -2°F; winds out of the west averaging 73 mph; visibility 0 miles, fog/blowing snow; windchill -38°F. Peak wind gust: 96 mph.

With four hours logged in the chamber, things up to this point have been tolerable for Fredrickson and Osborne. "It didn't seem that bad in the cave; I didn't feel cold yet," recalls Osborne. But time and temperature are tipping the scales in the wrong direction. As their body heat escapes and they exhale, the vapor from their breathing will not stay frozen on the granite. "It did eventually get damp in there," says Osborne.

In their book, Giesbrecht and Wilkerson discuss the challenge of water vapor management in the type of shelter Fredrickson and Osborne occupy: "Shelter should provide protection from moisture and conductive cooling. At temperatures below freezing, the moisture in exhaled air tends to form fast on walls of tents or snow that can drop down on the occupants. The frost may be melted by body heat and dampen the outer surface of clothing or a sleeping bag. Frost accumulation in shelters is difficult to prevent and can be limited only by decreasing water vapor within the shelter" (p.118).

Increased air flow would help the pair, but it's a double-edged sword given windchill levels, another variable Fredrickson and Osborne can't control or manage.

Mount Washington Observatory Surface Weather Observations (8:00 to 9:00 p.m.): Temperature -6°F; winds out of the west averaging 69 mph; visibility 0 miles, fog/blowing snow; windchill -43°F. Peak wind gust: 84 mph.

The chamber is a little damp, but conditions inside are still manageable. Fredrickson and Osborne are acclimatizing a bit to their cramped surroundings. "It had a summer camp feel," recalls Osborne. "Here we were staying up late, talking, keeping each other company out there in the wilderness."

The conversation is enriching, and a warm camaraderie develops between the friends, mitigating the cold that surrounds them. "We had in-depth and intimate conversations," says Osborne. "They were different from conversations we'd had before. We talked about our first loves, our first sexual encounters, and life in general." Both men are divorced and talk at length about why and how they may have failed. "Fred told a really good story of how he and Bette met," Osborne says. "He walked into the Cardigan Lodge wearing overalls and carrying a bowl of wax beans and that's when he first saw her."

Fredrickson recites favorite passages from Henry David Thoreau and Robert Frost. He is an avid reader of both, a passion he and Bette shared for many years. "As I child I learned to swim in Walden Pond," says Bette. "When Fred and I were married, I took him to Walden, and we walked to the site of Thoreau's cabin." More wintry times saw the couple sharing Frost's poetry. "Often when it was snowing like crazy and the dirt road hadn't been plowed, we'd hook up our horse, Zachary, to the sled, put on his string of brass bells, and off we'd go, reciting 'Stopping by Woods on a Snowy Evening' in unison."

For his part, Osborne chooses to contribute Bob Dylan lyrics. "I recited 'Tangled Up in Blue,' 'Like a Rolling Stone,' and 'Shelter from the Storm,'" he recalls. "'Shelter from the Storm' really spoke to me when I was going through my divorce." Those lyrics must certainly be speaking to him now: "In a world of steel-eyed death, and men who are fighting to be warm/Come in, she said/I'll give ya shelter from the storm."

Fredrickson eventually reaches his fill of Osborne's alpine recital, "Okay, I've had enough of Bob Dylan," he says. "It's time to get up and move around."

Mount Washington Observatory Surface Weather Observations (9:00 to 10:00 p.m.): Temperature -10°F; winds out of the west averaging 70 mph; visibility 0 miles, fog/ blowing snow; windchill -49°F. Peak wind gust: 82 mph.

Fredrickson and Osborne slide out of the chamber for the second time—and into chaos. "We got up between 9:00 and 10:00 p.m. to move, and the weather was absolutely raging," Osborne says. They are wrapped in their thin Mylar blankets, which emit a deafening vibration that sounds like a snare drum being struck hundreds of times per second. Their backs are to the wind, and they find it overwhelming to stand in the midst of such audible and physical power. Fredrickson adjusts his grip on his blanket ever so slightly, loses hold of one side, and watches as this cherished item is ripped from his other hand and disappears into the darkness. "I don't know how to explain it," Osborne says, "but there was a feeling of finality when that happened."

Disheartened, the pair retrieve their packs and remove additional clothing from them. After returning to the chamber, Fredrickson takes off his shell pants, puts on his three-season hiking pants, and replaces the shell pants over them. Osborne dons additional long underwear and socks. The clothing they are already wearing is damp, and they find that the additional layers are damp as well.

Mount Washington Observatory Surface Weather Observations (10:00 to 11:00 p.m.): Temperature -12°F; winds out of the west averaging 71 mph; visibility 0 miles, fog/blowing snow; windchill -53°F. Peak wind gust: 95 mph.

According to National Weather Service radar, the relentless snowfall finally ends around 9:00 p.m., and the frozen fog and clouds clear the ridge of the Franconia Range. Will the window be open for escape the next time Fredrickson and Osborne emerge from shelter?

Mount Washington Observatory Surface Weather Observations (11:00 p.m. to 12:00 a.m.): Temperature -14°F; winds out of the west averaging 74 mph; visibility 0 miles, fog/blowing snow; windchill -56°F. Peak wind gust: 91 mph.

The end of the snowfall allows state Department of Transportation plow operators to make progress with road clearing in Franconia Notch, as noted in their log: "Center of pavement partly bare. Moderate drifting. Heavy winds. Some icy spots."

Mount Washington Observatory Surface Weather Observations (12:00 to 1:00 a.m.): Temperature -16°F; winds out of the west averaging 77 mph; visibility 1/16th of a mile, fog/blowing snow; windchill -60°F. Peak wind gust: 96 mph.

Fredrickson and Osborne's remaining food, which consists of several Clif Bars, is frozen solid and inedible. The hot chocolate they've been sipping conservatively for the past few hours has also frozen solid. They have not eaten since sharing the Hershey's Bar almost eight hours before and have had nothing substantial to drink since downing chai tea when they first arrived at the outcropping. Their ability to stay properly fueled and hydrated to preserve warmth and help them eventually bail out across the ridge and down the mountain is fading.

"They really couldn't get any nourishment in them, which would have been very beneficial," says Todd Bogardus. "It certainly would have gotten their furnaces refueled. Their food was all frozen, their water was frozen, so there was clearly some misjudgment. A lot of people don't understand that food and water can freeze even on a day hike. Little techniques like stuffing things into the middle of your clothes or shaking your fluids every now and then can help keep them from freezing. When solid food freezes, it takes a lot of time to thaw out, unlike something like gorp, which is pliable. It's all good food until it freezes."

Mount Washington Observatory Surface Weather Observations (1:00 to 2:00 a.m.): Temperature -17°F; winds out of the west averaging 74 mph; visibility 1/16 of a mile, fog/blowing snow; windchill -60°F. Peak wind gust: 91 mph.

At about 1:00 a.m. Monday, the friends roll out of the chamber for the third time in ten hours to move around. Osborne is enthusiastic about what he sees. "The skies were clear. I could see the stars and the moon. It wasn't super bright, but it was a peaceful moment," he recalls.

The moon is in its waxing crescent phase with 13 percent illumination. It's not glowing by any means, but there's enough reflection off the snow for Osborne to see more terrain than the two have seen in almost seventeen hours. "It was idyllic," he says. "You could see the moonlight over the Pemigewasset Wilderness."

The two wonder if this might be their chance. "Should we make a run for it? Should we hike out?" Osborne asks. They deliberate on the landing as winds bellow through the now visible terrain around them and decide that a bailout at this point, in complete darkness, is too hazardous. Once again, they return to the chamber, where fatigue starts to take over.

Mount Washington Observatory Surface Weather Observations (2:00 to 3:00 a.m.): Temperature -18°F; winds out of the west averaging 77 mph; visibility 1/16 of a mile, fog/blowing snow; windchill -62°F. Peak wind gust: 94 mph.

The two friends lie next to each other in silence. They're digging deeply inside themselves to make it to sunrise—and a possible escape from their confinement. It's been twelve hours since the mayhem on the ridge that drove them into this cramped space. Other than during their three short exits from the chamber, their bodies have been in constant contact with heat-sapping stone. It's now gotten very damp inside, and their clothing has never had a chance to dry after hours of exertion on Falling Waters Trail and their time on the ridge.

Hypothermia has been lurking over their shoulders for most of the previous day and night, and it has finally found its way into the chamber. "My fingers were painful; they were way too cold," recalls Osborne. "And my feet felt like ice." This is evidence that his body is restricting blood flow to the outer extremities in order to keep his vital organs warm and functioning properly. Fredrickson may be experiencing similar effects of cooling, but he doesn't mention anything about it to Osborne.

In fact, Osborne believes Fredrickson is sleeping during several of these quiet hours. But that doesn't mean he's immune to the cold. He's been lying on freezing granite for hours and so has been continuously losing body heat to the rock below him. Although conductive heat loss alone is rarely a major cause of hypothermia, according to Giesbrecht and Wilkerson, it can worsen the cooling that is happening in other ways. The two have lost heat every time they've left the shelter into the bitter windchill. This is particularly true of Osborne, whose boots are not insulated for winter hiking.

Mount Washington Observatory Surface Weather Observations (3:00 to 4:00 a.m.): Temperature -19°F; winds out of the west averaging 75 mph; visibility 1/16 of a mile, fog/blowing snow; windchill -64°F. Peak wind gust: 90 mph.

Because Fredrickson and Osborne are losing heat they can't regain, they are now at a much higher risk of developing critical heat loss if they choose to bail out of the shelter and expose themselves to the severe windchill on their planned hike down. That risk is further exacerbated by their damp clothing. "They did try to put on what extra clothes they had, but that clothing had gotten wet because they didn't have plastic bags or anything in their packs to keep it dry," says Todd Bogardus. "It was a classic recipe for hypothermia."

What the two hikers are facing as they prepare to head outside is known as convective heat loss, a leading cause of hypothermia. According to Giesbrecht and Wilkerson, it occurs when air or water that has a temperature below that of the body contacts the skin, takes warmth from the skin, and then moves away. Depending on the temperature difference between the air and the skin, and on the speed of the air, the heat loss can be major. "Fortunately, clothing can greatly reduce this type of heat loss," write Giesbrecht and Wilkerson. "Insulating clothing forms small pockets in which air is trapped—the essence of thermal insulation—and windproof outer garments prevent displacement of air within and between the layers" (p.33). Unfortunately for Fredrickson and Osborne, wet clothing loses its insulating ability, leading to the dangerous convective cooling the authors describe.

In wilderness medicine circles, hypothermia is known as "the silent killer in the backcountry." If left unmanaged or untreated, it tightens its grip on the physiological and cognitive functions of its victims and methodically escorts them into oblivion. Hypothermia is cunning and opportunistic. It subtly exploits the smallest mistakes and is ruthless and unforgiving in its punishment. It is recorded as the official cause of death of numerous hikers and climbers in the White Mountains. Even those who are able to break free of its hold are often left with peripheral injuries—both physical and emotional.

The damage hypothermia inflicts is not restricted to the victims alone. Hiking companions, friends, family members, and rescuers will feel the emotional impact of that damage. In fortunate cases, when there is a survivor, that may involve compassionate care and learning to adapt to the victim's altered circumstances. But in worst scenarios, hypothermia can kill its victims, opening up a difficult path for those left behind.

As dawn approaches, Fredrickson and Osborne have not moved in four hours and will not until they leave their shelter when they attempt to self-rescue at sunrise. "We both dozed here and there, but there was no significant sleep on my part," says Osborne. Between shallow and short periods of sleep, each man retreats within himself. Active discussion slows, then stops. Suffering has now found its way in.

XIV
OVERDUE

"The woods are lovely, dark and deep,
But I have promises to keep,
And miles to go before I sleep,
And miles to go before I sleep."

—Robert Frost

Mount Washington Observatory
Monday, Feb. 11, 2008
4:09 a.m.

Mount Washington Observatory Surface Weather Observations (4:00 to 5:00 a.m.): Temperature -20°F; winds out of the west averaging 65 mph; visibility 1/16 of a mile, fog/blowing snow; windchill -63°F. Peak wind gust: 83 mph.

With updated weather models from the National Weather Service, weather observer Stacey Kawecki sits at her computer station and updates the Current Conditions, 24-Hour Statistics, and the all-important Forecast Discussion. Just as she did twenty-four hours earlier, Kawecki posts a cautionary message at the top of the Observatory's web page.

> **Windchill warning through 7 p.m. tonight. Windchill advisory 7 p.m. tonight–7 a.m. tomorrow**

The discussion that follows promises another long day of high winds and dangerously low temperatures, especially on the higher summits:

Low pressure moving into the Canadian Maritimes dragged an arctic cold front across the region, setting off snow and plummeting temperatures into the upper teens below zero. Strong high pressure descending from Canada is swiftly moving in, and as a result, the pressure gradient across New

England is significant, and winds have increased quite a bit. As the low continues to travel northeast, and remain close to the coastline, wraparound moisture will contribute to upslope snow shower activity today. However, with the high building from the west, the summits should see some clearing tonight, and winds will diminish overnight and through tomorrow. Another disturbance will send high clouds our way, on southwesterly flow, and temperatures will rise. With the diminishing wind, and increasing temperatures, windchill values will be improving. There is a windchill warning in effect through 7 p.m. tonight, and a windchill advisory in effect 7 p.m. tonight through 7 a.m. tomorrow. Today, freezing fog and blowing snow will cause whiteout conditions on the higher summits.

Franconia Ridge
4:30 a.m.

Fredrickson and Osborne are spending their last hours in their temporary overnight shelter. Had things gone as originally planned, Fredrickson would at this moment be unlocking the door to the building that houses the bus he's scheduled to drive this morning from Concord, N.H., to Boston's South Station. Once inside, he'd turn on the large overhead lights and see the Motor Coach International bus assigned to him. He'd enter the unoccupied dispatch office and check the log to confirm he had the correct bus and see if a note had been left with any specific tasks he'd need to do, such as meet another driver at Logan Airport or switch buses along the way.

Fredrickson would conduct a pre-trip inspection by doing a walk around the bus before boarding it. Then he'd walk down the aisle to make sure everything was ready. He'd start the ignition, crank the heat, and pull the bus out of the bay to run a pre-check of the vehicle's directional signals, lights, and flashers. He'd also "air up" the vehicle's air brakes. By 4:45 a.m., he'd have completed his inspection, and with the dash vents finally throwing off some welcome heat, he'd make the thirty-minute drive southbound from the corporate office and maintenance garage to the North Londonderry Transportation Center at Exit 5 on I-93. During the winter months, he would make it a point to arrive at this first stop fifteen minutes early so passengers waiting outside could get out of the cold.

North Londonderry Transportation Center
Monday, Feb. 11, 2008
5:15 a.m.

Gary Rasmussen stands at the curb, waiting to step onto the bus that will take him to Boston, where he works for the American Meteorological Society. It's 7°F, and winds are blowing hard and steadily out of the west/northwest at 13 mph, with gusts in the 20s. "The chill went right through you," he recalls.

The frigid air causes Rasmussen and his fellow commuters to turn their backs to the wind and anxiously count the minutes before their bus will arrive. The regulars look forward to the bus pulling up and the door swinging open, when they'll receive a warm "Good morning" from their regular driver for the past year, Fred Fredrickson.

"Fred was a good driver in that he was considerate of the passengers," Rasmussen says. "Opening the doors early was nice, especially in the winter, when it was so cold outside."

The following day, in a Feb. 12, 2008 post on his *Weather and Climate Community* blog, Rasmussen will describe Fredrickson as "[o]ne of the best Concord Coach drivers—always friendly, and always early…. Always, that is, until yesterday morning…. Not showing up, and not calling in, is not in character."

Sure enough, on this Monday, Fredrickson's bus doesn't arrive early, nor does it arrive by the time it is supposed to be departing for the Bay State. The ticket agent that morning tries calling Fredrickson on his cell phone, but there's no answer. He then tries calling Concord Coach Lines, but no one there knows where Fredrickson is.

Fredrickson's friend and coworker, Ernie Brochu, says everyone knew how reliable their friend was. "Fred was just one of those guys," says Brochu. "You didn't have to worry; he was going to be there." So Bill is both confused and concerned by his absence.

With still no sign of or word from Fredrickson, the 6:00 a.m. bus pulls up to the curb. Passengers from the two scheduled departures are now waiting. They line up and load onto the bus for a cramped commute to Boston.

While Fredrickson's absence is troublesome, it's still too early for anyone at Concord Coach to imagine anything dire. One missed route creates a ripple effect for bus routes, and steps must be taken to maintain continuity of operations. So, in the early hours, much of the immediate energy is being spent managing strategic problems.

"The assistant operations manager would have been looking at the schedule to see how Fred's bus would impact the day and start coordinating that," says Osborne. "That would be the priority. I was told later that an initial assumption was that Fred was probably stuck in his driveway because of the overnight snowstorm or had slid off the road on his way in and had no cell service. Everyone figured he'd call in eventually."

Osborne told the operations manager he spoke with on Saturday night where he and Fredrickson were hiking the following morning, but the operations manager is not working today. Ticket agent Christine Northrup, who encountered Fredrickson and Osborne at the Concord Transportation Center the previous morning, is working elsewhere at her full-time job. Other coworkers who may know that Fredrickson and Osborne had planned to hike over the weekend are not yet at work and won't be for at least a couple of hours.

Franconia Ridge
5:30 a.m.

Mount Washington Observatory Surface Weather Observations (5:00 to 6:00 a.m.): Temperature -21°F; winds out of the west averaging 66 mph; visibility 1/16 of a mile, fog/blowing snow; windchill -65°F. Peak wind gust: 85 mph.

It's bad enough if you yourself are in trouble. But it can feel even more excruciating if you are stuck and know you're considered missing. You know exactly where you are, but no one else does, and you have no way of notifying anyone. The passage of time increases not only your own fear but the fear of those down below who care about you. You want to put an immediate end to the suffering and speculation. You're exhausted, hungry, and cold, and your sense of urgency overpowers your need to be patient. You bypass calculation and move rashly toward what you perceive as resolution. Too often in these kinds of situations, acting more on emotion than on reason, you push ahead at your peril.

Both men are awake. For Osborne, this finally feels like a new day, one that offers the chance to get back home. The two both recognize the impact their absence is having, and will continue to have, on operations at the company. "Oh, they're looking for me down in Concord," says Fredrickson at 5:30 a.m. Half in jest, Osborne reacts to his own situation: "Goddammit, now payroll's going to be messed up." Even though he sometimes calls in to his office between 6:00 and 6:30 a.m. to check in with staff, he doesn't think it will alarm anyone at this point if he doesn't do it today.

Their discussion turns to who at work might connect the dots and sound the alarm. "We talked about who knew where we might be," recalls Osborne. "We're overdue, and no one has heard from us. Are they going to put two and two together?"

They identify Ernie Brochu and Steve Harbert as those having some knowledge of their planned hike. Brochu will be working in Boston today, so they believe Harbert is the likeliest friend to figure out that something went wrong on the hike.

Osborne is confident that it's only a matter of time before their colleagues determine they're overdue at work and call for help. He wonders briefly if maybe they should stay put but doesn't make the suggestion because he wants out of the situation just as much as Fredrickson does. "When the window was there, we felt we needed to take it, because there was a lot of exposure to the weather, and we needed to get down," he says. "We thought if we could get below treeline we'd be fine."

Sunrise is fifty-three minutes away, and the chamber is still an impenetrable shade of black. It's time for them to get up and prepare so they can be on the move the moment the sun breaches the ridgeline of the Presidential Range to the east. "I clearly remember checking my watch. It was 6:00 a.m., the time we agreed upon the night before to start the process of getting ready to hike out," says Osborne.

Fredrickson reaches into the darkness to his left and feels for each snowshoe. Finding both, he positions them flat on the floor of the chamber and starts to slide toward the exit. Osborne hears his friend suddenly stop moving. It turns out Fredrickson's motion has been halted by an alarming new variable.

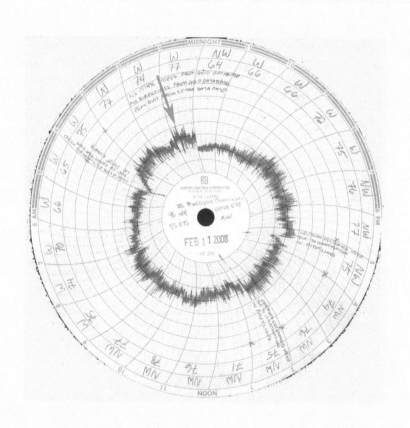

This is an image of the chart from the Hays Recorder at the Mount Washington Observatory on Feb. 11, 2008. The numbers in the outer rim represent the time of day, the average hourly wind direction, and the average hourly wind speed. The chart indicated a peak wind gust of 96 mph at 12:48 a.m. (see red arrow), and two more between 8:00 and 10:00 a.m. Winds throughout Monday were in the mid-to-high 70s, with gusts in the 80s and 90s.

XV
THE FINAL SHIVER

*"The problem with a steel boat is that the crisis curve starts
out gradually and quickly becomes exponential. The more
trouble she's in, the more trouble she's likely to get in, and the
less capable she is of getting out of it, which is an acceleration
of catastrophe that's almost impossible to reverse."*

—*Sebastian Junger,* The Perfect Storm

Franconia Ridge
Monday, Feb. 11, 2008
6:00 a.m.

*Mount Washington Observatory Surface Weather Observations (6:00 to 7:00
a.m.): Temperature -20°F; winds out of the west averaging 70 mph; visibility
1/16 of a mile, fog/blowing snow; windchill -64°F. Peak wind gust: 82 mph.*

Any thought of elation either man might have been anticipating
is suddenly dashed. In the five hours since Fredrickson and Osborne
last exited the chamber, strong sustained winds, combined with
hurricane-force gusts, have been at work on the opposite side of the
ridgeline. Heavy amounts of fresh snow have been extracted from the
windward side and deposited on the leeward side, where Fredrickson
and Osborne have been sheltering in place. Since 1:00 a.m., when they
retreated back into the chamber, the entrance has been buried in
approximately 18 inches of slab-like snow.

"Winds in any slightly sheltered spot like this one on the lee side
of the ridge are ideal for drifting, which starts to occur with winds at
around thirty to forty miles per hour," says Tom Padham of the
Mount Washington Observatory.

Fredrickson and Osborne are blindsided by this additional layer
of confinement. Although rattled, they are quick to turn on their
headlamps and seek a solution together. Osborne turns onto his left
side as much as he can, and Fredrickson, using his left arm, starts to
hook chunks of snow out of the heavy drift and into the shelter. "The
snow was packed right next to Fred," says Osborne. "For us to get
out, there was no place to move the snow except in between the two
of us."

Fredrickson slides the snow up and over his torso and piles it in the gap between the two men. As the pile of snow between them gets higher, Osborne's fatigue-fueled anxiety builds. "It was the most trapped and claustrophobic feeling I'd ever had," he recalls.

Once Fredrickson digs himself out, he sets to work to free his friend. On hands and knees, he scoops snow out of the entranceway, while Osborne pushes it out to him. Years later, thoughts associated with being temporarily buried alive still haunt Osborne. "I've had moments since then when I've thought what would have happened if Fred had perished during the night," he says. "There's no way I would have been able to get him out, and I was thinking that I would have likely died in there, too."

The physical and emotional effort required to extract themselves from the chamber is taxing, weakening them for the grueling hike out. "I think about all the energy Fred expended to get us out of there," says Osborne. "It was hard work for both of us and probably contributed to our decline later."

The pair's energy stores were already largely depleted before they had to dig out, so this couldn't have come at a worse time. In his book *Deep Survival: Who Lives, Who Dies, and Why* (Norton Publishing, 2003), author Laurence Gonzales explains what can happen to us when we're on the edge of exhaustion: "A survival situation is a ticking clock," he writes. "You have only so much stored energy..., and every time you exert yourself, you're using it up" (p.179).

Fredrickson and Osborne are probably operating on vapors at this point. They are without food or water and haven't had either for over twelve hours. Their bodies have been relying on fat reserves to generate body heat.

Standing together on the landing boulder, as their rapid exhalations freeze in the relentless arctic air, the friends pause to refocus and attempt to recharge. Although cold and fatigued, they are pleased to see a brighter sky than the one they were smothered by the day before. "We were in the sun, and it was a bright, blue winter sky," recalls Osborne." I can remember thinking, 'This isn't going to be a bad hike back.'"

Still, winds remain near hurricane force, gusts are belligerent, and the windchill level is homicidal. But even amid blowing snow that is moving through the air like millions of pieces of shredded packing foam, at least they can see. It's been sixteen hours since they've had such a calming sense of spatial awareness. The ridgeline behind them and the Pemigewasset Wilderness below are in view. Mount Washington and its surrounding peaks to the east are buried in blowing snow and cloud cover—but discernable. The range looks enraged from where they sit. If Mount Washington is the "Home of the World's Worst Weather," then Franconia Ridge is its guest house—smaller but equally undomesticated. The two hikers know they're not out of the woods yet, literally or figuratively, but once back up on the ridge, they'll at least be able to see the treeline that will point them downhill.

Fredrickson retrieves his snowshoes and struggles into each binding. "Fred eventually got his snowshoes on, but he had a lot of trouble doing so," recalls Osborne, who is having difficulties of his own. He locates his crampons buried in snow and finds he can't manage to attach them to his boots. "When we got up and started moving, my joints weren't working well," he recalls. "It was the coldest my feet had ever felt. I really couldn't feel them; they were like concrete. We struggled to get our boots firmly tied and do the other prep for hiking out. But I wasn't able to get my crampons back on because it wasn't possible for me to do fine motor activity." The gloves Osborne intends to wear are frozen solid, so Fredrickson gives him his mittens, and he himself puts on gloves.

The powerful low-pressure area of the day before is now in the Canadian Maritimes, and an arctic high-pressure area is now enveloping New England. The cold stretches far back into the Midwest.

Sometime between 6:30 and 7:00 a.m., Fredrickson and Osborne gingerly put on their packs and step off the landing boulder to execute their self-rescue. There's no conversation. Each has turned inward, well aware of the grind that awaits them. Despite their condition, which they were likely not completely aware of at the time, Osborne says, "Monday morning felt survivable. There was nothing at that point that signified death to me. Had we had reasonable shelter, a meal, and a sleeping bag, I think we would have been more energized. It still would have been really difficult to get back, but the outcome might have been different."

Uncharacteristically, Osborne finds himself out front on the walk across the slope back to the ridge trail. Fredrickson has started slowly.

"I was now the leader," says Osborne. "That was unusual, and I was concerned about Fred."

As Osborne reaches the exposed ridgeline, he collides head-on with the unimpeded wind. "I can remember getting up onto the ridge and saying, 'Holy shit, it's still windy, and it's colder,'" he says. He immediately pulls his goggles down over his eyes but realizes they have frozen. "It was obvious I wasn't going to be able to use them," he recalls. Fredrickson's goggles are frozen as well. Without goggles, the two will have tremendous difficulty coping with this new variable. Wind and cold at this level will wreak havoc on a hiker's exposed eyes.

In a few moments, Fredrickson joins Osborne on the trail. There's still no discussion, only motion. Fredrickson reclaims the lead position and heads toward the junction with Falling Waters Trail. Relieved to see his friend running point again, Osborne falls in. Winds are at their back as they move south. While predominantly out of the west, they are starting their shift to the northwest.

"As they get down toward Little Haystack, the winds are west/northwest, with some sheltering from the Kinsmans," says Tom Padham. "But there's also funneling taking place from the northerly wind. Funneling is enhancement of the wind due to the shape of the terrain, and Franconia Notch is a natural funnel for a northwesterly wind. As they make their way, they're likely experiencing wind speeds of about seventy miles per hour."

Concord Coach Lines
Concord, N. H.
Between 7:00 and 8:00 a.m.

Mount Washington Observatory Surface Weather Observations (7:00 to 8:00 a.m.): Temperature -19°F; winds out of the west averaging 74 mph; visibility 1/16 of a mile, fog/blowing snow; windchill -63°F. Peak wind gust: 91 mph.

While Fredrickson and Osborne move southward along the ridgeline, things at the bus company's corporate office are moving as well. Fredrickson's absence is now of great concern to his coworkers. According to Ernie Brochu, it is Craig Middleton who arrives at work and concludes that his friends might be in trouble. "Craig knew they were supposed to do a winter hike of Lafayette together," says Brochu. "He drove from the office over to the Concord terminal and found James's car still parked there. That was the red flag."

At around this time, the Franconia Notch Parkway is getting weather-battered once again. Road crews are doing what they can to stay ahead of it, but winds ripping down through the Notch are causing drifting in the roadways. At 7:55 a.m., Lincoln Police are called to The Flume area to deal with multiple vehicles off the road. Accident response and aggressive road treatment will continue throughout the morning and into the afternoon.

Franconia Ridge
After 8:00 a.m.

Mount Washington Observatory Surface Weather Observations (8:00 to 9:00 a.m.): Temperature -19°F; winds out of the west averaging 75 mph; visibility 1/16 of a mile, fog/blowing snow; windchill -64°F. Peak wind gust: 96 mph.

The winds have a soulless brutality to them. Gusts on Mount Washington are at or over 90 mph. Fredrickson and Osborne are continuously pushed by sustained winds and, without warning, violently shoved from behind by a force that makes a childhood bully seem gentle. They follow the narrow ridge southward.

According to Osborne, the walking is difficult, but "everything is okay at that point." The expansive views, invisible to them yesterday, no longer matter. Although he's wearing a balaclava, Osborne tries desperately to shield his face and eyes from the bite of the wind. The ridge levels off and widens. Little Haystack is in sight. At this point, Osborne estimates they are two-thirds of the way back. This would put them under a quarter of a mile from Falling Waters Trail and treeline.

But their pace is slowing even further as the cold continues to work through them, sapping energy. The wide gap that has separated these two on nearly every previous hike is now as narrow as the infinitesimal space between them back in the shelter. Cold has become the great equalizer. As they approach a large landform just north of Little Haystack, where the trail bears ever so slightly to the right, Fredrickson goes left—off the trail.

New Hampshire Fish and Game
District 2 Office
New Hampton, N.H.
8:30 a.m.

Having discovered Osborne's frost-entombed Chevy Cavalier, staff members at Concord Coach Lines immediately notify New Hampshire Fish and Game to report that their colleagues are overdue. At 8:30 a.m., Lt. Jim Goss contacts Steve Harbert at Concord Coach Lines to gather more information about the missing men. Goss is in charge of District 2 but is covering District 3 for Lt. Todd Bogardus, team leader of the Advanced Search and Rescue Team, who is off duty. According to the Fish and Game Incident Report, Harbert tells Goss that the pair had gone for a planned day hike over the weekend and hadn't been heard from or shown up for work. Harbert says he believes their intent was to ascend Falling Waters Trail, proceed north on Franconia Ridge to Mount Lafayette, and descend Old Bridle Path. He tells Goss that no one knows whether they departed on Saturday or Sunday, and no one has a copy of their itinerary.

After hanging up with Harbert, Goss contacts Conservation Officer Sam Sprague with information about Fredrickson, the vehicle he is driving, and the hiking plans they've been able to suss out. It will be up to Sprague to try to find the car the two men used to drive to the Notch.

The attempt to locate Fredrickson's car at a trailhead is the first step in this rescue attempt. "The first thing we have to do is investigate what we have, what's going on," says Todd Bogardus. "We have to find the vehicle, if it's even out there." The absence of a shared hiking itinerary is now causing a delay in the actual rescue efforts as officials work to fill in details. The difficult road conditions will add further delay.

In a Feb. 13, 2008 interview with Paula Tracy of the *New Hampshire Union Leader*, Concord Coach Lines President Harry Blunt said, "These guys were both bachelors. Normally when you don't show up at home when you're due from a hike, a search is begun by 8:00 p.m. or so, but it never happened. The sad part is that instead of the search beginning at 8:00 that night, it wasn't until about midday the next day before the search was on."

Todd Bogardus provides a technical perspective in line with Blunt's observations:

> Had they left an itinerary with someone, and New Hampshire Fish and Game had been notified [on Sunday], an initial response would have occurred because of the bad weather. Their vehicle would have been confirmed, and the investigative phase would have started. Initially, putting searchers on the trails may have occurred at least below treeline to locate any signs, but most definitely an early morning response would have been organized and under way much sooner If people were put on the trails the first evening, that would have broken out the snowpack sooner as well, which would have also sped up our access to treeline the next day.

Sprague, who at the time of the call is not in the immediate area of Franconia Notch, asks local law enforcement to check the trailhead parking lots in that area for a yellow Saturn belonging to Fredrickson. But local agencies are hampered by the weather and busy responding to accidents and other calls for service. State plow crews are primarily focused on the main thoroughfares and have not had the opportunity to plow out the ramps and parking lots of the Notch. High snowbanks from road-clearing operations and deep snow cover have made them inaccessible by vehicle anyway. Feeling the urgency of the situation, Sprague immediately heads to Franconia Notch to see if he himself can locate Fredrickson's Saturn.

Franconia Ridge
Approximately 9:00 a.m.

Mount Washington Observatory Surface Weather Observations (9:00 to 10:00 a.m.): Temperature -17°F; winds have shifted and are now out of the northwest averaging 77 mph; visibility 1/16 of a mile, fog/blowing snow; windchill -61°F. Peak wind gust: 96 mph.

Fredrickson and Osborne are not far from treeline. But factoring in what they've already endured and will continue to endure as they proceed, it might as well be miles away. Both men are exhausted.

Osborne is trying to keep his right eye from freezing shut, without much luck. For most of the traverse back, he's been squinting and turning the right side of his face away from the wind.

"Walking in even a sixty-mile-per-hour wind is going to drain you, and the longer you stay in it, the worse it's going to get," says Tom Padham. "It's also going to dehydrate you, because the wind is actually pulling moisture away from your skin and cooling you off more rapidly. It's why we have windchill values, because it's putting a lot of strain on your body. The stronger the winds, the greater the strain."

Dr. Murray Hamlet, an expert in cold-weather injuries, believes the two men were in the throes of a great physical struggle. "When the winds go up, the threat goes up, and your ability to defend against the cold goes way down," he says. "When they bailed out, they just didn't start from a good place body temperature-wise, especially with damp clothing and not having consumed food or water."

Following the left side of the landform, Fredrickson leads Osborne down the slope, where they tuck in beside a granite rock for a rest. Winds entering the Notch at Cannon and Lafayette are squeezed through the terrain and spill up onto and over the ridgeline. Winds, now even more powerful than they were when they entered the Notch, assault the pair in the pocket where they rest. Fredrickson, standing about 4 feet from the rock and more exposed than Osborne,

faces east toward the Pemigewasset Wilderness. His back is to the wind. Osborne has the rock at his back and is more sheltered than his friend. Both comment on how cold they feel.

Fredrickson hands Osborne his trekking poles so he can adjust his snowshoes. Before doing so, he delivers what Osborne now refers to as "the disaster conversation." Fredrickson's eyes lock onto Osborne's. "We're in some deep shit," he tells his friend. This is a gut punch to Osborne, delivered plainly and coming from a good friend and hiking mentor. It must have been excruciating to utter and terrifying to hear.

Fredrickson removes one of his gloves to make the adjustment to his snowshoes. Winds pouring over and around the landform snatch the glove from his gripped hand. It disappears toward the Pemi. Fredrickson makes no effort to replace the glove with a spare, even though Osborne knows he likely has additional pairs in his pack. Concerned, Osborne removes the outer shells of the mittens Fredrickson gave him earlier and passes them to his friend. Seeking to replace the missing shells, Osborne removes his backpack, only to find that his spare gloves are frozen. "It was so hard to move my arms; it was so cold," he recalls. Osborne puts the gloves on anyway and watches as Fredrickson tries to adjust a strap on his snowshoes. "He was completely unable to manipulate his fingers," says Osborne. Sure enough, Fredrickson makes no progress with the strap and stands back up.

What happens next seems surreal. "This gust of wind came and lifted Fred up off the ground," says Osborne, amazement still in his voice these years later. "It moved him a short distance south past me, and gently put him down to my right. It lasted maybe one or two seconds."

Osborne has thought a good deal about what that moment represented. "It was as gentle as could be, but I think it was Mother Nature saying, 'I'm still in charge.'"

In the process of being lifted, Fredrickson loses his right snowshoe. "It just wasn't working for him," says Osborne. "I retrieved his snowshoe and brought it over to him. Now the focus was on how he was going to get it back on. As he tried, his mitten shells were blown away, and he was left with only his liners on."

Fredrickson doesn't appear fazed by the loss of his mitten shells. "Oh, I'll be fine with just the liners," he tells Osborne. But his friend is worried, because Fredrickson is not sounding logical. In retrospect, it seems clear that Fredrickson is now entering the late stages of hypothermia, when rational thought becomes compromised. He can't get his right snowshoe on and so must abandon his left one as well, making it even more difficult for him to move on.

The two friends, now in the clutches of a full-blown crisis, hunker down at the granite rock. While both are having trouble marshaling rational thought, it is Fredrickson who's in a deeper state of decline. If they don't get moving soon, neither will move again. "I was insistent that we had to get moving, and that we had to get to the trailhead," Osborne recalls.

He makes a move to put on his backpack and is alarmed. "My arms were so frozen I couldn't get my backpack on. My shoulders were not functioning." Fredrickson cannot help him, because he is fighting his own battles. Making no progress and not wanting to carry his backpack in the wind, Osborne decides to leave it behind. He is mindful enough to remove his camera from inside and puts it in his jacket pocket, abandoning everything else.

"At the time, it felt bad to leave the pack because I'd done thirty-nine of the forty-eight peaks with it," says Osborne. "But other than the camera, I wasn't concerned about what was left inside it."

Fredrickson slowly ascends the slope with Osborne close behind. The pair rejoins the Franconia Ridge Trail and with it the unrelenting arctic winds. They descend southward along a short, gentle slope and step onto the final two-tenths of a mile to the trail junction and treeline.

"When we left the outcropping, I think we were in the full and maybe final throes of hypothermia," Osborne acknowledges. "I knew getting to treeline meant safety, but the idea of walking back, making a right turn, and walking another hundred-plus feet to the trees was unimaginable."

XVI
THE COLD GOODBYE

"There is a certain thrill to friendship, and there is certainly a certain thrill to friendship under risk, to shared risk. So, people have very profound emotions up to the point where it gets so dramatic that little is left."

—*Daniel Kahneman, author of* Thinking, Fast and Slow

Lafayette Place Parking Area
Monday, Feb. 11, 2008
Approximately 10:30 a.m.

Mount Washington Observatory Surface Weather Observations (10:00 to 11:00 a.m.): Temperature -14°F; winds out of the northwest averaging 78 mph; visibility 1/16 of a mile, fog/blowing snow; windchill -57°F. Peak wind gust: 91 mph.

Conservation Officer Sam Sprague parks his cruiser as far off to the side of the Franconia Notch Parkway as possible, climbs the high, sand- and salt-infused snowbank, and trudges through the deep snow into the trailhead parking lot. Although the setting appears peaceful, it's windy and bitterly cold here. The near-hurricane force winds are creating ground-blizzard conditions on the exposed slopes and ridgelines of the higher peaks surrounding Sprague.

As he reaches the top of the lot where it splits into two parking areas, his eyes are drawn to a single car parked in the north lot. Though it's covered in snow, he can see that it's a yellow Saturn sedan. Sprague is highly trained and has located vehicles under these circumstances many times before, so he remains calm and focused. It's obvious the car has been sitting here throughout the two-day storm. He makes his way over to it and brushes snow from the rear bumper, where he finds the New Hampshire license plate. It's definitely Fredrickson's car. At that moment, the preliminary investigation turns into a full-on rescue mission.

Concord Coach Lines
Concord, N.H.
Mid-to-late morning

Word of their coworkers' situation is making its way through Concord Coach Lines. Ernie Brochu is working at the Boston terminal when he receives the news. "I was getting a flurry of calls all morning. James's car was in Concord, and Fred's car was found in Franconia, so at that point we knew it wasn't good," he recalls. Christine Northrup, who worked at the Concord terminal the day before and was the last employee to see Fredrickson and Osborne, is shaken by what she learns. "One of my coworkers called and told me that Fred and James hadn't been to work," she says. "My stomach dropped. I was hoping everything was okay." Even though she is working elsewhere, Northrup stays tuned in. "I kept checking in with people to see if anyone had heard anything. I went home that night and watched the coverage of the search on the news."

Steve Harbert drives north to Franconia Notch to provide any additional information he can about his friends to New Hampshire Fish and Game personnel.

Franconia Ridge
Mid-to-late morning

Fredrickson is leading a painstakingly slow charge toward Little Haystack, and Osborne is feeling ambivalent about it. Without crampons on his boots, he frequently slips and takes painful falls onto the icy trail. "The wind kept pushing me over," he recalls. "I'd just fall. I didn't know it was coming."

Fredrickson is also falling frequently. At times, both men crawl because of the brutal gusts that seem to come out of nowhere. Osborne sees that Fredrickson has come to a stop ahead of him. When he reaches him, he notices his friend's eyes are frozen shut.

"I can't see!" Fredrickson yells over the wind. But Osborne notes again that he seems strangely unbothered by this latest crisis. Osborne guides Fredrickson's right hand onto his own left shoulder. He tells Fredrickson to keep his hand on his shoulder and to stay with him, that he'll guide him the rest of the way.

They are now on the upswing toward the summit of Little Haystack and nearing the junction with Falling Waters. Although they seem to be making progress, it's not long before Fredrickson loses physical contact with his friend. Osborne, himself deteriorating, walks a short distance before he realizes the disconnect and turns to see where Fredrickson is.

"I looked back, and Fred was crawling," he recalls. Having veered off the trail, Fredrickson is having great difficulty making his way.

"I walked back toward him," Osborne says. "By the time I got to him, he was on his right side in a fetal position with his back to the wind."

Osborne can barely bend at the waist to get closer to his friend, who is still wearing his backpack. He screams over the wind, "Fred, you have to get up!"

Nothing.

"Fred, we have got to keep moving, we're almost to treeline!"

Still no response.

"We've got to keep moving, Fred!"

Fredrickson responds by rolling from his side onto his back. As Osborne watches, his friend's hands clench into tight fists. "Oh, my

God, they're going to take my hands!" Fredrickson wails, as he holds his hands out in front of him. It is a moment of pure anguish and one that still deeply affects Osborne today. "Our hands make us human, and when Fred said that, it was as if his humanity was gone."

"Fred, you've got to get up!" Osborne pleads.

Fredrickson utters a moan and goes silent. Lying on his back, motionless, his head pointing in the direction of Cannon Mountain, he appears lifeless. The exposure and lack of movement will further thicken the blood slogging through his constricted veins, arteries, and vital organs. His ultra-lean body mass, which has allowed him to move fast on mountain trails, is now working against him. He has not been able to maintain a safe level of body heat and is now in critical condition.

It is impossible to know exactly what time hypothermia will claim Fred Fredrickson, but death is not far away. As he looks down at his friend, Osborne feels desperation take hold. "At that point, I felt there was no recovering from this," he says. "It was the end, and there was nothing else that could be done. I was sad about my friend. I was sad my life was ending, that this was how I was going to die. It was so clear to me."

Osborne sobs as he ascends the slope. He's making no effort to link up with Falling Waters Trail, which is now painfully close, or to even seek shelter. "It was a dead man's walk," he says. "I said to myself that I had done the best I could."

Before continuing, Osborne turns and looks back at his friend for one final goodbye. He walks past the trail junction leading down to Falling Waters, and past the summit of Little Haystack. Less than twenty-four hours ago, he and Fredrickson had stood there together, anticipating a long but exhilarating day hike. He walks aimlessly along the scrub line on the southeastern slope. "I said my peace to the world. I apologized to my mother, saying, 'I'm sorry, Mom, that it happened this way.' I went through a list of my regrets, one of which was never having raised a child."

Osborne's next thought takes the form of a vision. "I had this out-of-body experience, where all of a sudden I was up and I could see Fred," he recalls. "It was very clear to me. I was facing the Pemi Wilderness, and I could see Fred lying there. I could see my physical body walking off toward a little ledge, and I knew that was it."

He expresses surprise today that he doesn't remember feeling fearful in that moment. "It was peaceful. There was no pain, no worry, nothing," he says. "I knew that was the end. I'm not a religious person, but I do know there's a greater spirituality."

The vision is erased as Osborne drops into the snow and loses consciousness. Under tremendous duress, the cortex of his brain relinquishes responsibility for managing the situation. It hands control over to his primitive brain and switches off. As Osborne lies there alone on the mountain, it will be up to his primitive brain to keep him alive long enough for any hope of rescue.

XVII
INCIDENT COMMAND

*"When you're doing mountain rescue, you don't take a
doctorate in mountain rescue; you look for somebody who
knows the terrain. It's about context."*

—*Rory Stewart, British environmentalist*

Todd Bogardus Residence
Northern New Hampshire
Monday, Feb. 11, 2008
Around 11:00 a.m.

*Mount Washington Observatory Surface Weather Observations (11:00 a.m. to
12:00 p.m.): Temperature -12°F; winds out of the northwest averaging 76 mph;
visibility 1/16 of a mile, fog/blowing snow; windchill -53°F. Peak wind gust: 90
mph.*

Lt. Todd Bogardus, a nineteen-year veteran of New Hampshire
Fish and Game's Law Enforcement Division and team leader for the
agency's Advanced Search and Rescue Team, is on a welcome day off.
He's catching up on home tasks that tend to accumulate, given the
demands of his profession. Tall and lean, he exudes quiet confidence.
He's methodical in all he does, especially in his role as incident
commander on search and rescue missions.

Throughout the previous weekend, Bogardus has tried to keep
his instincts in check. He knew the weekend weather was going to be
extreme and hoped people would heed the warnings and avoid high
places. "The weather was forecasted probably a week in advance," he
says. "The forecasters said we'd have a major storm coming through
the weekend and to be prepared for it. They were on with this one.
They had it pegged for 2:00 p.m. on Sunday afternoon. It was going
to be serious: high winds, minus-twenty degrees, and large amounts
of snow. I just had this feeling the phone was going to ring at some
point."

Sure enough, his department-issued cell phone rings late Monday morning. Bogardus has been in this job long enough to know this probably isn't good news, and he's right. It's Lt. Jim Goss, who's covering Bogardus's district. Even on his days off, Bogardus is always notified if his team is needed for a major search and rescue mission, and he always responds.

Bypassing niceties, Goss gets right to the point. He has a case involving two missing hikers. The two men are overdue by at least one day, information on their hiking itinerary is sketchy, and one of their cars has been located by Conservation Officer Sam Sprague at the trailhead for Old Bridle Path and Falling Waters in Franconia Notch. Bogardus tells Goss he'll start making calls to coordinate an initial response and then head to the trailhead parking lot, where they'll establish an Incident Command Post. Then he rattles off tasks Goss can do to advance the effort.

As he stands in his kitchen and processes the challenge before him, Bogardus wonders about the missing hikers. "What were they thinking?" he asked himself. "This was predicted. Everyone knew this weather was going to happen." With the weather still dangerous, he is concerned for the crews who will be called upon to join the search effort.

But Bogardus knows the importance of staying objective and rational as he prepares to deploy personnel into extreme conditions. Now retired, he explains his approach to search and rescue during those years as team leader: "I certainly had concern for the victims, but we didn't want to create more victims. What got me through these incidents over the years was to tell myself I didn't put the victims there, but I was putting these people there to help them. They were my primary responsibility. I'd do everything I could to help people in trouble, but sometimes rescuers can't get there because there's just too much risk for them."

Depending on the scope of the mission, the coordination required for backcountry search and rescue in the White Mountains can be immense—and it can take time. The investigative phase alone can last for hours, even before the team leader can begin coordinating and executing a mission. This can create the false perception of a delayed response. "What people lose sight of is it's not like calling 911 on the pavement and the cavalry shows up in five minutes to take care of you," says Bogardus. "A search and rescue mission takes time to organize. You have to get enough personnel there, and then get them into search and rescue mode on the mountain."

The sixteen-member specialized Advanced Search and Rescue Team, which Bogardus leads, was formed in 1997. He is an original member and served as the assistant team leader at its inception. From there, he moved up to team leader in 2002. He is responsible for managing the state search and rescue program, leading rescue missions, and serving as the primary liaison to the many volunteer search and rescue teams that are mostly located in the northern part of the state. Bogardus has participated in hundreds of rescues up to this point, most of those in the White Mountains.

Conservation Officers from New Hampshire Fish and Game (NHFG) apply to join the team and, once accepted, are specially trained to go out with local volunteer teams to participate in and oversee missions. Each accepted NHFG member attends a three-day winter mountaineering course through the North Conway-based International Mountain Climbing School, and must meet and maintain stringent physical agility requirements. "We want people who want to be on the team and who will maintain standards to remain on it," Bogardus says. The entire team trains together three full days a year on various topics, including survival tactics, and throughout the year, individual members pursue additional training. The team is considered "winter ready" and "treeline-above" qualified.

Two members of the New Hampshire Fish and Game Advanced Search and Rescue Team on a search for a missing hiker on Mount Lafayette on Feb. 16, just five days after the search for Fred Fredrickson and James Osborne. The hiker was later located and safely evacuated by a Black Hawk helicopter.

Before he leaves the house, Bogardus contacts the head of NHFG's Law Enforcement Division, Col. Jeffrey Gray, to brief him on the situation. Gray will remain at headquarters in Concord, on call if needed, but confident that Bogardus and his team know what they are doing. "There's a lot of trust there," says Bogardus.

In addition to calling in ground search teams, Bogardus decides to attack this search by air. He contacts Col. Frank Leith of the New Hampshire Army National Guard (NHARNG) to request air search support. "I wanted a Black Hawk helicopter out of Concord," says Bogardus. "If they get up here and the conditions allow them to land on the summit, they can run search teams up to the top and speed up the whole process. As soon as they arrive in the search zone, they see if there's a possibility to land and drop teams."

Leith is the State Army Aviation Officer responsible for all Army aviation operations in New Hampshire, including search and rescue missions. He tells Bogardus that he'll identify a crew and send a Black Hawk to Franconia Notch as soon as he can.

For ground search support, Bogardus first calls Rick Wilcox, then-president of the elite North Conway-based, all-volunteer Mountain Rescue Service. Bogardus knows he's going to need climbers with the highest degree of expertise to handle the rugged terrain and exposure above treeline in these extreme weather conditions. He tells Wilcox the situation and what he needs and trusts Wilcox to select the right team. As usual, Wilcox wastes no time responding. He calls back shortly and tells Bogardus that MRS will send thirteen people.

Bogardus now has a total of twenty-one searchers lined up, the thirteen from MRS and eight from Fish and Game's Advanced Team, who are already responding to Franconia Notch. But he knows he's going to need more people to cover as much ground as possible, so he calls Allan Clark, president of the Pemigewasset Valley Search and Rescue Team (PVSART). "For the conditions on this one, I needed MRS to go with us above treeline, and Pemi and other teams to search up to the point of treeline and in sheltered areas," Bogardus explains.

The all-volunteer PVSART covers Franconia Notch and has a winter-ready team of personnel who have the requisite experience and equipment to operate in extreme conditions like these. Bogardus tells Clark he'd like his team to ascend the Skookumchuck Trail up to treeline.

Because of the weather, Clark knows he must be selective in his choice of recruits for this mission. He contacts one of his team leaders, Gordie Johnk, who says he's comfortable responding to the Skookumchuck Trail. Johnk then recruits two winter-ready team members to ascend the trail with him, and Clark informs Bogardus of the roster.

Bogardus isn't taking a scattershot approach in deploying personnel for this mission. He is thinking carefully about where he'll need particular skill sets that align with the mission's profile. The fact that so many volunteers are responding during a weekday is an example of the high level of commitment these teams feel to the search and rescue community—and to fellow hikers.

With personnel gearing up and heading for Franconia Notch, Bogardus gets in his department-issued Chevy Tahoe Blazer and drives to the Lafayette Place parking area, where he'll establish his Incident Command Post.

As Bogardus drives south on I-93 toward the Notch, he's getting a sense of just how difficult this mission is going to be for the teams who will be higher up. The entire ridgeline is in the midst of an intense ground blizzard. Not only is he thinking about the two that are potentially trapped up there, he's also thinking about the people he's asking to move toward them.

Lafayette Place Parking Area
Falling Waters Trailhead
11:45 a.m.

Mount Washington Observatory Surface Weather Observations (12:00 to 1:00 p.m.): Temperature -14°F; winds out of the northwest averaging 71mph; visibility 1/16 of a mile, fog/blowing snow; windchill -56°F. Peak wind gust: 88 mph.

Bogardus pulls into the parking lot and continues to take inventory of his surroundings. "The weather in the parking lot was a mix of blue sky and clouds," he recalls. "But there were high winds, and I already knew it was a lot worse up above. I didn't have a good feeling at all."

Goss and Sprague are already on site. The parking lot is only partially plowed, and Bogardus sees that Fredrickson's yellow Saturn is snowed in. Knowing he has a helicopter on the way, he contacts plow crews to do some additional clearing.

"I had the Department of Transportation plow the entire parking lot," Bogardus recalls. "It's large enough to land a helicopter, and to have the Command Post there, plus there's plenty of parking for the searchers. We had them plow the lower end of the lot for the landing zone."

The plow operators tell Bogardus that they only recall seeing the yellow Saturn parked there on Sunday. This is an important piece of information as Bogardus continues to determine whether Fredrickson and Osborne have been out for one or two days.

Bogardus contacts the Mount Washington Observatory by cell phone to gather additional information on current and forecasted conditions. "Although it's Mount Washington and a little higher than Mount Lafayette, the weather is very similar and will often hit Lafayette before it hits Washington, especially coming from the west," says Bogardus. "Information I can glean from them about weather on the highest summits isn't going to be exact, but it's going to be pretty accurate to the conditions we're going to see on Franconia Ridge. There were strong winds that day, and they could give me ideas of times when the wind would peak and when it would probably subside a little bit."

Bogardus reaches the Observatory's Brian Clark, a shift leader and meteorologist. "We didn't have any equipment in Franconia Notch, but our information could be interpreted as being applicable because of the similarities in exposure between the two ranges," Clark recalls.

With Observatory weather data in hand, Bogardus also contacts Cannon Mountain Ski Area. "Cannon gives me a ballpark on the weather in the Notch," he says. "If it's bad on Cannon, and it was, I know it's bad on Lafayette. So I've got Franconia Ridge sandwiched between Cannon Mountain and Mount Washington. I now have two weather observations available to me, and I know the ridge is going to be worse than Cannon."

Bogardus and Goss continue to gather information. "The planning process is constant, and so is the investigation itself," says

Bogardus. "Just as with a criminal case, there's a full investigation going on, but in the case of a search and rescue mission, it's meant to gather information to help us make informed decisions."

Concord Coach has supplied cell phone numbers for Fredrickson and Osborne, so Bogardus calls Sgt. Timothy Hayes of State Police Troop F for assistance in having their phones pinged. After working with cell phone carriers, Hayes tells Bogardus that the last activity on either phone was when they were talking with each other at 7:00 a.m. on Sunday as both arrived in Concord to meet up. "Pinging is not an exact science," says Bogardus. "Notches and valleys make it tough, but you've got to try it. If they'd taken a cell phone in one of their packs, it would have been helpful. They could have turned it on for a ping, but unfortunately and unbeknownst to us, they'd left their phones in the car."

Bogardus asks that the state's Emergency Services Incident Management truck be brought to the trailhead. The vehicle, which is the size of large box truck, is a mobile Incident Command Post that will allow Bogardus and Goss to manage the mission from a space designed specifically for that purpose. In addition to a desk and a small conference table, the vehicle has phone and radio technology, computers, and large monitors to allow them to monitor and communicate with air and ground personnel and the Mount

Washington Observatory, and to display maps of the area for planning and tracking. Managing a mission of this scope from the front seat of a Chevy Blazer isn't realistic, especially in these conditions.

Knowing what they have for air and ground assets, and with the mobile unit on the way, Bogardus and Goss continue formulating their strategy. "Having conducted numerous missions in that area, and looking at the weather patterns, we knew a westerly wind had been coming through most of the weekend," says Bogardus. "When people are up there and get into trouble, a lot of times they'll go off the backside [of the ridge] into the Pemi to seek refuge. It's a safety bailout. But if they go there, it's a no-man's land. It's a long way back out. That's one of the scenarios we were trying to figure out. Did they go off the backside?"

Bogardus is relying on both information and experience as he chooses how to proceed. "A lot of the attack strategy on this mission came from looking at the weekend's weather, the conditions that day, and past history," he says. "I'd done multiple searches on that ridge, and I also had a track record from really good leaders before me. Based on experience, I knew that people tended to end up in certain locations."

Bogardus and his colleagues also understand that hikers in distress will tend to behave in particular ways to extreme weather conditions. "We've learned from past rescues that when you walk into the opposing force of the wind, it's human nature to want to get away from it," says Bogardus. "Your mind is telling you that you're heading into danger, that going into the wind is not necessarily the thing to do. So, instinctively, people will retreat to where it's easier, and in a westerly wind, that's the leeward side. The wind physically pushes them into the Pemi Wilderness."

Hikers who bail off the ridge into the Pemi will likely get funneled down to the Lincoln Brook Trail, at the base of the Franconia Brook drainage. "This is a wilderness trail that's not that well marked or maintained," he says. "A lot of times, they go down that side and have a hard time getting out." With this in mind, Bogardus will direct two members of his team to take snow machines, which are being trailered in, to the Pemi Wilderness via the Lincoln Brook Trail. "If they were in there, our hope was to intercept them coming out through the valley."

But not every hiker reacts the same way, so Bogardus must allow for multiple possibilities. "The decision as to whether someone has decided to go leeward or windward is going to come down to time of day, conditions, and whether or not they're in a whiteout," says Bogardus. "The wind is a draining force on hikers, and the longer they're in it, the more energy they're going to have sucked right out of them. It's going to deplete them. That person may already be on the verge of teetering as it is, and so in deciding which way to go, they might be factoring in their ability to survive."

Bogardus realizes that if the two hikers decided to bail out on the windward side, it would have taken take them into Walker Ravine. "While it's not going to be easy on either side of the ridge, they're going to have more avalanche danger going into Walker Ravine," he says. "On the backside of the Pemi, there are a number of drainages that are all steep, and with the high snow load and the wind, there would certainly be avalanche risk going down there. Is it worth that to go into the trees or do they stay exposed on the summit?"

Goss is concerned about the risk to rescuers in Walker Ravine as well, especially if the search were to stretch into Tuesday and they had to send teams down both sides of the ridge. In a Feb. 13, 2008 interview with the *New Hampshire Union Leader,* Goss told reporter Lorna Colquhoun, "With all the snow we've had this winter, there was severe avalanche danger. We were pretty nervous about that."

Bogardus and Goss identify other points where they can put personnel in the hope of encountering Fredrickson and Osborne if they're bailing out on any of the main trails along the ridge. "We're trying to intercept them but also to backtrack and take every route that they could have gone on or bailed out to," says Bogardus. "We're not looking for people at this stage, we're looking for clues to lead us to people: candy wrappers, burnt maps from trying to start a fire, hiking gear, broken branches, tracks in the snow—anything related to people."

As members of the Fish and Game Advanced Team begin to arrive, Bogardus will provide them with their search assignments. Since they will be the first ground searchers on scene, they will take on the role of what are known as "hasty" search teams, which deploy immediately after an early briefing. When other teams and personnel arrive, they will be briefed on their assignments and deploy either by Black Hawk helicopter or on foot.

These are the assignments that will be given to each team, assuming that weather will prevent the Black Hawk from dropping rescuers on the summit:

New Hampshire Fish and Game (NHFG) Advanced Search and Rescue Team: Two members will ascend Falling Waters Trail to Little Haystack Mountain. (Designated NHFG-1).

NHFG Advanced Search and Rescue Team: Two members will snowmobile to Franconia Falls, then ascend Lincoln Brook Trail into the Pemigewasset Wilderness. (Designated NHFG-2).

NHFG Advanced Search and Rescue Team: Two members will ascend Old Bridle Path to Greenleaf Hut to treeline. (Designated NHFG-3).

NHFG Advanced Search and Rescue Team: Two members will ascend Greenleaf Trail to Greenleaf Hut. (Designated NHFG-4).

Pemigewasset Valley Search and Rescue Team (PVSART): Three members will ascend Skookumchuck Trail to treeline.

New Hampshire Army National Guard (NHARNG): Helicopter on arrival will transport Mountain Rescue Service (MRS) team members to the ridgeline, if possible. Then they will search the ridgeline, the backside of the ridgeline in the Pemigewasset Wilderness, and the high-priority trails and drainages within the search area, as weather conditions permit.

MRS team: Five members will ascend Falling Waters Trail and link up with the NHFG team and proceed to the ridgeline on Little Haystack. (Designated MRS-1).

MRS team: Six members will ascend Old Bridle Path and link up with the NHFG team and proceed above treeline on Mount Lafayette. (Designated MRS-2).

MRS team: Two members will ascend Liberty Spring Trail to Franconia Ridge. (Designated MRS-3).

The experienced search and rescue personnel who will comprise these teams are well aware that many factors are already conspiring to make this mission especially challenging. "Due to the conditions, the terrain, the time of year, you're just constrained in what you can do,"

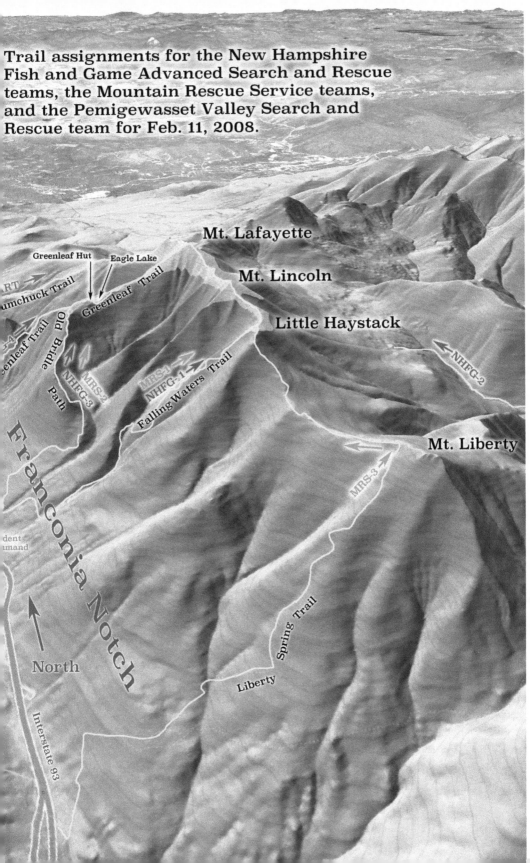

Trail assignments for the New Hampshire Fish and Game Advanced Search and Rescue teams, the Mountain Rescue Service teams, and the Pemigewasset Valley Search and Rescue team for Feb. 11, 2008.

Mt. Lafayette

Mt. Lincoln

Little Haystack

Greenleaf Hut

Eagle Lake

Greenleaf Trail

RT

umchuck Trail

Old Bridle Path

enleaf Trail

MRS-2

NHFG-3

MRS-1

NHFG-1

Falling Waters Trail

NHFG-2

Mt. Liberty

MRS-3

Franconia Notch

dent
mand

North

Spring Trail

Liberty

Interstate 93

says Bogardus. "You can only use so much terrain. You can't do line searching with such deep snow. You've got to cover all of the trails, circle the area, and move inward. We were trying to get into an area and look for clues, or anything that would lead us toward the victims. In this case, the searchers' job was to get up to the summit as fast as they could, but they were slowed down because they had to break trail. The mountains got loaded with snow that weekend."

Despite the bad weather and poor road conditions, some friends and coworkers of Fredrickson and Osborne, along with a few members of the press, gather in the parking lot. According to Ernie Brochu, Concord Coach's top executives, President Harry Blunt and Vice President Ken Hunter, are among those drawn to the scene that day. "Harry and Ken were very involved," says Brochu. "They jumped in Harry's car and drove up there."

Steve Harbert, who made the initial call to report his colleagues missing, arrives in the parking lot and meets with Bogardus to offer information that might be helpful to the search effort. His comments are recorded in the official Fish and Game Incident Report. Harbert tells Bogardus that he has hiked with Fredrickson and Osborne, but not in winter. He says Fredrickson hiked Falling Waters and across Franconia Ridge the previous weekend and told him he had had "a great trip." He also says that Fredrickson has hiked this same itinerary several times, in every season, and is "very familiar with the route." Harbert describes Fredrickson as proficient with a map and compass and adds that he recently took an ice climbing class to expand his winter skills.

Harbert adds that Fredrickson is in very good physical condition with no known health or medical concerns, but that he "would become colder faster due to his [low] body fat." Harbert is not sure how much or what kind of gear his two friends took with them, but he tells Bogardus that he doesn't think they were equipped to stay out overnight. He says Fredrickson wears glasses and might be wearing a bright blue or yellow jacket.

According to the report, Harbert says Osborne is younger than Fredrickson, stockier and slower but also physically fit with no known health or medical concerns. He adds that this was Osborne's first winter hike and that Osborne, who is likely wearing a blue jacket and leather hiking boots, "is always slow and cautious, being the last one, with others waiting for him."

Having gathered all the information they can, Bogardus and Goss brainstorm about contingencies and longer-term considerations. Even with the mission in its infancy, they know they must think ahead. "While we were waiting for teams to get up high, we were strategizing on scenarios around extracting the hikers should we find them," says Bogardus. "We were coming up with contingency planning and, as the day wore on, with the next day's plan. If we were going to be back here, where would we attack next? You do that throughout the mission and at the end of the night as you gather info from the teams coming out of the woods. You look at what worked, what didn't work, and what you need to go back to or modify."

XVIII
STATE MISSION

"In the case of pilots, it is a little touch of madness that drives us to go beyond all known bounds. Any search into the unknown is an incomparable exploitation of oneself."

—Jacqueline Auriol, French aviator

N.H. Army National Guard Aviation Support Facility
Concord, N.H.
Monday, Feb. 11, 2008
1:00 p.m.

Mount Washington Observatory Surface Weather Observations (1:00 to 2:00 p.m.): Temperature -12°F; winds out of the northwest averaging 75 mph; visibility 1/16 of a mile, fog/ blowing snow; windchill -53°F. Peak wind gust: 95 mph.

First Lt. Pete Cartmell hasn't left the ground yet, but he's already in mission mode. Ninety minutes ago his boss, Col. Frank Leith, called him at home about the search and rescue mission under way in Franconia Notch. Since that call, Cartmell has been focused on selecting his crew and preparing to fly. Although Cartmell is on a day off, most of the unit is away on annual training and a crew is needed now.

Cartmell doesn't hesitate to respond to his colonel, whom he is not alone in regarding as a legendary U.S. Army aviator. In 1970, at the direction of President Richard Nixon, Leith was awarded the Distinguished Flying Cross for his heroic actions while flying in a combat zone in Vietnam. Cartmell feels privileged to work for such an exceptional individual. "Colonel Leith is very humble, an amazing aviator, and a great boss and mentor," he says.

The New Hampshire Army National Guard has a memorandum of understanding with the New Hampshire Fish and Game Department that determines when the Guard is called to assist with a search and rescue mission. According to Leith, the Guard is involved when "there's a possibility of death or serious injury to a person or rescuer." The details of the memorandum are important because the Guard is a federal service branch. In order to participate in what is known as a State Mission, the crew must be put on State Active Duty.

"We have a very good relationship with Fish and Game, very streamlined," says Cartmell. "We call the aircraft the 'link-up,' because it connects directly with Fish and Game, so we designate one for the weekends. It's always configured for search and rescue, in case of a State Mission, and everyone knows where it is."

After graduating from Middlebury College in Vermont, Cartmell joined the U.S. Army in 1988. "I either wanted to go Special Forces or fly," he says. After getting married, Cartmell attended flight school and learned to fly helicopters. He left the Army in 2000 and moved to New Hampshire to be closer to family. That same year, he was hired full time by the New Hampshire Army National Guard as an instructor pilot and operations officer. He flew medevac missions in Iraq and Afghanistan for Operation Enduring Freedom, serving as commander of his medevac unit. By 2008, he had logged more than 3,000 hours of flight time, including a half-dozen search and rescue missions in winter conditions.

As Cartmell prepares for the day's mission, Staff Sgt. Matt Stohrer, who readied Black Hawk 031 for link-up on the previous Friday night, reports to the facility to join the crew. Like Cartmell, Stohrer is an instructor and will serve as one of the crew chiefs. Cartmell and Stohrer have logged many hours in the air together in combat environments overseas and in the skies over New Hampshire. "Pete is a phenomenal pilot, just incredible," Stohrer says.

Chief Warrant Officer Zach Lane will pilot Black Hawk 031 during the mission. After graduating from college, he joined the Army National Guard two weeks after the 9/11 terrorist attacks. "I could have gone in as a lieutenant, but I really wanted to be a Warrant Officer because their primary job is flying," he says. To become a Warrant Officer, you have to enlist in the Army, which Lane didn't originally intend to do. But he wanted to fly so badly that he chose to enlist, and he's been happy with that decision ever since.

Over time, Lane knew he had to learn more than how to fly an aircraft. "I told myself that if I was going to fly, then I was going to know how to fix them, so I became a flight mechanic," he says. He deployed to Bosnia after completing Basic and Advanced Training.

On returning stateside, he told his colonel he wanted to attend Flight School, and his request was granted in 2005. He learned to fly Black Hawks at the Eastern Army National Guard Aviation Training Site at Fort Indiantown Gap in Annville, Pa.

He was home for three days after graduating when he received orders to deploy to Iraq for Operation Enduring Freedom. "The whole one-weekend-a-month thing didn't really work for me," he says. "I was gone four and a half years out of my first six."

Lane entered Physical Therapy School in 2006 while still flying for the Guard. As of 2008 he had logged 600 hours of flight time. In addition to his overseas experience, he had flown search and rescue missions in the White Mountains in summer and winter. At that point, he was fifty flight hours away from achieving Pilot in Command status, which Cartmell already held.

Cartmell will serve as Pilot in Command for this mission. The plan is for Lane to do most of the flying and for Cartmell to handle the mission planning and briefing. "Your Pilot in Command is basically the quarterback," says Lane. "He's running the show, running the radios. The pilot's job is to fly the aircraft."

Staff Sgt. Allan Robinson serves as the second crew chief for the mission and will be under Stohrer's supervision. Robinson has been with the Army National Guard for eight years. Born in New Hampshire, he was on full-time active duty for the Army working on Apache helicopters when an opportunity arose to become a flight technician at the Army National Guard Aviation Support Facility in Concord. As of 2008 he had logged 200 hours of flight time in the Black Hawk.

Conservation Officer Delayne Brown also joins the mission and will serve as the Fish and Game liaison. He will assist the crew chiefs as needed and communicate with Incident Command on the ground via the technosonic radio installed in the aircraft. Brown began working for Fish and Game in 1997, first in the Wildlife Division. He became a deputy Conservation Officer in 1999 and was hired as a full-time Conservation Officer in 2002. A member of the Advanced Search and Rescue Team since 2004, he will be logging his first search and rescue mission from the air today. "I was really excited," he recalls. "I met up with the crew, they showed me how to use the harness, and buckled me in. I remember being amazed at how fast they can get to the scene."

With the crew on site, Leith pulls them together for a mission briefing. "Once the crew is set, the members and I determine if the weather is acceptable to initiate the mission," he says. "We will not initiate a mission if it poses a danger to the crew. Once the mission is initiated, the crew will make further determinations at the scene. Because the White Mountains have some of the worst weather in the United States, many of our final determinations have to be made at the scene, especially at night."

The main purpose of the briefing is to ensure that all the members of the crew understand what is happening and what the first steps will be. In this case, Cartmell tells them they'll fly to Franconia Notch, where two hikers are missing, land in the parking lot, and talk with Fish and Game officers. "Everyone has their own job, but we all work together to get the mission accomplished, and that's throughout the entire flight," says Stohrer.

After the briefing, Cartmell's crew gets to work gearing up for the mission while he meets with Leith for an additional confab about the mission parameters. "We could get a crew and get going within thirty minutes midweek, a little longer on weekends," says Cartmell. "We took a lot of pride in our ability to be responsive. We averaged a dozen calls a year. Occasionally we'd get called right out, but usually we were getting notified the night before for a mission the next morning. On this one, we were called right out."

Stohrer and Robinson don "Mustang Suits" for the mission. Insulated and bright orange in color, these flight suits will provide additional warmth as both crew chiefs look out their respective gunner's windows. They will also help in the event one of them has to be lowered on the hoist to assist ground searchers.

Each member of the crew is now focused on a specific task. Cartmell continues to work with Leith on a risk assessment; Robinson and Stohrer pull the aircraft out of the hangar, take a fuel sample, and assist Lane, who conducts a pre-flight check. Everyone is aware that meticulous planning is essential to success—and to safety. "You plan for the worst and hope for the best," says Lane.

XIX
DEPLOYED

"Technique and ability alone do not get you to the top; it is the willpower that is the most important. This willpower you cannot buy with money or be given—it rises from your heart."

—Junko Tabei, first woman to summit Mount Everest

Falling Waters Trail
Monday, Feb. 11, 2008
Early afternoon

Conservation Officers Mark Ober and Jeremy Hawkes are standing next to their cruisers, making last-minute adjustments to their gear. As each arrived at the Lafayette Place parking area, he backed his vehicle in along the northern edge of the lot, a customary practice for COs during search and rescue missions here. When teammates arrive, they'll do the same, until a long line of dark-green pickup trucks and SUVs dominate a significant portion of the lot. To curious onlookers, this protocol projects power and precision. To family and friends arriving in the lot, it shows that Fish and Game is taking this rescue seriously.

Because Ober and Hawkes are the first to arrive, Todd Bogardus assigns them the important Falling Waters Trail. His plan is to send the earliest, "hasty" teams up Falling Waters and Old Bridle Path, the two primary trails in the loop hike believed to be part of Fredrickson and Osborne's planned itinerary. Both these routes link up with the Franconia Ridge Trail.

If the Black Hawk is able to land members of Mountain Rescue Service (MRS) on the ridgeline, it will do so. If not, Bogardus will also send the MRS teams up Falling Waters and Old Bridle to link up with the hasty teams that have been deployed before them. MRS will move quickly because the trail will have been broken out by earlier searchers. Short of a Black Hawk ride to the ridge, this is the fastest way to get the highest level of expertise close to treeline. Once the teams link up, they will assess whether or not they are able to advance to the exposed terrain above treeline.

Before heading off, Ober and Hawkes, who've been on duty since 8:00 a.m., call their wives to let them know they're going to be home late. Without these check-ins, families and friends of first responders grow uneasy as the time on the clock moves further beyond shift's end.

With snowshoes on, the two make their way to the trailhead. Hawkes, who's been with Fish and Game since 2001 and the SAR Team since 2002, recalls seeing no tracks leading out from Old Bridle Path. "So we knew Fredrickson and Osborne didn't come down that way," he says. They report this important finding back to Bogardus by radio.

The teammates are carrying loaded 85-liter packs. Within the search and rescue community, Fish and Game's packs are among the heaviest. "We carry enough gear for us and for the victims if we find them," says Hawkes. Over the years, Conservation Officers have at times been forced to shelter in place overnight and provide care to a victim deep in the backcountry until a helicopter extraction or carry-out can be done the following day. Fish and Game requires a CO to carry specific gear, and he or she can decide to bring additional items based on personal preference.

In this case, Ober and Hawkes are each carrying a winter sleeping bag rated to -25°F; a sleeping pad; a bivouac sack; a stove; trekking poles; a GPS unit; a compass; maps; a portable radio; a radio harness; headlamps; a first-aid kit; a mountaineering axe; crampons; an avalanche probe and beacon; a portable shovel; extra clothing, including extra hats, socks, and gloves; Nalgene-insulated water bottles; Gatorade; a thermos of hot chocolate; and food for themselves and the victims. Both are wearing plastic mountaineering boots and Gore-Tex bibs, and they both have big puffy jackets, fleece jackets, balaclavas, Microspikes, and goggles.

Out of curiosity, Ober once weighed his winter-ready pack, and it came in at seventy-four pounds. "With what we were going into, I was glad to have what I had," he recalls. "Some team members will have things in their packs that others don't. I carry two bivy sacks and a Norwegian stove, whereas someone else may carry one bivy and a standard cookstove."

But though their pack contents provide them and anyone they might find with a high margin of safety, there's a trade-off. Falling Waters and the other targeted trails are covered in fresh snow. The trails are unbroken, and the snow is deep. At the start, the pace is manageable for Ober and Hawkes, but they know the snow will be much deeper in the higher reaches. Their heavy and slow approach is only going to get heavier and slower as the trail moves upward.

Still, at this early stage the hiking is straightforward, and the mission feels routine, especially for Hawkes, who's been on more missions than he can count. "I can remember thinking, 'This will be an easy mission,'" he says. "We'll go to the top and look around, find no footprints, and come back down. Quite frankly, when we got toward the top, I didn't think I'd need to dress that warmly because I didn't think we were going to be there that long. With the wind the way it was, even if Fredrickson and Osborne had walked there, we weren't going to see their footprints. They'd be erased. I felt that the big search for them was going to be the next day."

Skookumchuck Trail
Franconia Notch
2:00 p.m.

Mount Washington Observatory Surface Weather Observations (2:00 to 3:00 p.m.): Temperature -11°F; winds out of the northwest averaging 76 mph; visibility 1/16 of a mile, fog/blowing snow; windchill -52°F. Peak wind gust: 95 mph.

Allan Clark sits in his vehicle in the parking lot for the Skookumchuck trailhead. He's waiting for his crew of the three rescuers from the Pemigewasset Valley Search and Rescue Team (PVSART) who will participate in this mission. The team, which formed in 2005, traces its origins back to the search for a lost child on Loon Mountain and a rescue on Skookumchuck that required the participation of the Franconia and Sugar Hill fire departments, because Fish and Game was shorthanded. At the time, there was no volunteer search and rescue team on the western side of the White Mountains. If Fish and Game required assistance, they'd call the Androscoggin Valley Search and Rescue (AVSAR) team located on the northern side of the Whites, or Mountain Rescue Service in the Mount Washington Valley. Seeing a need, Clark and a small group took the initiative to form a team that would cover the area from Franconia Notch to the western side of Mount Washington's summit. This included Crawford Notch, Mount Jackson, and Mount Webster.

The team didn't rush to rescue, however. Through the fall of 2005 and into the spring of 2006, the founding members worked methodically to prepare a team. "We developed standard operating procedures and training," says Clark. "We wanted to make sure we were well prepared to assist Fish and Game. So we committed to six months of structured preparation. We practiced search work and carry-outs, and focused on having the proper attitude, respect, and professionalism."

Members of PVSART and New Hampshire Fish and Game belay an injured ice climber down the talus slope at the base of Cannon Cliff, February 2017.

The PVSART team participated in its first mission in April 2006 and was quick to earn the respect of Fish and Game's Search and Rescue Command and the Conservation Officers they worked alongside on missions. Today, the team averages between twenty-five and thirty calls per year. Most of these are carry-outs, but there is, on average, one missing hiker per year. A majority of PVSART's calls are in Franconia Notch on Old Bridle Path, Falling Waters, and Lonesome Lake Trails.

Bogardus has decided to send the PVSART team up the Skookumchuck Trail because of its proximity to Mount Lafayette. "We were in a low-priority area, but that trail needed to be checked, because it could have been an escape route for them off the ridge," recalls Clark.

The team will ascend Skook for 4.3 miles to treeline, at the Garfield Ridge Trail junction. AMC's *White Mountain Guide* estimates the hike will take three hours, forty minutes. Because of the conditions, Clark knows this is going to be a long and difficult grind for his crew. Responding Team Captain Gordie Johnk knows what awaits him. "Skook is the longest way up to Lafayette," he says. "It's gentle then steep, gentle then steep; it really surprises you. If you have the time, it's a great way up to Greenleaf Hut, but it's a loop that almost nobody does."

Johnk, a founding member of PVSART, has been hiking in the Whites since 1980. In addition to being a team member and volunteer firefighter, he works full time as principal of the Lafayette Regional School, a public elementary school located in Franconia. "I got the call at school and went right to Skook," he says. "Allan was there waiting." Clark will ask Johnk to lead the team up to treeline.

When Clark called him about the mission, they had a candid conversation about who Johnk would be comfortable going with. "Team selection is really important; you want to know whose ego is tucked away in their back pocket and who's is in your face. The most important thing is safety, and if that's not what your partner has in mind, see you later," Johnk says.

Johnk retrieves his pack, which is always in his vehicle, and ensures he's got everything he needs. "We carry enough to spend twenty-four hours out; that's the mandate," he says.

PVSART sets a particularly high standard for members of its "Above Treeline Winter Qualified" team members. To be eligible, candidates must have been on a PVSART team for at least one year and be a consistent responder to calls. They must demonstrate a successful history of winter hiking above treeline and show proof of winter-specific training. PVSART regulations also state that team members must own and be able to carry and use the following: crampons; ice axe; snowshoes; map and compass; shell jacket and pants; winter boots; adequate food and water; and requisite gear to keep warm and dry while moving and stopped.

In addition to the listed gear requirements, Johnk always includes personal favorites. "I bring Clif Bars and Snickers," he says. "I learned this from being out on calls with the Fish and Game officers. They had these great big Snickers bars. 'That's our energy,' they'd tell me." Johnk also brings hot tea, "tons of water," and Powerade drinks, all of which are in insulated sleeves.

While PVSART requires a high level of technical skills and competency in winter terrain, the group also places a high premium on personal qualities. Their directives state: "You must be able to trust the other members of this group with your life, and they must be able to do the same."

Johnk doesn't see much distinction between his role as team leader and member. "Yes, I'll take responsibility for the decision to turn around, but we all work together and look out for each other," he says. "If you've got some exposed skin up there, and it's starting to turn white, your teammate will see that and help you. It's kind of like the buddy system in firefighting."

The next to arrive is Matt Glarem, who joined PVSART in 2004 after moving to the area from Nevada, where he hiked extensively. He's spent a lot of time in the Whites, recreating and on calls for the team, and brings a good deal of backcountry winter experience with him. "I got the call at work and responded right away," he says. "The idea was to start the search before nightfall. I knew Gordie was level-headed and knew the trail systems well, so I was stoked to be out there with him."

Glarem is also feeling a sense of foreboding for those missing on the mountain. "When I got the call, I remember having this sinking feeling, knowing how rugged the weather system was going to be," he recalls. "I thought, 'These guys have got to be in tough shape.' We all knew this weather was coming. It was really well publicized."

The third and final member of the PVSART team, Irv Locke, works as a mechanic at Cannon Mountain Ski Area. He's been with PVSART for a couple of years and, according to Clark, "He's one tough guy. If I personally needed help, he would be one of the ones I would want."

Standing in the parking lot at the northernmost point of Franconia Notch, Clark and the team of rescuers are taking a direct hit from the wind and cold funneling into the narrow valley. As they're discussing the plan and what to expect, Glarem realizes he's made a critical oversight in his preparation. "It's the worst gaffe I've ever made on a call," he says ruefully. "I forgot my snowshoes. The snow was heavy, and we knew there was more on the way. I offered to go home and get them, but Gordie said we should start without them and see what happened." Deeply disappointed in himself, Glarem is grateful that Johnk and Locke have remembered their own snowshoes and could break trail ahead of him. "Thankfully, I wasn't post-holing," he says.

N.H. Army National Guard Aviation Support Facility
Concord, N.H.
2:10 p.m.

When First Lt. Pete Cartmell joins his team in the Black Hawk "link-up," his co-pilot Zach Lane tells him that the aircraft is ready to go. Cartmell then gets approval from the tower for takeoff.

At 2:10 p.m., the three burly tires of the Black Hawk leave the ground. The 80-plus-mph winds generated by the rotor wash away any remnants of snow lying on the tarmac below. The snow clouds spinning in circles through the rotors look like inverted whirlpools.

Standing just outside the hangar door are Col. Frank Leith and the other Army National Guard personnel, all of whom are as deeply invested in the mission as the crew members themselves. They look on as the aircraft rotates on its axis. Lane adds more power to the engines through the collective, adjusts the foot pedals to compensate for it, and with his right hand eases the cyclic forward. The nose of the aircraft dips slightly, the tail rises, and the Black Hawk moves forward, gaining elevation as it goes.

Leith and other onlookers feel the vibration of the engines and rotor rotation pushing against their chests. Residents inside their homes lining the base and those in the shadow of the copter's flight path hear the "thump, thump, thump" as the Black Hawk pushes north along the I-93 corridor toward its Area of Operations in Franconia Notch. As Matt Stohrer looks out his gunner's window and down at the snow-covered fields of East Concord, he wonders if there might be a young child gazing skyward, completely mesmerized by the passing helicopter—just as he was not all that long ago.

Stohrer's brief daydream is interrupted as Cartmell breaks the silence and gets his crew talking. "As we were inbound up to the Whites, we started talking about what we were going to do when we got there," Lane recalls. "We'd first check to see if we could land rescue teams up top and then, after landing and briefing with Fish and Game, we'd run them up there if we could and then start our grid pattern."

They also discuss the transition from search to rescue if the hikers are found. "We talked about whether we'd try to land or try lowering Matt on the hoist," says Lane.

Lincoln Brook Trail
Franconia Notch
2:13 p.m.

Conservation Officers Heidi Murphy and Mike Eastman start their department-issued Ski-Doo touring snow machines in preparation for their trip deep into the Pemigewasset Wilderness. Once under way, they'll follow an old logging road for close to 3 miles before reaching a bridge that can only be crossed on foot. They'll then don snowshoes for a 6-mile hike along a wilderness trail that parallels the east branch of the Pemigewasset River.

"Command thought the hikers might have gotten blown off the eastern side of the ridge by the westerly winds, and they wanted us to snowshoe up in there in case these guys were there," says Eastman. "Because no one had been up in there at all, they also wanted us to break a trail for them, in case they made it down, so they could hike out."

Because Murphy and Eastman are headed into such a remote location, Officer Herb Karsten of the National Forest Service Law Enforcement Division parks his cruiser at the Hancock Trailhead high up on the Kancamagus Highway to provide radio communication support for them and for the Mountain Rescue Service team assigned to climb Mount Liberty.

Murphy finds the conditions tolerable at that point. "It was cold on that side, but it wasn't really windy because we were sheltered," she recalls. "Once we started walking, it was pretty good."

The two remove the rear seat cushion of their snow machines and tie down their large packs and snowshoes for the ride in. They've made this trip into the Pemi together before.

Old Bridle Path
Franconia Notch
2:15 p.m.

Conservation Officers Mark Hensel and Brad Morse start up the trailhead and walk onto the Old Bridle Path for the 2.9-mile ascent to Greenleaf Hut. The average hiking time to the hut is two hours, forty minutes. If they end up continuing to the summit of Mount Lafayette, it will take approximately one hour more. "The plan was for Mark and me to hike up Bridle to Greenleaf and wait there," Morse recalls. "They didn't want us to just keep going above treeline once we got there because of the conditions, so once we got to the hut, we were to check in to see where things were at."

Hensel has been a Conservation Officer since 2000. Because of the extensive alpine experience he brought with him, he was immediately appointed to the SAR Team. "Mark was our strongest guy," says Morse, years later. "He was, hands down, the best hiker we had."

Morse, who spent twenty-one years in the U.S. Army, fourteen of those as a member of Special Forces, was hired by Fish and Game in 2004. Already a paramedic, he was brought onto SAR before the end of his trainee year.

Both are well versed and comfortable operating in remote environments in winter conditions. They'll follow an established plan they've used during previous missions. "We stop every twenty to thirty minutes to do a quick check on each other and to hydrate and eat," Morse explains. "We do that every time we go out. That day, we knew MRS might eventually come up behind us on the trail, but we made sure to find a manageable pace."

Hensel and Morse are wearing snowshoes and taking turns breaking trail. They have packed for any contingency. "We had everything," says Morse. "We knew they were somewhere on that loop trail. We were pretty sure they were up there at least overnight, so we knew if we got to them, they'd either be hypothermic or dead, so we were prepared to stay the night if we got to them."

Airspace over Franconia Ridge
Incident Command Post
2:50 p.m.

As Black Hawk 031 approaches the Franconia Ridge, Matt Stohrer notes an unfortunate change in conditions. "The weather was good when we left Concord," he recalls. "But I remember getting to the Notch, and it was really windy and cold, with eighty-mile-per-hour gusts." Using the technosonic radio, Cartmell contacts Bogardus, who's now in the Incident Command Post with Lt. Goss, informing him that the helicopter is four minutes away.

Bogardus asks him to check the feasibility of dropping teams on the summit of Haystack. "It's faster for us to start from the top and work our way down," he explains. "If we can drop rescuers, they're up there in ten minutes."

Lane brings the Black Hawk as close to Haystack's summit as he can and quickly determines that the downdrafts are too strong and unpredictable, and visibility too poor, to attempt a landing on the summit. Cartmell informs Bogardus that "it's not going to happen."

Bogardus doesn't balk at the news. "If the Black Hawk guys tell me they can't do something, it can't be done," he says.

He instructs the helicopter crew to land at the Lafayette Place parking lot and meet him in the Command Post for a briefing about where they should search. "An initial face-to-face meeting before they start searching is important because things can change by the time they arrive here," he explains.

Bogardus then leaves the mobile unit and meets with the eleven members of MRS who are waiting in the parking lot to see if they'll be flying or hiking to the ridgeline. Given the situation, he sends the MRS teams up Falling Waters and Old Bridle Path on foot.

Earlier, two members of MRS, Steve Dupuis and Tim Martel, decided they would prefer to get moving, so they volunteered for the Liberty Spring assignment. "Everybody wants to fly in the Black

Hawk, but it hadn't shown up yet," recalls Martel. "I can remember standing in the parking lot and thinking, 'This sucks; let's just go.' It was so cold standing and waiting for the helicopter. I was thinking they wouldn't even fly at all when they heard what the winds were up there, so I was really impressed to find that they did fly."

Bogardus is mindful of the toll the conditions will take on his teams and monitors their status closely. "Everybody was complaining about busting trail going up," he says. "It was slow going, and we still had subzero temperatures and high winds." He and Goss understand that individuals and even teams might reach a breaking point in their ability to go on, so they continuously assess short- and long-term considerations. "Throughout the day, the teams were relaying the conditions and what was going on, and we were trying to determine if we had enough personnel, if we needed to call in more, if there was something else we could try."

Lane lands the Black Hawk in the parking lot near the Command Post and shuts down the engines. The crew of five exits and joins Bogardus and Goss inside for the briefing. Bogardus tells the crew what he knows of the missing hikers, what's been done so far, what trails the ground teams are covering, and where they're currently located. "Todd was an unbelievable professional," Cartmell recalls.

Using the large monitor located in the mobile unit, Bogardus shows them where he'd like them to search and why. "Fish and Game always had a grid identified for us to maximize search efforts," Stohrer says.

Bogardus asks the crew to do a check of the Falling Waters Trail up to the ridge and cross over to search the Pemi Wilderness. Once those areas are cleared, he directs them to work their way toward Mount Lafayette and, after clearing the mountain, to search the western slopes of the ridge on its opposite side.

Cartmell has worked with Bogardus on previous missions and trusts his instincts. "Todd understood very well about the windward and leeward sides," Cartmell says. "Oftentimes, the windward side will be a little easier to sweep back and forth on and search. On the leeward side, the downdrafts can be tremendous sometimes, and we can't be effective in those conditions, even with a Black Hawk."

XX
POINT LAST SEEN

*"What strikes me the most about Mount Washington and
the Presidential Range are the unique and vibrant
communities that thrive on and around this mountain, in
particular the rescue community."*

—*Joe Klementovich, Mountain Rescue Service*

International Mountain Equipment
North Conway, N.H.
Monday, Feb. 11, 2008
Early afternoon

Before MRS team member Tim Martel arrives at the Lafayette
Place parking lot and heads up the Liberty Spring Trail with fellow
MRS member Steve Dupuis, he unwittingly lands on a key piece of
information that will help Todd Bogardus advance the rescue mission.
While hanging around the house on this cold winter day, he receives a
cell phone call from MRS member Joe Lentini. "Hey, Tim, want to go
for a hike?" Lentini asks.

"Sure, where are we going?" Martel asks.

"Franconia Ridge," Lentini responds.

"Who are we looking for?" Martel inquires, well aware that this
isn't a friend's invitation to go on a day hike.

Lentini tells Martel they'll be searching for two missing hikers
and asks that he meet two other MRS team members at International
Mountain Equipment in North Conway, the site of the International
Mountain Climbing School, where MRS stores its gear.

Martel is in his sixth year as a member of the MRS team. His
passion for the mountains was instilled in him by his father, Dick,
who—as yet unknown to his son—was on Falling Waters Trail the
previous day, where he encountered Fred Fredrickson and James
Osborne.

Tim started climbing with his dad when he was five years old at

Rock Rimmon Park in Manchester and on the slabs at Pawtuckaway State Park. "We'd go fishing and hunting; we were an outdoor family," he says. Tim built on the skills instilled in him by his father and took his climbing to the next level after graduating from high school. In college, he was a climbing leader in the outdoor program and was assistant instructor for a mountaineering course. He also worked as a caretaker at Harvard Cabin in Huntington Ravine, where he met members of MRS who were either guiding or rescuing there. Seeing that he was highly proficient in an alpine environment, they invited him to join the team.

After talking with Lentini, Martel gets his personal gear, which is always ready to go, and makes the drive to downtown North Conway, where he greets his two teammates, Charlie Townsend and Alain Comeau. The two are grabbing extra gear from the team's designated closet before heading to Franconia Notch with Martel. Most MRS team members have a key to the store, allowing them to retrieve what they need at any hour.

Townsend, a veteran of the team, has been climbing in the Whites since the late 1960s. He attended summer camp there, where he developed a passion for hiking and climbing. In 1982, after graduating from college, he established roots in the Mount Washington Valley. "I was always trying to get here," he says, so he decided it would be a good idea to just relocate. Townsend started guiding in the area early on and established relationships within the climbing and rescue community. He taught at the Eastern Mountain Sports Climbing School in 1984 and earned his Emergency Medical Technician certification before joining the MRS team. "The climbing community here is especially well connected," he says. "Going out after meetings and on callouts, I've gotten to know people I wouldn't have gotten to know otherwise. There's a mutual respect among team members. You trust their judgment."

Martel recalls a time when this camaraderie was especially evident: "I can remember a rescue we did on Mount Washington in extreme winds and cold," he says. "There was so much force in the wind we had to turn away to breathe. After finding the two victims, we got back into the snowcat, and we all looked at each other. Then everybody put a hand on each other's cheek. Here we were, a bunch of grown men checking each other for frostbite because it's impossible to know if you have it. It was this really cool cohesion that you don't typically see in groups."

Comeau, also a forty-year veteran of the team, has been climbing since the 1970s. He started guiding and eventually also moved to the valley. In addition to climbing and guiding, he spent five years as a flight instructor at the Portland Jetport in Maine. "I eventually had to choose between flying or climbing," he says. Climbing won out. Comeau became an instructor examiner for the American Mountain Guide Association before launching his own guiding service and joining MRS.

Mountain Rescue Service grew out of an accident in the very same area where Martel, Townsend, and Comeau are heading. "Back in the 1960s, there was an incident on Cannon Mountain where two climbers died," says Rick Wilcox, the founder and first president of MRS. "Based on that accident and a similar one, the Appalachian Mountain Club Search and Rescue Committee decided there needed to be a more specialized team." That team was incorporated in 1972, and by 1976 had completed enough missions to become the go-to crew for the most challenging search and rescue efforts.

There are strict criteria for joining the MRS team. "Team members have to have year-round climbing skills and ice- and rock-climbing skills," says Wilcox. "They also have to live in the area and be available, and they have to be very familiar with the terrain— particularly the cliffs. We have to be confident that none of our members will become part of the problem."

Wilcox adds that MRS team members must have additional qualities to really make the grade. "Just because you're a really good climber doesn't mean you're going to be a really good rescuer," he says. "You have to have the mentality to want to help other people." Team members are the first to acknowledge that they're not immune to mishaps while out recreating. "We've rescued ourselves nine times," he says.

The MRS team has worked hard to build relationships with the National Forest Service and New Hampshire Fish and Game. "It's a very unusual situation in New Hampshire, with law enforcement and volunteers working together," says Wilcox. "Fish and Game are really good people and really good at what they do. They'll ask us for advice at times, and when they're doing a search, they may send us to certain areas that require a higher skill level."

Members of Mountain Rescue Service and Snow Rangers from the United States Forest Service return to a Mount Washington Observatory snowcat after rescuing three stranded climbers in Huntington Ravine on Mount Washington, February 2013.

Wilcox is clearly proud of the team he helped form. "They're as good as it gets," he says. "Occasionally, they want to go over the limit, and we have to hold them back, but I think there's a lot of common sense within the team. Certain conditions present extreme danger to our team members, and the only time we even consider attempting a rescue is if there's a chance the person is alive and [we know] where to find them. If we know there is a very low probability of saving somebody, the search becomes secondary to the team's safety."

The SAR Working Group, a collaborative team of representatives from Fish and Game and the volunteer teams that participate in rescues, meets monthly throughout the year to talk about the safety of rescuers. According to Wilcox, the group discusses what should be considered reasonable risk in terms of the conditions, the terrain, and the capabilities of those involved in the search.

The issue of rescuer safety came to everyone's attention on Jan. 25, 1982, when MRS lost one of its own during a search and rescue mission on Mount Washington. Albert Dow was killed when he and his partner were caught in an avalanche. "It was a horrendous tragedy for the rescue community," recalls Wilcox.

Dr. Frank Hubbell, founder of Stonehearth Open Learning Opportunities (SOLO), was present at the accident scene. "Everything changed when Albert died," he says. "After that everybody thought MRS was done, that they were going to dissolve it, but it was just the opposite. The team members decided it was time to ramp up their training. Rick Wilcox came to me and said, 'So I understand you have a Wilderness Medical Training course at Pinkham Notch next week. All of Mountain Rescue Service will be there.'"

Before Dow's death, volunteer rescuers were not covered by workers' compensation. Through a change in the state statute, they are now considered state employees when activated by Fish and Game or the Forest Service for a search and rescue mission. "People have been injured on rescues over the years," says Wilcox. "Being insured in the rescue community was something good that came out of Albert's tragic death."

Now ready to head out, Martel, Townsend, and Comeau load gear into the back of Martel's Volvo 850 wagon and take Route 302 toward Crawford Notch and Franconia. "My car was running like shit on the drive over," recalls Martel. "Because it was so cold, the gas pedal was getting stuck, so I had to tap it with my toe to get it unstuck. It was that cold."

Anyone might think that discussion during a ride to a rescue call will be entirely mission focused, but that's not always the case. Sometimes team members use the opportunity to catch up on each other's doings and news going around the hiking and climbing community. "Every time I got together with Alain, we talked about what projects he was working on, because he always had Special Operations guys he was guiding, and sometimes they'd do night training that was cool to hear about," says Martel. Comeau once told him, "One night, I took three buckets of water, put them on the cliff, and had teams go rescue them. Whichever team had more water in their bucket won."

Martel and his passengers are just about to enter Franconia Notch when he decides to check in with his father, who he's hoping is at home. "I called my dad when we were pretty close to pulling into the lot. He spends so much time in the Whites, I wanted to make sure he wasn't one of the guys we were looking for," he says. He feels a tinge of relief when his dad answers the phone.

"Hey, Dad, we're going out to look for some missing hikers, and one is in his mid-fifties. I just wanted to make sure it wasn't you," he says.

"Well, it's not me. Where are you going?" his father asks.

"Franconia Ridge."

"I saw them! Those guys didn't make it down?" his father replies.

Dick Martel recalls the moment his son made him aware of the situation. "I knew right away [that they hadn't gotten down], because on the way down Falling Waters, the weather was turning rotten," he says.

Dick tells his son about his encounters with the two hikers on the previous day, and Tim says he'll put his father in touch with Incident Command so he can relay all he knows to the leaders of the rescue effort.

Tim Martel understands the significance of his father's knowledge for the mission. "I knew it was a big deal, because it was

Tim Martel and his father on the summit of Cotopaxi, the second highest summit in Ecuador, April 2008.

going to zero in our search to the area last seen," he says. "We weren't going to have to send people up Cannon."

Townsend is riding in the passenger seat listening to his teammate's reaction to the call. "It was just a random thing," he says. "Driving to Franconia and getting this piece of information because of a family phone call—it was too freaky. It was a key link, and you usually don't have that."

He's also taking note of the weather in the Notch. "By the time we got over there, we were thinking, 'Man, this is some serious weather,'" Townsend recalls. "You have this initial feeling of judgment, asking yourself, 'What were they thinking?', and then you realize they were probably doing the exact same stuff we were when we'd been out in that kind of weather."

When Martel pulls into the Lafayette Place parking lot, he immediately seeks out Todd Bogardus. "You're going to want to talk to my dad. He was up there yesterday and saw the guys," Martel tells him.

Bogardus gets on the phone with Dick Martel, who walks him through the previous day's events. "If you're looking for them, there's a stockier guy in a red shirt and a thinner guy," he says. He describes the yellow car he saw Fredrickson and Osborne in when he arrived in the parking lot and his two encounters with them on Falling Waters Trail. He also tells of passing hikers just before treeline and encountering a solo hiker on the summit of Little Haystack at 11:18 a.m.

"Just so you know," he tells Bogardus, "the trail to Shining Rock was not packed out, and the Old Bridle Path had not been packed, so there's a pretty good chance no one was on that trail that day because the weather was so nasty."

The information is a boon to Bogardus. Even though they don't have an exact itinerary, they can focus the rescue effort more tightly. "He gave us a good starting point," he says. Through an eerie coincidence, Dick Martel has provided Bogardus with a critical piece of information: the point last seen.

XXI
GRID

"On Franconia Ridge we don't want you to bail out to the east into the Pemi Wilderness because we may never find you again. And to the west in Walker Ravine, there are slides and drainages, and it's pretty rugged country. Unless you absolutely have to bail out, there's no good option. You've got to get over to either Lafayette or Little Haystack."

—*Allan Clark, Pemi Valley Search and Rescue Team*

Airspace over Franconia Ridge
Monday, Feb. 11, 2008
3:05 p.m.

Mount Washington Observatory Surface Weather Observations (3:00 to 4:00 p.m.): Temperature -11°F; winds out of the northwest averaging 74 mph; visibility 1/16 of a mile, fog/blowing snow; windchill -52°F. Peak wind gust: 94 mph.

On orders from Incident Command, Black Hawk 031 lifts off from the parking lot to start searching. Overcast conditions have turned the sky the shade of a ping-pong ball. A thick canopy of frozen fog and swirling snow obscures a large swath of the Franconia Ridge.

Snow pouring out of the tall trees in Walker Ravine is being blown upslope and swallowed by clouds. These updrafts, generated by the prevailing winds as they interact with the terrain, push the Black Hawk along as it follows the contours of the slope just over Falling Waters Trail. Four of the five crew members on board know all too well that things on the other side of the ridge are going to be much angrier than they are here. Winds and terrain are conspiring to create turbulence at the ridgeline and over on the leeward side of the range. Pilot Zach Lane tightens his grip on the cyclic and readies himself for the inevitable tug-of-war that awaits him up ahead.

Pilot in Command Pete Cartmell informs Incident Command that Falling Waters Trail is clear of any signs of the missing hikers and that they're heading to the eastern side of the ridge. Little Haystack's summit is hidden, but the southern ridgeline is partially visible up to Mount Flume. Lane picks a spot in between Haystack and Mount Liberty where visibility is most favorable and threads the helicopter through it and over the ridge. He hugs the terrain and slowly follows the slope downward.

Because of the well-established history of hikers bailing out off the eastern side of the ridge and into the Pemigewasset Wilderness, Lane makes this a primary focus of their search. His goal is to keep the Black Hawk low over the terrain and establish a grid pattern, allowing the rest of the crew to look for signs of the missing hikers. Hovering 50 to 100 feet over the terrain, Lane positions the Black Hawk just beyond the base of Little Haystack and points the nose of the aircraft northward into the wind in the direction of Mount Lafayette.

Once the aircraft reaches a speed of between 16 and 24 knots, it achieves what is known as Effective Translational Lift, allowing it to move forward, low and slow, over the terrain. As it moves, Cartmell searches from the cockpit, Matt Stohrer and Allan Robinson from the gunners' windows, and Delayne Brown from the rear jump seat. "I'm primarily looking at the controls," says Lane about his role as pilot. "I'm just trying to stay on a certain heading to make sure I'm flying an accurate grid. It's the other crew members who are looking out and

Staff Sergeants Matt Stohrer and Allan Robinson search for Fred Fredrickson and James Osborne from the gunners' windows on Feb. 11.

searching."

Once the aircraft arrives near the base of Mount Lafayette, Lane turns the Black Hawk 180 degrees. This is referred to as "turning the tail," because the aircraft is moving so slowly. Now pointing southward back toward Little Haystack, Lane can ease up on the power and take advantage of the tailwind to fly back the way he came, maintaining a grid pattern, until he reaches his starting point. Lane flies this back-and-forth pattern until he's confident that he's covered the necessary ground. "We're basically flying grid paper," he says. "We're as low as we can get. We want to be able to see the ground, but we don't want to be so low that we create a whiteout."

Black Hawk 031 flying over the Falling Waters trail earlier in the day on Feb. 11.

Flying a Black Hawk in the mountains is all about power management. It's important to know the direction of the wind and the weight of the aircraft in order to maximize efficiency. The pilot positions the nose of the aircraft into the wind whenever possible. This provides more lift and requires less torque, which means better fuel management. As the aircraft climbs a slope, more power is required. Counter-intuitively, if it is pointed into the wind, it actually uses less fuel. This strategy is helpful in the event of an emergency, such as an engine failure, because the aircraft will retain more power in reserve in case it needs to access it.

When the potential exit points off the ridge and the surrounding terrain are cleared, Lane positions the Black Hawk toward the west, keeping the nose pointed in the general direction of the wind. Brown radios Incident Command to keep them apprised of the crew's progress. Staying just high enough off the terrain to avoid creating a whiteout and to maintain a viable escape route in the event of trouble, the Black Hawk climbs the slope up toward Little Haystack's summit.

This phase of the grid search brings the helicopter closer to the ridgeline and the turbulence that's cascading over its leeward side. Brown is sitting secured to his seat along the back wall of the rear cabin, experiencing his first flight over the winter Whites. "It was terrible weather, and I was doing my job, but I was holding on with a death grip," he recalls.

The higher the aircraft travels up the slope, the bumpier the ride becomes. "The Black Hawk was getting tossed around quite a bit," says Brown. "I'm sure it's normal for an experienced crew, but the gusts that come over those ridgelines are insane. You drop fast; it feels like a thousand feet in a second. I eventually acclimated to it, but it was pretty intense looking down at black-and-white tundra for hours."

Conservation Officer Delayne Brown flying with the Black Hawk crew on Feb. 11.

On reaching the cone of Little Haystack's summit, Lane is careful to keep the aircraft below the cloud canopy that's draped over the ridge, stretching all the way over to Mount Lafayette. Looking out in all directions over the monochromatic landscape, the crew is laser focused on finding the slightest anomaly. "When they're searching, they're not only looking for people, they're looking for the small stuff, because the small stuff leads you to the big stuff," says Bogardus.

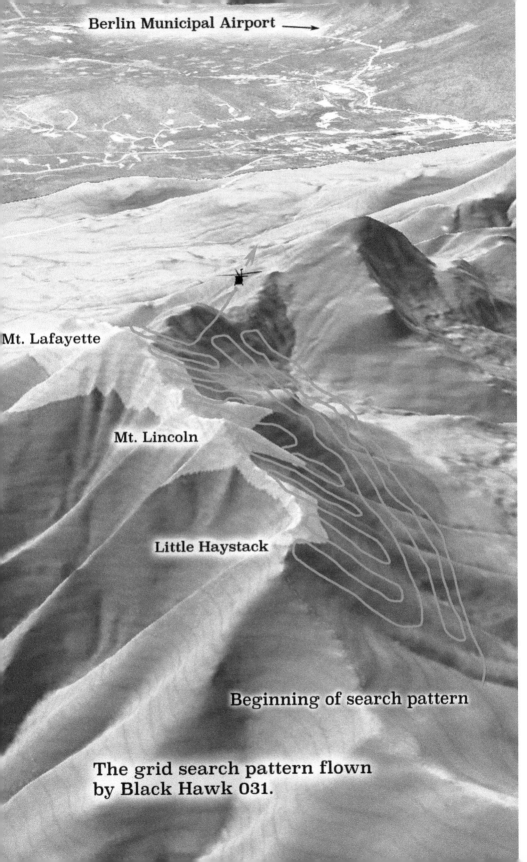

Berlin Municipal Airport →

Mt. Lafayette

Mt. Lincoln

Little Haystack

Beginning of search pattern

The grid search pattern flown
by Black Hawk 031.

"They're looking for tracks, debris, and gear."

Stohrer adds that nothing they come across is ever dismissed. "We're looking for prints in the snow. From a hundred feet up, it's hard to tell if the prints were made by humans or animals, so we follow them all. Once we clear the tracks, we resume the grid search pattern."

From his Command Post, Bogardus realizes the ridgeline isn't getting searched as it would be on a blue-sky, low-wind day with lots of good visibility. "They had to stay at lower elevations for much of the search pattern because they couldn't stay on top for long with those winds," he explains. "They would poke their head up and then drop back down."

The Black Hawk's crew members are doing their very best. But the poor visibility on Little Haystack's summit, where Fredrickson and Osborne are lying, makes it impossible for them to detect any signs of the stricken hikers.

In addition, by the time they are searching on Lafayette, the aircraft is running low on fuel, and Lane will soon need to break off and fly north to the Berlin Municipal Airport in Milan to top off its two fuel tanks. So the efforts of the Black Hawk crew will, at this point in the mission, be stymied by weather. "The conditions definitely hampered the air search," acknowledges Bogardus.

XXII
WRECKAGE

"They are the survivors of a night without heroes, though surviving that storm may have been heroic enough; for the storm cut short all choices but the final one, between life and death—choices for which no rules exist, not for them, not for any of us on mountains of our own, in storms we cannot foresee, storms that catch us with no warning."

—*Mel Allen, "Making the Final Choice on Katahdin"*

Little Haystack Summit
Monday, Feb. 11, 2008
4:30 p.m.

Mount Washington Observatory Surface Weather Observations (4:00 to 5:00 p.m.): Temperature -9°F; winds out of the northwest averaging 75 mph; visibility 1/16 of a mile, fog/blowing snow; windchill -49°F. Peak wind gust: 94 mph.

James Osborne is motionless. The only thing moving is the snow dancing across his frozen clothing. His body acts as the foundation for a growing snowdrift that further envelops him the longer he lies here. Fred Fredrickson, lying some 100 yards away, has died.

The origin of this tragic scene remains debatable. Did it begin when their plans were first hatched? At the trailhead? On the ridgeline? Regardless of when or where it began, the final site of the wreckage is here.

Because of the precarious conditions up high, Black Hawk 031 could only flirt with the ridge and is now moving past Mount Lafayette toward Berlin Municipal Airport to refuel. Ground searchers are closing in on Fredrickson and Osborne, but it will be hours before they emerge from the small trees onto the ridge.

Osborne is, of course, oblivious to what is being done on his behalf. As he lies unconscious, his body is trying desperately to maintain its core temperature despite the absence of caloric intake. His viscous blood is being shunted away from what his brain, now in contingency mode, considers to be low-priority areas: his arms and legs. His core and head are the last vestiges of warmth. Without warm blood circulating through them, his outer extremities will get even colder, causing cells and muscles to freeze. This will inevitably lead to varying degrees of frostbite.

As all this proceeds, Osborne's body is forced to enter starvation mode, dissolving muscle and fat to generate calories. Because he is unable to move or shiver, this is an inefficient way to retain warmth. He is burning many more calories than he would if he were able to move around and eat.

Because Osborne is also dehydrated, his kidneys are unable to filter the toxins that result from the breakdown of fat and muscle. Unable to urinate, he cannot excrete these toxins from his system, so they will continue to build and inflict damage on his vital organs.

Meanwhile, the cold begins to act as a tourniquet, cutting off critical blood flow to Osborne's muscles. This causes necrosis, the death of cells and tissues within his body. His liver is in overdrive, trying to clean his now compromised blood. As the enzymes in his blood increase, he will be at high risk of cardiac arrest.

Osborne is in need of immediate intervention if he is to survive. But it's also true that if he is suddenly jolted or moved without care, he will become highly susceptible to ventricular fibrillation that could lead to a heart attack.

XXIII
COHESION

"A team is not a group of people that work together.
A team is a group of people that trust each other."

—*Simon Sinek, author and speaker*

Falling Waters Trail
Monday, Feb. 11, 2008
5:00 p.m.

Mount Washington Observatory Surface Weather Observations (5:00 to 6:00 p.m.): Temperature -12°F; winds out of the northwest averaging 77 mph; visibility 1/16 of a mile; fog/blowing snow; windchill -54°F. Peak wind gust: 90 mph.

Twilight's glow weakens as the murky hue of the churning night sky establishes itself over Franconia Notch. The last vestiges of daylight retreat to the west behind the sheer granite wall of the Cannon Cliffs, taking with them the ability to detect subtle signs of the two missing hikers. The trees lining Falling Waters Trail are absorbed in darkness, but Steve Larson, a member of Mountain Rescue Service since 1979, is undeterred. He knows his purpose and is committed to it. "Fish and Game tries not to call us, but when time is of the essence, they call. I knew that if we didn't do it that night, there would be nothing left to save," he says.

Larson and four fellow members of the team designated as MRS-1, Jim Surette, Chris Noonan, Alain Comeau, and Charlie Townsend, ascend the trail at a disciplined pace. "It's important to not overexert yourself," says Surette, a twenty-year veteran of MRS. "You don't want to be sweating bullets in the winter." Rick Wilcox, who was president of MRS at the time, underscores the necessity of a steady gait during a lengthy search. "Pacing yourself, that's the difference between an experienced climber and an inexperienced climber, especially if you know you're going to be out all night," he says.

Larson is the designated leader of this five-member team. There's a hierarchy within MRS, but it is informal. Usually, the team leader will meet with Fish and Game's Incident Command, learn what needs to be done, choose a crew, and brief each member on the assignment.

Larson is mild mannered and highly respected within the search and rescue community. "Steve doesn't act as a selfishly driven, goal-obsessed climber," says fellow MRS team member Jeff Fongemie. "He moves carefully, taking the time to keep watch over his teammates, looking for frostbite, and talking about each step as a team. I think of Steve as the guy who can often figure out practical solutions to the problems the team is facing."

Because of the hard work Conservation Officers Mark Ober and Jeremy Hawkes have done to break trail ahead of them, these five are able to move over the terrain efficiently. "It was pretty cold and nasty, and we knew that if these guys had been out for a couple of days, it was serious," says Surette. "One of the things MRS does really well is to move steadily in the mountains and improvise. I'd be surprised if anyone had more than a thirty-pound pack."

The light weight of an MRS pack is in sharp contrast to the heavier packs carried by other teams, but there is experience and logic behind the standard. "Anytime you go out, you need to be able to take care of yourself, but you've also got to have enough extra gear to lend to the team effort," says Larson.

Every ounce in an MRS backpack is chosen with purpose, whatever the season. Some of the contents are required and others are left up to individual discretion, as outlined in the organization's written standard. Members are told to be prepared for spending at least twenty-four hours in the field in all conditions. The choice of food and drink is left up to the team member, as is any gear that might provide comfort if the team needs to bivouac overnight. But, say the guidelines, "keep in mind the need to tend to the patient as well as to yourself for this extended period of time. Choose your own level of suffering; but do not become a liability!"

The MRS regulations stipulate that the weight of personal gear should not exceed thirty pounds, so team members are instructed to choose the lightest and most durable equipment in the following categories, and they often choose to pool gear to address mission-specific requirements:

• Pack: 3,500-4,000 cubic inches. This pack should only be two-thirds full with personal gear; the extra space may be necessary for carrying group or patient gear.
• Footwear: mission specific
• Microspikes, crampons, ice axe
• Avalanche equipment (beacon, probe, shovel)
• Snowshoes (if ground conditions and location require)
• Insulated pants, coat, wind shells, gaiters, face mask, ski goggles (2 pair), fleece neck-up, balaclava, gloves, extra mittens, extra socks.
• 1-quart water bottle in insulated parka and one half-quart thermos (full with hot drink)
• Map, compass, pencil, small note pad, GPS, bright headlamp with extra batteries
• Chemical heat packs, personal basic first-aid kit, lighter, whistle, chem-light stick, multi-tool
• Bivy gear (mission specific): foam pad, lightweight down sleeping bag, bivy sack, stove, one freeze-dried meal, and hot drink mixes. Consider what the patient may need when found.
• Minimum personal technical gear. This is your own toolkit: basic alpine harness, helmet, ascent device, 3 large pear-shaped locking carabiners, 4 non-locking carabiners, belay device, 2 cordelettes, 4 slings, Prussik slings, a sharp knife.

Because MRS members are known for their experience and top-level skills, they are able to head up with relatively light packs. Still, says Charlie Townsend, all the well-chosen gear is sometimes no match for the weather conditions in the White Mountains. "You have to have incredible respect for these mountains," he says. "I've climbed in other places all over the world, and once my climbing partner shouted at me through some Alaskan storm, 'Wow, this is almost as bad as that time on Mount Washington!' I hope I never lose that little edge of fear, which is how the respect manifests itself."

Townsend's humility is well placed. But it's also true that he and other MRS members have accumulated so much experience in difficult terrain and full conditions that it takes a great deal of adversity to set them back—and they know when that point has been reached. "For us, it's so easy to be in the terrain; we're so comfortable there," says Larson. "Every one of us is operating within our limits. We all spent so much time climbing before we began participating in search and rescue. We also work as a team. We ask a lot about how others are doing, checking people's faces for frostbite, things like that. It works very well. If we're not okay, we turn around. Nobody thinks of himself as a hero on MRS, and none of us are doing anything heroic. We're just operating in our comfort level. We wouldn't have necessarily gone out on that day, but someone asked us to, so we did, and that situation didn't really take us beyond what we're comfortable doing."

Comeau, who trains military special operations personnel in mountain practices, stresses the importance of a cohesive team: "It's nice when you get a tight-knit group. When you show up and things are really bad, you want to know who you're with. We go out all the time together. Some of us have been working together for forty years. We grew up climbing together, hiking, and doing rescues all that time. So, if someone has any doubt whatsoever, we don't debate it. We turn around. We all read each other's minds. We're on the same page."

Noonan, a forty-year member of MRS, recognizes the risk associated with a team that's pushing far beyond its capacity. It takes a good deal to test an MRS team's capacity, but team members are discouraged from pushing too far. "The first rule in all search and rescue scenarios is don't become a victim," says Noonan. "It all depends on the group you're with, how comfortable everyone is. If someone feels it's too extreme, that's enough. But most everybody on the team has a lot of experience above treeline, so they feel comfortable in pretty bad conditions."

Decades of accumulating perspective and wisdom in the backcountry have also translated to empathy for those who are being searched for. "On the one hand, you've got the rescuers, and on the other hand, you've got the victims, and we're really not that far apart," says Larson. "Some of us on MRS have been rescued for various reasons and the victims are out doing exactly what we do. Even if you look at us on a spectrum of skill and experience, we were all there once. To me you have to embrace these people going out and having their own adventure. You can't wait for them to be experienced, because you can't be experienced without going. You've got to pay your dues."

Like his teammate, Townsend understands the small degree of separation between him and those he seeks to help. "It doesn't take much," he says. "Any little element—a shifting wind direction or a stumble or a twisted ankle—can be really serious. At MRS, we're not a medical provider but rather a transport service. Most often, the priority is to get people out of the elements so a medical professional can work on them. In the bitter cold, we don't want someone to die of a broken ankle because we don't move them quickly enough to shelter and warmth. Hypothermia is the biggest concern."

Usually, rescuers set off with very limited information about the location and condition of those they're seeking. But their loved ones at home are working with even less information and can do little but wait and hope for the best. "When these guys go out in extreme conditions, Steve and his teammates don't know anything other than 'I have to be in such and such and place, and I have to be prepared,'" says Larson's wife, Tricia. "And we wait. It's kind of a family affair. Worry is in the back of your mind, especially on those really severe winter nights." Tricia vividly recalls one occasion when her husband arrived home in the early morning hours following a winter rescue shivering uncontrollably because the conditions were so extreme.

Now in the darkness, headlamps illuminated, the team of five are at the higher reaches of Falling Waters Trail. With a measured and fluid ascent, they have steadily closed the distance between them and Ober and Hawkes, who continue to break trail, creating the trough they hope will lead rescuers to victims.

Franconia Notch
Liberty Spring Trail
5:00 p.m.

Meanwhile, the two members of the MRS-3 team, Steve Dupuis and Tim Martel, are ascending the 2.9-mile Liberty Spring Trail toward Mount Liberty (4,459 feet) in case the two missing hikers summited Little Haystack and headed south. They have encountered a lone hiker, who tells them he summited Liberty and saw nothing, but they choose to continue upward anyway. If they don't find Osborne and Fredrickson on top, they'll follow the ridgeline northward toward Little Haystack.

Overhead, Black Hawk 031 arrives back in the Area of Operations after refueling at Berlin Airport and begins a grid search pattern on the western side of the ridge at Profile Lake. Pilot Zach Lane flies southward down to Liberty Spring Trail, then turns the tail and flies northward above Greenleaf Trail. Lane continues this back-and-forth pattern over the flatter portions of the terrain until it begins to rise toward Franconia Ridge. On his fifth sweep, Lane arrives at the southern end near Liberty Spring Trail. At this point, he begins a new pattern, hooking left, and following the contours of the terrain, west to east, up to the ridgeline. On reaching the ridgeline, he turns the tail 180 degrees, points the Black Hawk west, and follows the terrain back down to the base of Franconia Notch. He will continue this west-to-east/east-to-west pattern northward until he reaches the summit of Mount Lafayette.

Martel and Dupuis are happy to be moving. "I remember it being extremely cold at the trailhead, and it seemed to get colder and colder as we went up the trail," says Martel.

Dupuis started climbing and hiking in the White Mountains in 1986. In 2001, he joined MRS and currently serves as president, succeeding Rick Wilcox. "I was lucky to have a handful of older mentors on whose coattails I road during my early years in the mountains," says Dupuis. "Those men instilled in me a couple of crucial things: always leave an itinerary with dependable people; and, realize that turning back when things get really bad is always the right choice, because there are many days when the mountains don't want you there."

Dupuis's experience has taught him to navigate the unpredictability of the White Mountains. "When things get really bad, I make a point of keeping calm, managing any fear that might crop up, and working through the problems in front of me logically," he says. Anytime Dupuis is in the mountains, even for the day, he is prepared to stay out for twenty-four hours unassisted, equipped with "a small kit of stuff that is hardly noticeable to carry."

The two are far from any support and will need to hunker down if one becomes incapacitated or weather conditions worsen. "I was carrying gear to bivy, if we needed to: a small stove, fuel, food, a shovel, a small foam pad, a sheet of plastic, and a hundred feet of cord," says Dupuis. "I also had a thermos with a hot drink. It is a much lighter kit than most people would be comfortable with in the conditions we are called out in, but it's functional. We were prepared to dig in and stay in a snow cave. It would not have been a comfortable night to stay out, but it would have been manageable."

For his part, Martel is carrying a bivy sack and a relatively light sleeping bag. "I roll with a little bit lighter bag because I figure if I'm in it, I'm also going to be wearing my puffy jacket and puffy pants, which make the bag much warmer," he says. In addition, he carries a basic first-aid kit, a stove "which probably wouldn't have worked in those conditions," a thermos with a mixture of hot chocolate and coffee, and a second thermos of boiling water, energy bars and gorp, and an avalanche beacon in the event Fredrickson and Osborne have bailed out to the west where the snow load is heaviest.

Like his teammate, Martel has benefited from valued mentorship. "After MRS meetings, Charlie (Townsend) and Joe (Lentini) used to test us over a beer at Flatbread Company in North Conway," he recalls. He's gained a lot of knowledge about the nuances and unique challenges that exist throughout the region from being out with these and other veteran members of the team. But he credits another mentor as well: "Mount Washington has taught me a lot about knowing my limits," he says wryly.

Dupuis and Martel are making good time as they approach the Liberty Spring tent site. Martel typically hikes at a measured pace to avoid sweating and the need to continuously hydrate. But today he finds he can move fast and not overheat. "I wasn't sweating a lot, so I didn't need to drink that much," he recalls. Part of the reason for this is his high level of fitness. "We have a strong foundation of fitness at MRS," he says. "It's built through years of being on trails and guiding. Our legs are always ready to go."

But these two also know where their limits are. "We know where that line is," says Martel. "Everybody on MRS has that mindset. Yes, we're more willing to accept risk than the average recreationalist, but we know what we're capable of and what our backup plan is."

They also know the importance of paying attention to variables. "People don't always know what a variable is," says Martel. They think, 'I'm going to do this because I've done it many times before without a problem.' But how many variables are affecting that person on that particular day? Cold, snow, an unbroken trail, a bad weather forecast? Those of us who go out to rescue someone understand how these variables can pile up and create unmanageable risk. Pushing a little bit further to get the job done is acceptable, but taking unnecessary risks is not. The variable you don't account for usually gets you."

High up on the trail, the two stop to make gear adjustments. Martel is struck by the amount of clothing he is already wearing, and they haven't even reached treeline yet. "I had on my puffy jacket and puffy pants," he recalls. "My jacket was the warmest one Wild Things gear made at the time. My pants were down-insulated and inside a lightweight shell pant. I had all of that over a one-piece Gore-Tex suit. and under that a one-piece stretch fleece suit and base layers. I was also wearing plastic expedition boots, knee-high gaiters, a neoprene face mask, and heavyweight gloves that I've worn at 6,000 meters. We were walking uphill with all our layers on, and I was not warm, or even remotely comfortable."

Pemi Wilderness, Old Bridle Path, Falling Waters Trail
5:45 p.m.

Like Dupuis and Martel, Conservation Officers Heidi Murphy and Mike Eastman are also operating as a pair and without any trailing support. They are on the opposite side of the ridge, in the Pemigewasset Wilderness on relatively flat ground and not all that far from their snow machines. They have been deployed to that area in case Fredrickson and Osborne have chosen to bail out in that direction. But they are not encountering any signs that this has occurred.

Elsewhere, other teams are slowly making upward progress amid waist-deep snow. Conservation Officers Mark Hensel and Brad Morse are just below Greenleaf Hut on Old Bridle Path and have linked up with two members of the MRS-2 team, Bayard Russell Jr. and Sam Bendroth.

Hensel, Morse, Russell, and Bendroth radio their location to Incident Command. They are advised to continue to the hut but are told not to go above treeline because the weather is too bad. The four other members of MRS-2 are close behind. "I remember walking up the trail with the team, looking and exploring all of the little side trails that lead to views just in case they went in there," says Fongemie.

Back southward, on Falling Waters Trail, the five-member MRS-

1 team, led by Steve Larson, catches up with trailblazers Hawkes and Ober, who are exhausted from pushing through deep snow for over four hours.

At this point, the teams operating in Franconia Notch that evening comprise hundreds of years of collective alpine and rescue experience. And all of it is making its determined way toward Fredrickson and Osborne.

XXIV
GAUNTLET

"In every walk with nature one receives far more than he seeks."
—*John Muir*

Skookumchuck Trail (3,000 feet)
Monday, Feb. 11, 2008
6:10 p.m.

Mount Washington Observatory Surface Weather Observations (6:00 to 7:00 p.m.): Temperature -11°F; winds out of the northwest averaging 76 mph; visibility 1/16 of a mile, fog/blowing snow; windchill -52°F. Peak wind gust: 93 mph.

Gordie Johnk and his two Pemi Valley Search and Rescue (PVSART) teammates might as well be off grid. He's tried to reach Incident Command numerous times to check in, but to no avail. "We lost phone reception, and my radio wasn't working either," he recalls. "It was really cold. We were on the Fish and Game direct frequency, but we weren't getting through."

Although they're cut off from radio contact, the trio continues upward. The hiking higher up is arduous and draining. "The reflective blazes on the trees were only ten inches off the snow, because there was just so much," says Johnk. "They're usually over our heads about seven feet up the tree."

Matt Glarem is shocked by the depth of the snowpack as well. "It was so deep that we'd have to stop and lean down to our hips or even our knees to look for the blazes on the trees," he says. "In many cases, the blazes were completely covered by the snow or at snow level."

The ski tracks they're following end abruptly. Whoever cut them must have heeded the deteriorating weather and turned back. Johnk has been enjoying the packed trail assistance, but that's gone now.

"Nobody was up there," Johnk recalls. "We were breaking trail through fresh snow. There was no sign that anyone had come that far."

Close by, Black Hawk 031 completes its final grid pattern over the northern portion of Franconia Notch. Pilot Zach Lane points the aircraft due south to head "back to the house." Lane recalls the moment their mission concluded. "We searched until we were told by Incident Command that the weather was too dangerous, and we were called off," he says.

Crew Chief Matt Stohrer is disappointed to be leaving the Area of Operations but is philosophical about the decision. "Getting called off was pretty status quo for me, because I had done so many of these before," he says. "Your adrenaline isn't pumping at that point because you're just searching, which makes it a little easier to turn away."

Greenleaf Hut
Old Bridle Path
6:20 p.m.

South of Johnk and his team, Conservation Officers Brad Morse and Mark Hensel and two MRS-2 team members, Bayard Russell Jr. and Sam Bendroth, arrive at Greenleaf Hut. It has taken them four hours to reach this point. Under normal hiking conditions, it would take approximately two hours and forty minutes. The rescuers have worked hard to break through heavy fresh snow and recognize the risk the wind and cold now pose as they approach treeline. "We stripped off our wet base layers and put on dry clothes, and then our heavy mitts and goggles," recalls Morse.

They are soon joined by the remaining four members of MRS-2, Jeff Fongemie, Joe Lentini, Joe Klementovich, and Rob Adair, on the leeward side of the hut, and the group starts discussing next steps. "We thought that if we didn't find them, there was the possibility of two people staying up there overnight. In that case, we'd pool our gear for the two guys we'd leave behind, and the rest of us would descend," recalls Adair.

Bendroth and Russell offer to stay at the hut. "We considered sleeping there, assuming that we'd be called out again in the morning anyway," says Russell. Bendroth doesn't have overnight gear, but steps up anyway. "Other team members had the gear, so I volunteered to stay," he recalls. Keeping Bendroth and Russell, both of whom are expert alpinists and rescuers, at a location high on the mountain will serve a number of purposes. If new information about the missing hikers is received and relayed to them, they'll be able to respond quickly. If Fredrickson and/or Osborne arrive at the hut, they'll have immediate support. And Bendroth and Russell will be in a position to get an early start the following morning.

With a plan in place, the rescuers decide to enter the hut to get out of the extreme cold, but they hit a snag. "We tried and failed to get into the main living space of the hut, which was locked," recalls Fongemie. "But we were able to access the basement. It's a cold, dark, and dirty space, but we figured we'd use that as an emergency shelter if needed."

Lincoln Brook Trail
6:25 p.m.

Five miles into their 9-mile assignment, Conservation Officers Heidi Murphy and Mike Eastman arrive at a brook crossing at Lincoln Branch. The running water is a godsend, since both have consumed all the water they've brought with them. Eastman recalls the welcome but risky refueling station. "We filled our bottles in the brook and talked about our chances of getting giardia," he says. "We were just so thirsty. We'd gone through our Nalgene bottles quickly making the hike out there." Suddenly, their radios squawk and they hear the sound of Todd Bogardus's voice. He feels they've gone far enough and wants them to head back to the trailhead. Murphy and Eastman acknowledge the instruction and head back to their snow machines.

"The moon was so bright in that spot, we turned off our headlamps and used the illumination to navigate," says Eastman. "We actually had a nice hike out." Still, he and Murphy can't help but think about the challenges others are facing on the other side of the mountain above them.

Falling Waters Trail
Shining Rock Junction
6:35 p.m.

Conservation Officers Mark Ober and Jeremy Hawkes are cooked. Just prior to reaching the junction to Shining Rock they are overtaken by the five members of MRS-1. That team continues moving upward, while Ober and Hawkes stop at Shining Rock Junction to rest. "It was dark as hell, and we were just dying," recalls Hawkes.

To get a sense of the difficulty of the work they've been doing breaking trail, it has taken the pair five hours to reach this point, a hike that, in normal conditions, would take half that time. Focused and driven, Ober has taken on the lion's share of the work. The pair initially took turns breaking trail, but Ober took over completely at some point. "There was a lot of snow from the night before, so the trail wasn't packed out at all," he recalls.

Their effort is not lost on the members of MRS-1. "We've got to give them credit for breaking trail, that's for sure," says Jim Surette. And teammate Chris Noonan adds, "Their work made it much easier for us to get up there quickly."

Ober is strong and maintains a solid level of physical fitness, but the immense effort required to push through the knee-high snow has taken a toll on him. "Snowshoeing with a heavy pack is not uncommon for us at that time of year," he says. "But I hadn't hiked in a while. Our normal rate of speed is two miles per hour, so it should have taken us three to four hours at most, but it took much longer."

During the pause at the junction, Hawkes takes the opportunity to make some adjustments. "I remember adding a layer, and I removed my pack briefly because it was so heavy," he says.

But the pauses are brutal for Ober, so much so that he finds himself unable to perform self-care. "My pack was so heavy; it was something like seventy-four pounds," he says. "I didn't want to take it off because my back was all sweaty, and I didn't want to get cold. So in my thick-headedness, I wasn't drinking enough on the way up." Rather than remove his pack, Ober resorts to leaning against a tree to get some relief.

While they rest for these few moments, the light from their headlamps bobs violently up and down, slashing lines through the total darkness. It is snowing, and they can hear the wind's guttural howl as it assaults the summit of Little Haystack above them. They envision the five members of MRS-1 huddled at treeline. They must get moving to provide support if the five decide to step out into open terrain. Hawkes resumes hiking, and Ober straightens up from his deep bend at the waist and follows behind his friend. The steep terrain, brutal conditions, and lack of hydration, combined with the heavy pack that holds enough gear for Ober and anyone he might find, will continue to deplete him with every step he takes.

Skookumchuck Trail
7:00 p.m.

The ascent of the three-member PVSART team, Gordie Johnk, Matt Glarem, and Irv Locke, up the Skookumchuck Trail mirrors that of Ober and Hawkes over on Falling Waters. "You're talking to each other a lot at the lower levels. You're all chatty. And then at around four thousand feet you're in your own head," says Johnk. "It's one foot in front of the other until you yell, 'Next!', and the next person in line takes the front to break trail."

As they move up, the blazes are getting harder to find. Glarem is thankful to be with Johnk and Locke, both of whom know the terrain. "Those two guys had a pretty good sense of the trail," he says. "They were remembering trees they thought had a blaze on them but were caked in snow. The higher we got, the harder it was to find the trail, but we took our time and kept checking in with each other."

Because Glarem doesn't have snowshoes, Johnk and Locke break trail through the lower and middle portions of the climb. But, eager to contribute to the effort, Glarem takes the front as they get higher on the mountain. "I was putting a lot of weight on my poles, and the snow was mid-calf to knee high," recalls Glarem. "I was sweating heavily. We were working so hard. At one point, we stopped for a break, and I put on dry socks. We were taking off layers as we hiked, but as soon as we stopped, we were putting everything back on."

The trio reaches approximately 4,400 feet, just before the point where Garfield Path heads to Mount Lafayette. Johnk is growing concerned about the state of his team and the extreme conditions. "The weather was not good," he recalls. "It was brutally cold, and the wind was howling. As we were hiking up, the trees were bending over and pulling up part of the ground, and in winter that's saying something."

Glarem recalls how angry the wind sounded. "It was nukin' up there. The wind was blowing so hard, and the spindrift was swirling all around us. Without exaggeration, I'd say it was roaring."

The team huddles together to assess the situation. "We were right at treeline in the scrub pine but not exposed," recalls Johnk. "We could feel and hear the wind, and it was really hard to have a conversation. I can remember taking my gloves off to get something to drink out of my pack. That was the wrong move. It was so cold."

Glarem yells to his teammates, "Is anyone cramping?" Locke indicates that he is.

"How long has it been going on?" Glarem asks. "About forty-five minutes," Locke replies.

"Uh, oh," Glarem thinks to himself and immediately takes action.

"I got into my pack and took out electrolyte tablets, dissolved them in water, and gave him the water," Glarem recalls. "I knew that if we were cramping already, we had to get off the mountain."

Johnk arrives at the same conclusion as Glarem. His own hands are cold from removing his gloves, Glarem's feet are wet, and Locke is cramping from dehydration. "Does anyone have a problem turning around?" Johnk recalls yelling. There is immediate consensus.

"When you get into a situation like that, you need to get a feel for how people are faring, and they need to be honest," says Johnk. "They were good guys, they were strong, they'd been in adverse conditions before. We weren't at our limits at that point, but we all wanted to turn around before we reached them."

Johnk is finally able to get through on his radio to Team President Allan Clark, who is parked at the trailhead to monitor his team. "We're turning back, my call," Johnk tells him.

"Understood," replies Clark, who trusts his team to make the right decision. They are up there in it, and he knows they aren't making the decision lightly.

"We had radio reception at the top, so we knew the hikers hadn't been found," says Glarem. "We were feeling bad because we hadn't cleared our trail. Once we made the decision to go down, we all layered up and just hauled ass. We walked down that hill really fast."

Years later, Glarem still feels the weight of their decision. "We weren't talking about it, but I can tell you I was really heavy-hearted on the descent," he says. "Those guys could be up there dying. They could be on the trail, and we had to turn around. But it was the right thing to do."

Down at Incident Command, Todd Bogardus and Jim Goss are monitoring the deteriorating weather conditions and the status of the teams they have deployed. Bogardus knows the longer he keeps them up high, the greater the risk of something going wrong for the people he's sent out.

"All the crews were attempting to get higher, but it was really difficult because of the snow load, the wind, and the poor visibility," Bogardus recalls. "It was getting too dangerous. At one point, I felt I was going to have to bring all the teams back down. We were probably reaching the cusp of that decision. I always ask the teams to do what they can, but they're the ones up there, and they have to make those judgments as a team."

With a few teams so close to the ridge where Fredrickson and Osborne might be found, Bogardus decides to let the mission play out a little while longer.

XXV
IN EXTREMIS

"These things we do, that others may live,"
—*United States Air Force pararescue creed*

Treeline on Falling Waters Trail
Monday, Feb. 11, 2008
7:10 p.m.

Mount Washington Observatory Surface Weather Observations (7:00 to 8:00 p.m.): Temperature -11°F; winds out of the west averaging 75 mph; visibility 1/16 of a mile, fog/blowing snow; windchill -52°F. Peak wind gust: 92 mph.

Steve Larson's finely tuned alpine instincts tell him it's time to stop. As he does so, Alain Comeau, Chris Noonan, Charlie Townsend, and Jim Surette, who are lined up single file behind him, follow suit. No one speaks a word. There's no need, because what happens next is standard practice for the Mountain Rescue Service (MRS). Sheltered among tightly packed spruce trees, the five rescuers, designated today as MRS-1, remove their packs. Each retrieves a big puffy jacket, an additional clothing layer or two, a balaclava, and goggles.

After passing Conservation Officers Mark Ober and Jeremy Hawkes near Shining Rock Junction, MRS-1 has been tasked with breaking trail to treeline. They've already encountered deep snow in the more exposed areas of the trail, and they know their sheltered walk below treeline is about to morph into a colder trek. "You work up somewhat of a sweat, so you try to manage heat loss up to that point," says Larson. "But the wind is howling, and you know that once you get into it, it'll be harder to stop and get more clothing on."

Larson cups his gloved hand and slowly raises it skyward. When it reaches a point just above the scrub trees, his entire arm jolts backward as it absorbs the northwest wind's lethal punch. Two feet above their heads and a few steps beyond where they're standing are conditions that few people ever encounter. "When you're in high winds above treeline in the White Mountains in winter, it's as bad as any place in the world," says Chris Noonan. "You feel like you're in outer space, and you realize there's no margin for error."

Alain Comeau, who is not new to these conditions, recalls times when he's had to crawl on his hands and knees to make any progress. "Until they've experienced it, people don't know how *bad* bad really is," he says.

Down in the base of Franconia Notch, Todd Bogardus and Jim Goss sit at their workstations in the mobile command center. Their eyes shift back and forth between maps and monitors that show the locations of their teams. The base radio in front of Bogardus has, for the most part, remained silent. Radio discipline during winter missions is critically important because of the difficulty of communicating with teams above treeline and the speed with which batteries in the rescuers' radios drain when exposed to arctic conditions.

Bogardus maintains a stoic demeanor, but he's feeling a tremendous weight on his shoulders. "My biggest concern was the safety of everyone going in," he recalls. "That was paramount. They all knew they needed to relay conditions back to me, and I might make the decision to pull them. They also knew they were empowered to turn around if conditions got to be too much for them. I trusted their judgment because they'd all been in these situations numerous times before, and they all knew what they could do—what was worth it and what was not."

The silence in the control room is broken by an incoming radio transmission from MRS-1: *We're at treeline and we want to push to the summit for a quick search!*

Bogardus and Goss can hear the wind roaring in the background. The message goes on to say that, after reaching the summit, the team will likely need to bail out and not make an attempt to search the ridgeline.

Go! Bogardus responds.

Once MRS-1 has the green light, balaclavas are pulled up and over mouths and noses, clear-lensed goggles are dropped off foreheads to cover vulnerable eyes, and packs are shouldered. "Without speaking or discussing a formal plan, we all knew what we'd do," recalls Larson.

"We'd fan out to cover as much ground as possible and work our way to the summit of Little Haystack."

Larson leads the team on the narrow trail and, like skydivers funneling out of the side door of a plane, one by one they leave the security of the stunted trees and head into the howling wind. The onslaught pins the outer layers of their clothing against their bodies, and the high-tech fabric responds with a loud and continuous "rrraaappp!"

"Visibility was terrible," recalls Larson. "With blowing snow, the headlamps don't help much at all. You're just seeing this wall of darkness and snow. You can't see beyond the beam. I can remember thinking, 'This is crazy; how can we possibly do this in these conditions?'"

When they break treeline, Larson expects to see a cairn at the entrance to the trail, but there is none. "How the hell are we going to find our way back in?" he thinks to himself, deciding that they'd just have to hope to find their crampon marks on the way back and follow them down. At this point, he can't let that concern derail the mission. "You know what you can deal with and can't deal with," he says. "We probably could have found our way back to the trail if we needed to, and if we couldn't, we could have just forced ourselves into the pucker brush and at least gotten out of the wind."

But Charlie Townsend has something else in mind. As he emerges above treeline, he drives the spike end of his mountaineering axe into the frozen snow at the entrance to the trail and leaves it there. Earlier that day, when Townsend learned of the location of the search, he was already thinking through the multitude of variables that could put the team at risk. "It's difficult to find the trail entrance at that spot even in good conditions," he says. "I'd had trouble in the past, so I wanted to mark it that night so we could find our way back down. Missing that one turn can change a fairly normal winter experience into a full-on epic nightmare. You can find yourself post-holing through scrub trees. You know there's a trail somewhere very close to you, and you could be off by just ten feet. But that's as bad as being off by ten miles."

As they move slowly forward, Comeau breaks slightly right of Larson and takes a more direct line toward the summit of Little Haystack. Using the rock-lined trail for reference, Noonan takes the position farthest to the left in order to do a wider sweep around the backside of the summit cone. Larson stays to the left of Comeau, Surette stays just behind both, and Townsend fills the small gap between Larson and Noonan. Each rescuer needs to stay in visual contact with those closest to him so the link between them can be maintained.

The team advances upward, and Townsend is finding it increasingly difficult to keep the man on each side of him in sight. "It doesn't take much to lose contact in swirling snow and wind," he says. Thinking back on the night, Larson acknowledges, "One of us could have disappeared up there."

Back at treeline, Jeremy Hawkes stops, turns around, and watches as the beam from Mark Ober's headlamp dances across the snow-encased trees lining each side of the narrow trail. It's a picturesque moment amid dire circumstances. Hawkes continues to walk toward the faint lights of the MRS-1 team ahead of them, deciding against adding layers of clothing before breaching treeline. He feels confident this is going to be a short sweep of the summit cone and a quick return back down. "Our mission was to cover the trail and then go to the summit to check for any signs of the hikers," he recalls.

Following behind his teammate, Ober is beginning to feel the effects of the conditions. "I was drained when I reached treeline," he recalls. "That's when I really started to feel it. I was thinking to myself, 'Holy crap, I'm tired.'"

Meanwhile, MRS-1 has fanned out for their search of Haystack. Jim Surette walks across the ridge trail that lies just north of the summit cone and continues east. As he scans the terrain in the shrouded light of his headlamp, he detects a consistent pattern of indentations in the snow. They are tracking parallel to him and headed south. Frozen footprints.

Because visibility is almost nonexistent, Surette is only able to see a couple of the imprints at a time, but he can tell they're leading downhill off the backside of the summit cone. At this point, he's close to becoming separated from his teammates and calls out to them. "I was far enough away that I wasn't sure they could hear me when I yelled to them," he says. "I was basically on my own. I didn't want to lose the team, but I really didn't want to lose those footprints, either. I felt like I had to stay on them, so I decided to follow them down."

Noonan is on the ridgeline just north of the junction of the Franconia Ridge Trail and Falling Waters Trail and tracking east in the direction of the Pemigewasset Wilderness. Townsend, Comeau, and Larson are nearby. Townsend does hear Surette yelling and senses his teammate is on to something. But he's also worried about losing sight of him.

"Come on back, come on back!" Townsend yells to Surette. But Townsend can tell by his friend's body language that he's committed to whatever he's following.

At this point, Noonan is approximately 100 feet below the summit of Little Haystack, on the eastern side of the trail. His gaze is drawn to a brief flash of light just beyond the reach of his headlamp. It looks like light glazing off reflective material. Sure enough, it's a backpack. As he gets closer, he spots a bright yellow jacket and a motionless figure lying on his right side. Although he won't learn who it is tonight, Noonan has found Laurence "Fred" Fredrickson.

Noonan kneels at the victim's side to check for signs of life. The hood of Fredrickson's jacket is pulled down over his eyes, and his face mask sits just below his nose. His right arm is bent at the elbow, and his right, gloved hand is curled in a fist and positioned near his face. His left arm is bent at the elbow and lies across his lower abdomen, and his left hand, inside a glove liner, is curled in a fist with the left thumb fully exposed. Fredrickson's upper and lower torso are in a straight line as if he were standing erect. His arms and legs are rigid and frozen. When Noonan pulls Fredrickson's face mask down below his chin, he can see by the skin color, texture, and accumulated frost that his face is frozen solid. He attempts to elicit a response but receives none.

"He had clearly died," Noonan says. "Everyone else was near the top, so I signaled for them to come to me."

In a matter of minutes, the situation has completely changed. "The victim is lying there as Jimmy Surette is finding tracks in the snow, and it becomes pandemonium," recalls Larson.

"It's not pleasant when you find someone like that." Comeau adds. "With the weather and the environment and everything that's going on, it's not like you have time to sit there and consider what you're seeing. Things are just happening; things have to be done. So any emotions or reactions will come later, as you reflect back on it."

There's an old adage in wilderness medicine concerning the treatment of a hypothermia patient: You're not dead until you're warm and dead. But there are exceptions, and Fredrickson's case is one of them. "You have to weigh the weather situation, the duration of the patient's experience and exposure, their clothing, and whether the patient has any signs of life," explains Dr. Murray Hamlet, an internationally recognized hypothermia expert. "In this case, the rescuers had no chance of resuscitating him. You can in fact be cold and dead."

Dr. Frank Hubbell, founder of Stonehearth Open Learning Opportunities (SOLO), agrees with Hamlet. "[Fredrickson] cooled off much faster than his hiking partner because he had exhausted all of his energy stores," Hubbell says. "He didn't have twenty-four hours of glycogen stores in his system. He didn't have the insulation or the energy reserves, so he lost the ability to shiver. His heart stopped, and therefore his blood stopped flowing. If you grab hold of a person's arm and it contracts, that person is alive because it takes life to contract a muscle. If you grab hold of an arm and it's stiff and you can't straighten it out, you have no ability to resuscitate the person; he's done."

Surette is unaware of what his teammates have discovered. Careful to keep the frozen footprints he has spotted directly in front of him and hoping his teammates are keeping eyes on him, he works his way southeast down the slope behind Little Haystack. The footprints end abruptly and are replaced by a snowdrift that has almost completely enclosed the torso of a man lying on his back. Loose snow swirling up the windward slopes and depositing on the leeward side are in the process of burying the torso completely. Surette has found James Osborne.

Operating in minimal light, deafened by the bellowing winds, and essentially disconnected from his team, Surette walks toward the man whom he fully expects is dead. He bends at the waist and illuminates the man's face with the beam of his headlamp. Snow blows across Osborne's cheeks, eyes, and nose, but there's not so much as a twitch to be seen. Surette places his gloved hand on Osborne's shoulder and presses down.

"Hey, buddy," Surette says in as gentle a manner as he can manage.

Osborne responds with a low, guttural moan that shocks Surette, who can still visualize the moment. "He really didn't look alive," he recalls.

This new discovery has greatly complicated an already complex situation. Now rescuers—in complete darkness, extreme conditions, and at great distance from medical care—are faced with a live victim who's critically ill. Surette tries desperately to alert his teammates for immediate assistance, to no avail. "I remember yelling my head off trying to signal someone, but there was no communication in that moment," he says

Dr. Horace Henriques, at the time a trauma surgeon at Dartmouth-Hitchcock Medical Center (DHMC) in Lebanon, N.H., offers some insight into what Osborne might be experiencing as he meets his rescuer. "At that point, the only things really working are his vital and primitive neurological functions," he explains. "He'd see the light of the rescuer's headlamp and be stimulated by the sound of the rescuer's voice. Things would be going from light to dark and dark to light, and his brain might interpret that he's in the wilderness. The hand touching him would signal help, and at that moment he may know he's going to make it. In a primitive way, he may realize he has a rope to grab on to and that's why he moves and groans. He couldn't imagine how he was going to get out of this and, all of a sudden, there is a touch. As he gets more and more stimulation, his brain realizes he's part of a process that's going to save him, and that he needs to help participate in that."

In retrospect, Todd Bogardus acknowledges that Surette's discovery of James Osborne, alive and capable of rescue, was an unexpected stroke of good luck. "During this whole mission, while the two hikers were missing, it snowed a lot. So we assumed any tracks that Fredrickson and Osborne made would disappear under fresh snow or be blown away by the high winds—unless we got lucky and the tracks froze. And that's exactly what happened."

Little Haystack
7:30 p.m.

When Fredrickson is found, Jeremy Hawkes radios down to Incident Command to inform them that one of the hikers has been located and is lifeless and frozen. He tells them that he and Mark Ober are staying with the victim, while MRS-1 follows the frozen footprints of what they believe to be the second hiker.

"Our batteries on all of our electronics were dying or freezing fast," recalls Hawkes. "I can remember using my portable radio to call down information. It was difficult to keep it warm under my jacket so it wouldn't freeze."

As members of MRS-1 walk in the direction where they last saw Jim Surette, Hawkes looks on with trepidation. "I was scared for them," he recalls. "I know they have a lot of experience, but I always feel it's my responsibility to ensure that everybody up there is going to be okay. They were going off trail, and if you go off trail up there, one minute you can be walking across a rock up to your ankles in snow, and then you can fall in between scrub trees and you're up to your chest. I'm trying to make decisions, and yet these people are more capable than me on a mountain. I made sure I kept a light on them so they'd know where to come back to. It was so windy that I was worried their own footprints would be swept away."

In an effort to get warm, Ober and Hawkes rock back and forth and jump up and down while they watch over Fredrickson. Ober is clearly struggling. Exhausted and dehydrated, he recalls thinking, "I'm beat. I'm cooked." The winds are taking a toll on their sweat-dampened clothing, and Hawkes scolds himself for his lapse in judgment back at treeline. "The MRS guys were smart. They put extra clothes on at treeline. That's the one thing I would have done differently," he admits ruefully. "I just thought we'd be moving around enough to stay warm."

Standing with his deteriorating teammate, Hawkes finds himself fighting his own battle with the elements. "My eye just froze shut!" he yells to Ober. Although exhausted, Ober knows they've got to make rapid adjustments. "We've got to get our goggles on!" he tells Hawkes. For the first time since stepping onto Falling Waters Trail over six hours ago, Ober takes his backpack off. The feeling of relief is instantaneous but short lived as the wind and cold drive the sting deeper into his sweat-soaked upper torso.

The two know they need to add layers of clothing, but that is a huge physical challenge above treeline in full conditions. Hawkes retrieves his goggles and puffy coat from inside his pack and is alarmed to find his range of motion significantly impaired. "I took layers off to put much warmer ones on, and when I did, my right arm wouldn't straighten out enough to get it into the sleeve," he recalls. "It was like all of a sudden I lost muscle. The cold had never caught me like that before. Finally, as I moved around trying to get my stuff on, my arm straightened out. It was strange how things were happening up there."

Because his muscles are also seizing up, Ober elects to put on a shell jacket along with his goggles. "I remember just being extremely cold without my puffy jacket on, but I didn't know if I'd be able to get it on by myself the way I was feeling," he says.

When they notice the MRS-1 team converging over something they appear to have found in the snow, Hawkes comes to the unwelcome realization that the mission will probably run much longer than he anticipated—and prepared for. He tells Ober he's going to move toward the team in an effort to get an idea of what's transpiring and that Ober should stay put so both can act as beacons back to the trail. "Jeremy took off, and I'm standing there near the summit freezing my ass off," says Ober.

Larson, Comeau, Noonan, and Townsend arrive as Surette is removing snow from Osborne's body. Surette shouts to them that Osborne is alive. "It was clear that Fredrickson was dead, so when we realized Osborne was alive, albeit comatose, all our effort went into giving him his best shot at survival," says Larson. "We did what we could to shelter him from the wind and provide what we had for additional warmth. We formed a wall around him as a windbreak."

"Usually when a person is that cold and you try to move them or carry them out, you cause the heart to fibrillate, so often they can't handle a carry-out," says Comeau, as he recalls the challenges they were facing.

Given that Osborne is severely hypothermic, the rescuers know any movement carries high risk. According to Giesbrecht and Wilkerson's *Hypothermia, Frostbite, and Other Cold Injuries,* "A hypothermic heart is particularly susceptible to ventricular fibrillation. Minor irritants fully tolerated by the heart at normal temperatures ... can cause a hypothermic heart to fibrillate. Once a cold heart fibrillates, restoring a normal rhythm with electrical shock is usually impossible" (pp.26-27).

But given the conditions, rescuers also know their hands are tied. "We tried to be gentle with him, but there weren't a whole lot of options," says Surette. "We tried to do as little damage as possible."

Townsend removes his pack, retrieves his spare down jacket and bivy sack, and Comeau radios down to Bogardus: *Second subject located within 300 feet from victim 1, and 200 feet south of summit of Little Haystack. Victim 2 alive, severely frozen!*

James Osborne lying unconscious in bivy sack while rescuers form a windbreak with their bodies.

As soon as Bogardus gets the message that there is a survivor, the mission shifts into even higher gear. It has now become a full life-saving mission with much greater urgency.

XXVI
WHEELS UP

"We are more fulfilled when we are involved
in something bigger than ourselves."

—*John Glenn, 2009 commencement address,*
Ohio State University

Little Haystack Mountain
Monday, Feb. 11, 2008
7:40 p.m.

Charlie Townsend stands over James Osborne while his teammates prepare him for a carry-out. Osborne continues to emit haunting groans and, though unconscious, attempts to sit up. "I straddled him and grabbed him by his belt and picked him up," recalls Townsend. With Osborne partially suspended in air, team members wrap him in Townsend's spare down parka and unzip the bivy sack. "You can't warm him, but you can keep him from getting much colder," explains Townsend. "So we got him inside the bivy bag and placed the bivy on a foam pad."

When Hawkes hears that MRS-1 has found the second hiker and that he is alive, he is shocked. "I can remember thinking as I'm hearing it, 'What are the chances?' and realizing just how close to the trail entrance both of them were," he says. According to Larson, they were no more than 100 yards from the shelter of treeline when they were found. But neither Hawkes nor Larson is aware at this point of the long ordeal the two hikers had endured before they collapsed.

Hawkes tells Ober, who is shivering mightily, about the surviving hiker. They had walked to the spot where Fredrickson lay, but now move toward Osborne so they can help decide how to proceed. When they arrive, they find Osborne inside the bivy sack and out of view, but they know he's in dire straits and are not sure he will survive the rescue attempt.

Meanwhile, it's becoming ever more clear that Ober himself is in trouble. His dehydration has brought on debilitating leg cramps that are working their way up into his lower torso. "Mark was bent over, mentioning pain in his legs," recalls Hawkes. "I could tell it was bad. When we stopped moving, that's when it got worse. He hadn't been drinking water and was dehydrated, and he was mad at himself for it. I gave him some hot chocolate, but he wasn't really coming out of it."

With a rescuer experiencing such a degree of difficulty, the situation has grown even more serious. "Ober was really hurting, just losing it," recalls Larson, "It was clear that he was on that fine line where he was barely able to care for himself. I became really concerned about him and about our situation. We were above treeline, in horrible conditions, with two victims, no carry-out litter, and potentially only six rescuers if Ober were to go down."

Ober still berates himself for his mistakes in judgment and says he learned important lessons from the experience. "I didn't know how cold I was until Jeremy saw that I wasn't responding to what was being said," he admits. "My biggest takeaway from the mission is the importance of fluids. I now make it a point to stop and drink more than I used to."

The MRS-1 team understands what is happening to Ober and helps him put on his puffy jacket, which immediately brings some relief. "It seemed like the wind calmed down, and I began to feel warmer," says Ober.

The longer the team and Osborne stay exposed to the conditions, the more danger they'll be in as well. Hawkes radios to Bogardus to ask what they should do and stresses that the situation is now urgent, both for Osborne and for the rescuers, who are all getting cold from inactivity. The rescuers are not optimistic that Osborne can survive a carry-out without a litter, even over the 100 yards or so it would take to get him to the shelter below treeline, but that might be their only option.

Bogardus recognizes that time is of the essence and calls all the search teams back to Incident Command so they can organize a ground rescue. At this point, with the winds so brutal, Bogardus assumes there will have to be a carry-out, so he enlists the help of additional search and rescue personnel from Fish and Game, the Pemi Valley Search and Rescue Team (PVSART), and Androscoggin Valley

Search and Rescue (AVSAR). These added rescuers are instructed to come to the trailhead for a briefing.

Ridgeline between Little Haystack and Mount Lincoln
7:45 p.m.

Steve Dupuis and Tim Martel, the two members of MRS-3, work their way along the 1.8-mile ridge trail northward toward Little Haystack. They're ascending a gradual rise but the closer they get to Little Haystack, the steeper it will get.

"As we hit the ridge and headed north, the trail was unbroken and beyond boot-deep, even with snowshoes on," says Martel. "Once we got going, the snow became thigh-to-waist-deep. We were taking turns breaking trail, and I can remember being completely gassed, and my heart was racing. We'd alternate breaking trail, but I never got what I would call warm or sweaty. The temperature gave me a lot of concern for anyone who'd just spent twenty-four or so hours outdoors. Even if they had gotten themselves below treeline and dug a hole to climb in, it would have been brutal."

As they approach Haystack, Dupuis and Martel suddenly hear the radio call informing them of the discovery of the two victims. "We really wanted to help and started working even harder to get there," says Martel. They know Bogardus is calling everyone back to the Command Post but believe they're close enough to the victims to make it there directly. So, they radio down for permission to continue along the ridge.

"You guys know where you are. If you think you can make it, go for it," replies Bogardus.

With clearance to move toward Haystack, Martel and Dupuis continue to grind. "There wasn't much conversation between us," says Martel. "We talked about how difficult it was and how cold it was, but we were just pounding it out, because we both knew what the goal was."

Larson remembers the effort put forth by Martel and Dupuis to attempt to reach Little Haystack in time to help. "Those two guys were killing themselves to get to us," he says. "Unlike us, who had a trail broken out for us, they busted the trail all the way across the ridge."

Incident Command
Falling Waters Trailhead
7:55 p.m.

Todd Bogardus knows that the odds of Osborne's surviving a carry-out down Falling Waters Trail, an effort that would last well into Tuesday morning, is almost impossible. So he calls the Army National Guard in an attempt to get a helicopter back into play.

"We have [the two hikers], and it's life or death," he tells Col. Frank Leith, who approved the early use of Black Hawk 031 for the mission. "Can you try?" Bogardus asks.

Without hesitation, Leith tells Bogardus he'll try to pull the same crew back together for an attempt at a rescue. Bogardus, in turn, radios up to Hawkes to let him know the helicopter will be dispatched to Haystack.

"What's the wait time?" Hawkes yells into his radio.

"About twenty minutes," estimates Bogardus.

Concerned that the aircraft will not be able to effect a rescue in the extreme conditions above treeline, Bogardus continues to gather personnel for a possible ground carry-out. He has no choice but to plan for a worst-case scenario.

Up on Little Haystack, Hawkes looks skyward and isn't optimistic. "I can remember thinking, 'Nope, they're not going to be able to do it; there's no way,'" he recalls. "The wind up there was ridiculous and there was cloud cover. The cloud cover would now and then break, and you could see the stars for a second, but then it would sock right back in. I've been on these missions before with similar conditions, and they've told us they can't fly."

While they wait for the Black Hawk, the seven rescuers maintain their shoulder-to-shoulder half-circle barrier around Osborne. Rocking back and forth, they try to protect him from the arctic blasts of northwest wind and keep each other warm.

N.H. Army National Guard Aviation Support Facility
Concord, N.H.
8:00 p.m.

Mount Washington Observatory Surface Weather Observations (8:00 to 9:00 p.m.): Temperature -12°F; winds out of the west averaging 72 mph; visibility 1/16 of a mile, fog/blowing snow; windchill -53°F. Peak wind gust: 92 mph.

First Lt. Pete Cartmell is in the midst of wrapping up his post-flight duties and preparing to head home when his cell phone rings. It's Col. Frank Leith, letting him know that Fish and Game wants a helicopter back in Franconia Notch and that it's now a life-or-death situation. "They know exactly where the hikers are, and if they're not extracted by air, it's unlikely the one survivor will make it through the night," he says. "Obviously, you don't have to go back up there if you're tired or you think the conditions are too bad," Leith adds. "But I'm letting you know they've found them."

As the Pilot in Command of Black Hawk 031, Cartmell already knows what he wants to do, but he has his crew to consider. "Anyone on the crew at any time, even during flight, can say, 'I'm done; we're not doing this,'" he explains. "But you really want to have that conversation on the ground and no place else, if you can."

Cartmell recognizes that encouraging candor from subordinates is challenging, given the hierarchy of military authority. "You do it through training, so junior personnel see what productive communication is supposed to look like. Then, if they see something way outside of that model when they're on a mission, they should feel comfortable expressing their concern," he says. "But it's a hard pattern to break, and there are still those times when personnel will defer to the senior person."

When he locates Zach Lane, Matt Stohrer, and Allan Robinson, who are engaged in various phases of task completion as each prepares to leave for the night, Cartmell gets right to the point:

"The colonel called. They found them," he says to his crew.

"Where?" asks Stohrer.

"On top," Cartmell replies.

No one needs an explanation of where the "top" is. Each crew member can still imagine himself back over the ridgeline, the very place they spent all day unable to see. "We all did a double take," recalls Stohrer. "We had just left there because the weather was poor, and we couldn't even get up top, and now.... But no one said we shouldn't do it. We all took a deep breath and said we'd do the mission, but we knew it was going to be dangerous."

The crew's intensity after they have considered and accepted the challenge shifts immediately to the mission. Zach Lane expresses what is likely in the minds of all his crewmates when he recalls thinking, "We have a good crew, so let's go get this done. Let's go get this guy on the mountain. And we don't want to leave the rescuers up there, either."

This second call to action, says Stohrer, meant "it was game time for us." Each crew member knows exactly what to do and begins the methodical preparation for takeoff. "Your adrenaline's pumping because you know that you have to perform and that there's a lot of risk involved," he says. "We have to go to the very top, where it's coldest because the winds are most extreme, in order to do our job. If we don't do our job effectively, we risk our lives, the lives of the ground team, and certainly the life of the person we're trying to rescue."

Cartmell calls Leith to let him know his crew is fully invested in their new mission but adds, "If conditions aren't favorable, we'll have to abort."

"Mission approved," Leith replies.

Stohrer and Robinson pull the refueled aircraft out of the hangar, and Lane takes his seat in the cockpit to start his pre-flight checklist. Cartmell and Leith spend a few minutes on the phone conducting a risk assessment for the mission. After assessing the equipment, terrain, and environmental factors, with weather being the most critical, they move on to the human factors involved, that is, the level of experience of the crew members and their track record of working together. It doesn't take them long to reach agreement that the level of competence and trust among these crew members is very high. They have worked together before and respect each other's skill and common sense.

Cartmell will serve as Pilot in Command again for this second Haystack mission. "As a team, we work through our specialties to get the job done," says Stohrer. According to Cartmell, serving as a Pilot in Command requires judgment and maturity. "The Army says it's trusting you to go out and do things the way you've been trained to do them, not to screw around. Just because they're giving you the keys to the Ferrari doesn't mean you get to go out and do what you want with it, and that's a hard thing. Army aviators need to be young, but they've also got to learn to be careful. That machine is incredible, and it's easy to get in trouble with it."

One of the roles of a Pilot in Command is to see beyond the initial risk assessment and stay alert to the need to adjust for unforeseen variables. "Risk assessments are great," says Cartmell. "But they're static. They're snapshots of what you think or what you may know at the very start. Once you start the mission, it becomes dynamic. One of the things inherent in military aviation is that you have to learn to make good decisions as things develop, or deteriorate, while the mission is in progress."

Cartmell joins co-pilot Lane in the cockpit of Black Hawk 031, where both have already spent most of the day, and together they run through the rest of the pre-flight check. Behind them, Stohrer and Robinson are securing themselves into their gunner's seats. Lane is preparing to fly the aircraft on this leg.

The green light is given for Black Hawk 031 to lift off. As Lane pulls up on the collective and back on the cyclic, the 16,000-pound aircraft loses contact with the ground. "We headed right up there, because they had the hikers and we had a coordinate," says Lane. The goal is to get there as quickly as possible. "Whenever we had combat wounded in Iraq, we used max power to get there as fast as we could, and that's what we did with this one," Stohrer recalls.

As they leave the ambient lights of Concord behind them, the crew flips their night vision goggles down from their flight helmets. The two-monocle system provides for a 40-degree field of vision, and that's if they've been adjusted perfectly. "It's like looking down a toilet paper tube," says Lane. "If you're looking straight ahead and want to see what's going on at three o'clock, you have to turn your head to that position. There's no peripheral vision. On nights with a lot of illumination, it's really clear and you can see a lot. You do have to get used to the lack of depth perception, but that just comes through experience and training."

Stohrer and Robinson are in the rear cabin preparing for what they might encounter when they arrive at the summit of Little Haystack. "As an air crew member you've always got to be ten minutes ahead of the mission," says Stohrer. "I was preparing the hoist and making sure the Stokes litter was prepped, but we just didn't know what we were going to find. I remember saying to Allan, 'Hey, we announce when we're going to do everything and make sure we get a call and response.' It's always good to refresh that protocol with the crew because everyone gets task-saturated. With your adrenaline pumping, you can stop thinking."

Interior of a Black Hawk helicopter operating at night.

Call and response in an aircraft, just like communication within teams on hard ground, is essential in managing risk and removing ambiguity during a mission. "Everything we do, everything we can think of, we're going to announce and get acknowledgement for," says Stohrer. "Because Army aviation is inherently dangerous, and every mission is a team event, communication is essential. There are multiple calls we use, but just about every action during the flight is announced and acknowledged to ensure the entire crew knows what's happening."

Lane is careful to fly the aircraft below the cloud ceiling, at approximately 1,500 feet above ground level. "That night we couldn't just pop up to five thousand feet and cruise up there because the cloud ceiling was so low," he says.

Out of his right-door window, Lane sees the tempered lights of the town of Lincoln, casting their glow on the low cloud cover that hovers above this popular ski town. No one is out and about on a night like this. The Black Hawk enters the southernmost point of Franconia Notch and, as it passes by The Flume, Lane banks the helicopter slightly right. Relying on his night vision goggles, he chooses a spur that lies between Mount Liberty and Little Haystack and follows it upward toward the ridgeline.

"We had to weave through the terrain down low to stay below the cloud ceiling, and then we snaked our way up the mountain," says Lane. "We hoped we wouldn't punch into the clouds and go 'whiteout,' which would have required us to navigate by Instrument Meteorological Conditions (IMC). If you go full IMC, you're not really in trouble, but one guy has to transition inside and start flying instruments like a commercial pilot, and you have to be really careful not to smack into a mountain."

About halfway between Mount Liberty and Little Haystack, the Black Hawk reaches Franconia Ridge. Lane banks the aircraft slightly left and follows the ridgeline northward toward their objective. Cartmell keys the technosonic radio and notifies Incident Command: *Guard 031 arrival on station and searching for rescue team.*

Bogardus offers a concise acknowledgment and lets the Black Hawk crew get back to work. As Lane follows the apex of the ridgeline just off to the eastern side, Stohrer picks up two prominent beams of light below moving slowly northward toward Little Haystack. "We started searching for the rescue team from the south slopes," Stohrer recalls. "When we made it up on top, we came across the first two. Headlamps are easy to see with night vision goggles, which magnify the light even in low visibility."

Lane draws the Black Hawk in closer to the ridge so the crew can identify the two figures below them. It's Steve Dupuis and Tim Martel of MRS-3, who are just over one-eighth of a mile from the summit of Little Haystack and continuing to drive through deep snow in the hope of reaching their teammates.

Lane eases the cyclic forward in the direction of the GPS needle and, shortly thereafter, arrives at their objective: *Guard 031 arrival Little Haystack.*

"The conditions were pretty terrible," says Lane. "Winds were gusting at seventy knots, and the temperature was like seventy below zero with the windchill."

The conditions at the summit are much worse than they were during the flight from Concord. Even with night goggles, says Lane, "visibility was garbage, maybe a half-mile. It was pretty bad, with snow and gusts."

Lane is worried about sending a hoist line down from the top of the mountain with such high wind gusts coming up the slope. Such strong gusts would give the aircraft quite a jolt and endanger team member Matt Stohrer, who'd be down below on the other end of the hoist line. "I was nervous about that, because I would have had to make a lot of corrections with the controls to keep things secure," says Lane.

Stohrer, too, is understandably concerned about the conditions. "The turbulence was like a roller coaster. At forty to fifty miles per hour it's not bad, but seventy-mile-an-hour gusts bounce you around in the back of the aircraft. Still, we also knew that was part of the mission."

As the Black Hawk creeps along the leeward side of the southern slope of Little Haystack, Stohrer looks out of his gunner's window and detects multiple headlamps. "When we came across the second group of rescuers, it was obvious they weren't searching," he recalls. "They were trying to protect someone."

Since liftoff in Concord, it has taken the team thirty-six minutes to reach the summit of Little Haystack, four minutes less than it took to get up there earlier that day. Cartmell notifies Incident Command: *Guard 031 located rescue team Little Haystack.*

XXVII
MOUNTAIN WARFARE

*"A soldier lives always for the next battle, because he knows
that before it arrives, impossible changes can occur in his favor."*

—James Michener

Summit of Little Haystack
Monday, Feb. 11, 2008
8:36 p.m.

Having located the rescuers, the helicopter crew has to decide
how it's going to proceed with the evacuation. "The snow was so high
on parts of the summit that you could only see the tops of the trees,
and we didn't know how compacted it was," says Lane. "What if we
tried to land and sank right into the snow?"

The initial plan is to drop Stohrer down on the hoist so he can
assess the situation. But without even opening the cabin door, Stohrer
and Robinson realize that a hoist rescue is completely out of the
question. "There was blowing snow and extreme wind gusts," says
Lane. "There was too high a risk. If you put a crew member down on
a hoist in those conditions, he could be run into the side of the
mountain or into a tree. It's also time consuming to prepare the
patient to be hoisted up, and the patient can end up spinning in the
litter."

Although not ideal, landing the aircraft is less risky, so that
becomes the new plan, and Cartmell begins to look around for a place
to land. But that, too, is looking questionable. As strong northwest
gusts buffet the aircraft, Lane inches the Black Hawk back and forth
along the eastern and southeastern slopes of the summit cone. The
uneven terrain below them is visible to him one second and gone the
next, as blowing snow and low clouds blast over the summit.

Lane recalls the frustration he felt when it was looking unlikely
they would be able to touch down. "Pete's looking left, and I'm

looking right," he says. "We had to land, and we didn't think we could hover over the terrain because the winds were just too strong. We were getting blown around everywhere. We finally realized we were going to have to try to land on the top of trees. So we began trying hard to find a suitable place."

Lane suddenly sees a little opening in the trees and tells Cartmell he thinks they should nose right about 20 degrees and try to land.

"Yep, I see it," replies Cartmell. "That looks good to me. Let's just set it down. We'll get it light and get these guys out fast."

It was indeed a landing spot—but not an ideal one. "The area had a big enough open space for us to fit the main fuselage on," says Cartmell. "It also became clear enough so we could actually see it."

Standing just off the southeastern side of the summit and shoulder to shoulder with other rescuers trying to protect James Osborne from the wind, Conservation Officer Jeremy Hawkes watches the helicopter key in on a landing zone. "I could hear the Black Hawk coming," he recalls. "When that thing came out of the clouds, it seemed to come down slowly, and then they found that one spot where they could land. I still wasn't sure they'd stay."

Down at Incident Command, Todd Bogardus is looking skyward as the Black Hawk arrives on Haystack. "When they showed up, the winds died down and the skies parted," he says. "We had a little lull in the weather right then. It was one of those moments when you think, 'This was meant to happen.'"

Cartmell decides to land the aircraft himself, with no objection from Lane. "I took it in for a couple of reasons, the first being experience," he explains. "I had done this a number of times and was confident being on the controls. I also had a better view of the landing zone, because everything was happening out of the left side of the aircraft, and Zach was positioned on the right side."

While he guides the Black Hawk down, Cartmell radios Stohrer in the rear cabin and walks through his intentions. "Matt, I'm going to kick the tail to the right," he tells him. "We're going to put the aircraft down, and I'm going to keep the power in [the rotors]." Given the unpredictable terrain encompassing the landing zone, Cartmell will essentially be hovering.

Stohrer then starts to do some planning of his own. "I explained to Allan [Robinson] that, on landing, I would exit the left cargo door with the Stokes litter and return with the victim," he says. "I had to be clear about everything I was doing in the back, because it could directly affect what the pilots were doing at the controls."

Warren Lyons, a rotary-wing flight instructor at the Eastern Army National Guard Aviation Training Site at Fort Indiantown Gap in Annville, Pa., explains the importance of Stohrer's communication protocols: "If Matt slams a door or drops something in the back and doesn't announce it, the pilots up front are going to start getting really paranoid about things. They're up front thinking, 'Okay, what's going on with my systems?'"

Now in control of the Black Hawk, Cartmell kicks its tail to the right, which points the aircraft's nose directly into the wind. This creates a natural airflow through the rotor discs of the helicopter, which will then require less power to stay airborne, allowing Cartmell to keep some power in reserve.

Lyons explains the series of maneuvers Cartmell performs as he approaches the landing zone: "You always make sure you're landing into the wind. In this case, Pete already knows where winds are coming from, but there are all sorts of eddies and currents interacting with the terrain that he needs to keep in mind. The most important thing in landing where there's snow, sand, or dust is that you land into a headwind."

The crew recognizes that a snow cloud could form and reduce visibility as the Black Hawk gets closer to the ground. By turning into the wind, Cartmell is mitigating that risk. But since he plans to keep power in the rotors, there's still a chance a cloud could develop. The crew chiefs in the rear will monitor this as they hang out the gunners' windows and communicate with Cartmell if they see one forming.

Stohrer knows the importance of keeping Cartmell informed of anything that might impact the pilot's ability to see. "You want to get the aircraft down on the ground before a cloud reaches the cockpit," he says. "The problem on Little Haystack was that we never really landed; we hovered. The thing that saved us is that everything up top was frozen over. We experienced ice-packed snow blowing around, but by hovering, we could dissipate the swirling snow before it formed a cloud."

As Cartmell moves the Black Hawk into the airspace above the landing zone, the wind is both a blessing and a curse. "Wind can be very helpful because it will push the clouds off the summit," he explains. "In this case, it gave me a gap in the clouds to go down through." But Warren Lyons explains the downside of the strong headwind Cartmell is contending with: "It is literally pushing the aircraft backward as Pete comes down, so he'll need to work hard to maintain forward motion."

Stohrer is positioned in the left gunner's seat, directly behind Cartmell, and Robinson is in the right-hand seat. As the pilot approaches the landing zone, the two men open their gunner's windows and lean out in order to perform what is known as airspace surveillance. They'll scan left to right and up and down for any obstacles that might impede the landing. Pilots can't always see directly underneath the aircraft, so the two are also ensuring that the helicopter is not about to land in a hole or on something that could penetrate it.

When the surveillance is complete, Cartmell initiates his descent. "Our approach was very slow, very deliberate," he says. "We were not racing to get in there. Our searchlight was on and everything I needed to see was illuminated. We went in at an angle because it was windy."

Cartmell is communicating with his crew about the wind direction and the various contingencies they have to be alert to. What will they do if a snow cloud forms? What is their escape route if the landing fails or they lose an engine? How much power can they expect to need? Crew members must all be on the same page with these possibilities so they can react quickly if a new plan is called for.

"The biggest thing you worry about in those conditions is engine failure," says Lane. "If we had lost an engine, we wouldn't have had single-engine hover capability that night. We'd either have had to go down and land or peel off and dive down the mountain to get our airspeed up."

With this and other hazards to consider, Lane, a veteran pilot with many hours logged in combat situations, calls this "a flight I'll never forget." It is definitely a high-risk mission. "You're not worried about guys shooting at you in the White Mountains," says Lane. "But you are worried about something bad happening. It was very stressful. It was freezing cold, but I was still sweating."

Cartmell further decreases his airspeed as the Black Hawk slowly loses altitude. He's descending at a rate of 40 to 50 feet per minute while Stohrer calls out their distance to the landing zone.

"Pete, there are trees poking out of the snow below us," Stohrer informs Cartmell.

"Okay, we're not going to go down that far," Cartmell replies.

In addition to checking the airspace, Lane keeps an eye on the GPS in front of him to monitor the aircraft's airspeed and slope angle. "I can remember the last part of the approach and landing," he says. "Pete was really threading a needle."

On the ground below, Jim Surette and his teammates watch as the blazing searchlight gets closer. "There were a lot of questions in our minds," he says. "We were wondering how it was going to work and whether they'd be able to land. It was so dark—pitch black."

Black Hawk 031 approaches the landing zone while rescuers prepare to move James Osborne.

Through the lenses of his night vision goggles, Cartmell can see the rescuers' reflective gear and headlamps. "I was concentrating on landing, and I knew they were a safe distance away from where I planned to go," he says.

The 64-foot aircraft is now hovering just above the tops of the scrub trees that are poking out of the deep snowdrifts below. Stohrer can see that there's more work to be done to get the Black Hawk into a position that will allow him to exit.

"Pete, I need you to slide left more. You're only going to be able to put the left wheel down. I'll call you in," advises Stohrer.

"I had complete trust in Matt to direct me to bring the aircraft where he needed it to be," says Cartmell. "And he had complete trust that I would get it there, and it would stay. We had trained for this."

At last, with his entire upper body hanging out of the side, Stohrer is confident they're over the best location for the Black Hawk to make contact with the surface of the snow. He tells Cartmell he can now lower the aircraft, and Cartmell executes.

"He just kind of set it down because the snow was so deep," says Lane. "You could see the tops of the trees poking out, but Pete is setting it into the snow. We're not actually landing, because when you fully land, you put the collective fully down and the aircraft is, essentially, in neutral. So, Pete is still applying just the right amount of power to keep the aircraft light enough so we don't stick in the snow, but heavy enough so we're not going to bounce around."

The hover Cartmell intends to maintain brings its own challenges, but it's the safest option in the circumstances. "If we had tried to land fully and had sunk into the snow, we could have potentially rolled the aircraft over," Lane says.

Members of Cartmell's crew and rescuers on the ground continue to marvel at the skill Cartmell displayed on Haystack that night. "Just the fact that he was able to come down the way he did," says Stohrer. "We had no idea what was under the snow."

"We couldn't believe the helicopter was just staying there," recalls Mark Ober.

South of Little Haystack, still trying to reach their fellow rescuers, Tim Martel and Steve Dupuis watch as the Black Hawk passes over them and initiates its landing. "I was really impressed,"

Mt. Lafayette

Mt. Lincoln

Approximate location where Pilot in Command Pete Cartmell placed Black Hawk 031 relative to Osborne and the rescuers.

Fredrickson

Little Haystack

Osborne →

Landing Zone

Falling Waters Trail

Fredrickson's body was discovered only 150 feet from the entrance to Falling Waters Trail, and Osborne was found approximately 200 feet away from it. Had they reached the trailhead, they would have found shelter below treeline.

says Martel. "We could see the ground team's headlamps. We could hear the helicopter coming in. There was enough snow in the air that you couldn't see the helicopter clearly; you could only see the halo created by the landing lights and snow in the air. It was pretty amazing."

Once he's confident he has the hover under control and the crew tells him the way is clear, Cartmell radios to Stohrer: "You're cleared to get out Matt. Just make it fast."

Stohrer unbuckles from his seat harness and radios the crew: "Opening left cargo door, grabbing litter, going off-line."

"Roger that," Cartmell replies.

As Stohrer opens the door, frigid air pours into the rear cabin. He grasps the plastic litter, sits down on the floor, slides to the edge of the door opening, and disconnects his Internal Communications System. He is now completely on his own.

Pilot in Command Pete Cartmell lowers Black Hawk 031 to its hover point.

XXVIII
TWELVE MINUTES

"Step aggressively towards your fear—that is the step into bravery."
—Jocko Willink, former Navy SEAL and author

Little Haystack Summit Cone
Monday, Feb. 11, 2008
8:40 p.m.

Mount Washington Observatory Surface Weather Observations (8:00 to 9:00 p.m.): Temperature -12°F; winds have shifted and are out of the west averaging 72 mph; visibility 1/16 of a mile, fog/blowing snow; windchill -53°F. Peak wind gust: 92 mph.

With his legs hanging over the side of Black Hawk 031, Matt Stohrer sits at the lip of the open left cargo door and looks out into complete darkness. As he prepares to launch himself into the snow, one hand grasps the plastic Stokes litter and the other the edge of the doorframe. Just above him, the main rotor system roars because, as planned, Pete Cartmell is keeping the power in to maintain the aircraft's hover.

Even with the ear protection built into Stohrer's flight helmet, the roar of the wind creates a sensory overload he hasn't experienced before. Through his night vision goggles, his eyes try to find some frame of reference in the space in front of him. Nothing. All that's visible to him are the eerie green hue of the snow-covered terrain and intermittent dark smudges created by the tops of the scrub trees that have yet to be buried.

Slowly, Stohrer turns his head to the right and looks north in the direction of the rescue team. They are approximately 150 yards away, but he has no idea of the distance because the goggles reduce his depth perception. He sees the line of lights of the seven headlamps as they stand watch over James Osborne, who lies encased in a bivy sack on the ground in front of them. Then he turns his head back to center and looks down at the ground to gauge his landing spot. The left tire of the aircraft, locked in place by the parking brake, barely touches the snow as Cartmell holds the hover. "How is he managing that in this wind?" Stohrer thinks to himself. Then, "Time to do this."

With his hand planted on the doorframe, Stohrer pushes down and thrusts himself forward and out. The soles of his boots meet the snow, but his downward momentum continues. When he finally stops, he finds himself chest deep in snow.

"I remember seeing the crew chief drop into deep snow, which was weird because we were not in deep snow where we were," says Jeremy Hawkes. "When I saw him disappear, I realized how hard it was going to be to get Osborne onto that helicopter."

Stohrer has become the victim of a classic White Mountain terrain trap. Snowfall has accumulated, covering clusters of waist-high krummholz trees. Their branches, thick with needles, prevent snow from penetrating, which creates empty pockets down to their base. Unlucky winter hikers, backcountry skiers, and snowboarders who venture even slightly off trail can find themselves in chest-deep or even chin-deep snow that can be alarming and exhausting to extract oneself from.

As he tries to determine the best way to get himself out, Stohrer makes sure he's got a firm grip on the Stokes litter. "I had to worry about the rotor wash kicking the Stokes up into the rotor system," he says. "Then it would have blown away."

Stohrer knows he needs to move. Using his free arm in a sweeping motion, he shoves waves of snow from out in front of him as he drives each leg forward. He is essentially swimming through the snow, knowing that with each leg thrust he could drop down even deeper. "I was trying to look under my goggles for better depth perception," he says. "It was really disorienting for me until I got to the rescuers. As I moved forward, I would flip my goggles up and it would be pitch black, so I'd flip them down to reorient myself and try to figure out where the rescue team was."

It takes Stohrer approximately six arduous minutes to reach Osborne and the team. By that time, his blaze-orange Mustang suit is caked in snow.

MRS-1 team member Steve Larson recalls the moment Stohrer

makes contact with them. "He was wearing combat boots and probably a couple of layers under the Mustang suit," says Larson. "But with the windchill what it was that night, he was not prepared to be out in those conditions."

"Back then, it was our responsibility as crew members to bring our own gear on missions," says pilot Zach Lane. As it turns out, the crew's experience on this mission resulted in changes in protocols for Black Hawk teams engaged in winter rescues in the White Mountains. "We learned a lot from that mission and from the debriefing we did afterward," he says. "At the time, the ground guys didn't have cold-weather survival gear, and we didn't have survival kits on board. I had a jacket, but if the Black Hawk had gone down, I probably wouldn't have survived the night with the gear I was wearing. We now have extreme-cold-weather clothing and 'go bags' with survival gear on board."

Once Stohrer joins the team, Larson tells him they have one victim in critical condition and a Conservation Officer, Mark Ober, who is hurting. He tells Stohrer he would like those two to be put on the helicopter. Then the aircraft can return and retrieve the body of Fred Fredrickson. Stohrer agrees readily with this plan. Though it will be a challenge to attempt two trips, Stohrer knows that Osborne needs urgent help, and he doesn't believe it is prudent to wait for the rescue team to retrieve Fredrickson, given the precariousness of the hover and the need for immediate care.

Larson briefs the other rescuers on the plan and tells Ober he needs to go on the helicopter. "Mark was having trouble standing, and if he actually went down, it was going to be a big problem," recalls Larson. "He was in a downward spiral. They were trying to give him something to eat, and he kept trying to rise to the occasion, but his tank was just empty. I felt he had to get on that helicopter."

Other rescuers can see the excruciating pain Ober is in, even as he keeps insisting on staying with the team and completing the mission. Jeremy Hawkes attempts to coax him onto the aircraft, but Ober is adamant about staying. It is Steve Larson who manages to change Ober's mind by assuring him that the best thing he can do right now for the team effort is to get on the Black Hawk and get help for himself. Ober finally acquiesces. "I give him credit for acknowledging his situation and getting on the helicopter," Larson says. "It really helped the team."

Larson is also thankful for the effort Ober put forth on behalf of the mission. "He and Hawkes were ahead of us and broke trail the whole way," he says. "Ober did a huge amount of the work, and he never took his foot off the pedal."

Turning to James Osborne, rescue team members line up on each side of him, and each grabs a handful of the bivy sack. Together, they raise him off the ground and carefully place him onto the Stokes litter.

Off in the distance, Pete Cartmell continues to hold the Black Hawk in a hover. "I was really consumed," he says. "My attention was split between hovering, keeping the Black Hawk as stable as I could, looking down the valley, and listening to communications. I could see clouds and ice fog coming in. You've got to be careful with night vision goggles, because they help you see through most of the bad weather conditions. Then, all of a sudden, you can't see anything at all. We had all our lights on, and I could still see down the valley, so I knew I could sneak my way back down if I needed to. And being on top isn't the worst thing in the world, because you can go straight up if you need to."

While Cartmell holds the hover, and Stohrer and the ground teams prepare Osborne to be lifted into the helicopter, Lt. Todd Bogardus is on his phone at Incident Command updating the family members of the missing hikers. "I advised them that we believed both had been found," he says. "I was reasonably sure these were the missing hikers we were searching for, since we had no knowledge of anyone else being there."

Trevor Fredrickson remembers the effect the news had on him and his family. "We got the phone call, and it was rough because they told us they had found two people and one of them was alive. We didn't know if it was James or my dad."

As the search has unfolded well out of their control, members of Fredrickson's and Osborne's families have been trapped in their anxiety. Bette Fredrickson recalls seeing the "Missing Hikers" image on the news late that afternoon. "I was very worried, but I still felt they would be okay," she says. "Did I think they were going to get out of it unscathed? No. Did I think Fred would die? No."

Susan Pelfrey, Osborne's mother, heard the news in the early evening. It was Osborne's colleague, Steve Harbert, who called and gave her contact information for Incident Command. Despite her fears, she was able to provide Bogardus with critical pieces of the puzzle. "She told me they went out on Sunday, not Saturday," says Bogardus. "If they'd been out two nights, it would have changed the scenario and been an even more drastic situation than it already was. She also knew James had bought crampons, so we knew we might find crampon tracks. It was a wealth of information. Being a mom, she was concerned, but she was willing to give as much advice as she could. She was probably feeling helpless, as a lot of family members do."

Up on Little Haystack, the five members of MRS-1, Jeremy Hawkes, and Matt Stohrer carry James Osborne toward the hovering Black Hawk. Mark Ober follows closely behind. It is a very challenging carry as the group moves into the deep snow that hampered Stohrer's initial approach. But it is a much better alternative than carrying Osborne out via the Falling Waters Trail.

Approaching the helicopter, the rescuers find that the whirling rotor blades and the double engines are extremely loud. Without ear protection, their ears are ringing. Stohrer instructs them to approach the aircraft from the side and to be mindful of the rotors spinning over their heads, especially since the terrain is so uneven.

They reach the open cargo door and, with the assistance of Robinson inside, lift the litter up onto the lip. As carefully as they can, they rotate Osborne out of the basket and onto the floor of the rear cabin. "With hypothermia, it's very dangerous to move people," says Stohrer. "We were mindful of that, but we were also in a cabin that was completely dark, so we had to take extra care." During all this, Cartmell is having to work extra hard to keep the Black Hawk steady.

Alaska's *Cold Injuries Guidelines* state that the ideal temperature for the interior of a helicopter carrying a hypothermic patient is 82°F. The interior temperature of Black Hawk 031 is nowhere near that ideal. Unlike a medical transport affiliated with an urban medical center, the military aircraft is not equipped for such a situation.

Before the Black Hawk lifts off, Stohrer tells the rescuers that they'll fly to Littleton, get Osborne to the hospital, and then fly back to get the second victim.

It has taken twelve minutes to get to this point from the time Cartmell started his hover. That may seem like a remarkably short time, given the difficulty of the conditions, but it has been a long wait for Cartmell. "It was exhausting mentally," he will say years later. Warren Lyons is less restrained in his assessment: "Twelve minutes holding like that is a freaking challenge," he says. "To have been able to keep that aircraft from settling down or taking off—because the winds were pushing it to take off—is an incredible feat."

At 8:48 p.m., Cartmell lifts the Black Hawk off the ground, and Lane radios Incident Command: *Guard 031 picked up 1 pack (rescuer) and 1 patient. En route to LRH (Littleton Regional Hospital).*

Bogardus then informs the hospital of the helicopter's impending arrival.

While the helicopter was in hover mode, Lane was already preparing for the flight to Littleton Regional Hospital. He obtained the GPS coordinates for the route and the distance to be covered. Once they are back in the air, Cartmell turns the flight controls back over to him.

Lane flies north at approximately 500 feet above ground level to stay below the cloud ceiling. Meanwhile, Cartmell manages their remaining fuel by doing calculations on his kneeboard, a small notepad attached to his right thigh. Among the questions he is trying to answer are: How much fuel do we have left? Do we have enough time to come back and get these other guys and make it back to Concord, or are we going to have to go to Berlin Airport to refuel? How much fuel are we burning per hour?

"Every aircraft is a little different," says Lane. "They all have different personalities and burn fuel differently, too."

While Lane flies and Cartmell crunches numbers, Stohrer explains to Robinson what will happen on arrival. When they get to the hospital, he will exit by the left door, go around to the nose of the aircraft, and open the right door. He asks Robinson to help him and the emergency room staff put Osborne onto a gurney.

In the dim light of the rear cabin, Stohrer, Robinson, and Ober watch over Osborne, who is still inside the bivy sack. "The ride was bumpy and quick," says Ober. "Every now and then, Osborne would move and moan."

Although semi-comatose, Osborne has likely sensed that something is happening. "He'll be stimulated by being moved," explains retired trauma surgeon Dr. Horace Henriques. "There's relative calmness for him in the helicopter—white noise, the sound of rotor blades. After a while, his brain will ignore it, and he'll be back into his dream."

Soon, Cartmell and Lane can see the lights of Littleton to the right and, just to the north, the glow of the overhead lights that line the large parking lot and helipad at Littleton Regional Hospital. Pointing the nose of the aircraft into the wind, Lane pinpoints his landing zone and starts his angled approach to the helipad as Cartmell wraps up his fuel calculations. He has determined that they'll have just enough to make another run to Little Haystack to pick up Fredrickson, fly back to the hospital, and return to base in Concord. He radios Incident Command: *Guard 031 arrival Littleton Regional Hospital.*

XXIX
CRITICAL

"Nothing burns like the cold."

—*George R.R. Martin, author of* A Game of Thrones

Littleton Regional Hospital
Monday, Feb. 11, 2008
8:55 p.m.

Mount Washington Observatory Surface Weather Observations (8:00 to 9:00 p.m.): Temperature -12°F; winds out of the west averaging 72 mph; visibility 1/16 of a mile, fog/blowing snow; windchill -53°F. Peak wind gust: 92 mph.

Dr. Richard Merrick has seen a wide range of illnesses in the Emergency Department (ED) over the course of this cold winter day. The ED treats approximately 11,000 patients per year, and Merrick has seen thirty since his shift began earlier this morning. Thirty patients in a single day is considered "high normal" for this twenty-five-bed, critical-access hospital located in northern Grafton County, just east of the Vermont border and a stone's throw from Franconia Notch. Until tonight, the ED has dealt with a typical list of ailments and injuries for this time of year: slips and falls on ice, skiing accidents, flu, cough, cold, and pneumonia have all presented here either by walk-in or ambulance.

But the patient who has just arrived by air has Merrick on high alert. Just minutes ago, the ED received word from New Hampshire Fish and Game of an incoming Black Hawk helicopter carrying a severely hypothermic male. The hospital staff has been hearing about two missing hikers and the search for them on Franconia Ridge through word of mouth and news updates. They assume this is related.

There is much to do to prepare for the arrival of a patient in such critical condition. According to Natalie Kennett, clinical director of Critical Care Services, the staff would be making sure the trauma bay was set up with the necessary equipment to receive the patient and discussing how best to initiate treatment on his arrival.

As it turns out, the ED is full that night, so the staff also has to develop a plan for handling the care of the other patients. This involves dividing up tasks and determining which staff members will focus on the critically ill arrival.

There's a television monitor at the nurse's desk in the ED that shows the nearby helipad. Tonight, however, the monitor isn't necessary to track the aircraft's arrival. "It was a roar like a train coming down the tracks at you, like the roar of a chimney fire," says Merrick. "I'm used to seeing DHART (Dartmouth-Hitchcock Air Response Team) helicopters. Seeing a Black Hawk coming in during a snowstorm is intimidating and awesome. It was dark, the winds and snow were blowing. The lights outside the hospital were creating a weird aura that wrapped the aircraft in a kind of halo. Everything looked surrealistic."

Merrick is no stranger to aviation. Besides being a rock and ice climber and a skier, he is also a pilot who flies hang gliders and other soar craft. Still, he is mesmerized by the power and presence of the large, rotary-wing copter. "A Black Hawk landing on your helipad is not an everyday thing," he says. "I've seen a lot of aircraft in my life. This thing coming in on a winter night looked alien—even aggressive."

But, in fact, the Black Hawk is exactly what's needed for this mission. "DHART wouldn't have flown in that weather, not in a million years, and they shouldn't," says Merrick. "This guy was an impressive pilot. He came in and parked this huge beast in a tiny little heliport, and he brought it down in a blizzard. How could you not be impressed by that?"

Zach Lane sets the Black Hawk down inside the 70-by-70-foot fence that surrounds the helipad. As Merrick says, there's not a lot of room to spare. Pushing down on the collective, he takes the power out of the main rotors but keeps them spinning. Then he gives the all-clear for Matt Stohrer to exit the aircraft to retrieve the stretcher. Mark Ober and Allan Robinson wait inside the rear cabin with James Osborne, who continues to show intermittent signs of life.

As he drops down off the aircraft, Stohrer is surprised to see no one waiting outside with a stretcher. "When we were in Iraq, we'd land at the combat hospital, and there was always a litter team there ready for us," he says. "I felt like I was in the Twilight Zone. We land, this guy's urgent, and I'm there alone in the parking lot in my blaze-orange suit."

Stohrer will understand later that the ED staff is following established hospital protocol. They are waiting inside for the helicopter to land and shut down its engines, but Lane has kept the engines on and the rotors spinning in order to head back out quickly. "The eighty-mile-per-hour rotor wash pushes down and fans out," says Kennett. "In the winter in particular, there is salt, sand, and dirt flying around the helipad and parking lot that can lacerate a cornea. That's why we keep staff inside."

Stohrer approaches the sliding doors and depresses the switch to alert ED staff. The doors slide open, and Stohrer walks inside and down a short hallway into the brightly lit ED, where he sees a nurse.

"We've got someone who needs to get in here ASAP," says Stohrer. "He's urgent."

He retrieves a gurney from the hallway and removes the mattress, blanket, and sheets, leaving only the metal base. With the main rotor system of the Black Hawk still running, anything on the gurney will be ripped off. He exits the building and approaches the open right cargo door of the aircraft, where Robinson and Ober are waiting to assist with moving Osborne onto the stretcher. With as much care as they can muster, the three slide Osborne onto the gurney. Then Stohrer and Ober wheel him inside and into one of the ED's two trauma bays, where two nurses and Merrick are waiting. Stohrer delivers a concise synopsis of what has occurred with Osborne, who has not been officially identified at this point, and then returns to the aircraft, while Ober remains behind to get warm and hydrated.

At 9:04 p.m., nine minutes after arriving, Black Hawk 031 lifts off and heads back toward Little Haystack Mountain, where the rescue team waits with Fredrickson.

Merrick, who has been at the hospital since 2000, is board certified in general surgery, family medicine, and emergency medicine. As an Emergency Department physician, he has treated several life-threatening hypothermia cases, most of which have been brought by rescue teams from the White Mountains. He describes Osborne's arrival as "a classic ER train wreck," says Merrick. "The patient hasn't received any medical attention yet, he is very ill, unconscious, and extremely cold. We don't know his name or anything else about him. He's in a bivy sack and still wearing his winter gear. All we know is that he's a hiker, and he's been picked up off the mountain."

As the nurses prepare Osborne for treatment, Merrick approaches Ober, who is slowly pacing back and forth outside the trauma bay.

"I heard there's two of them," Merrick says.

"Yes," replies Ober. "We don't think the other one's alive. He's completely frozen."

Merrick reenters the trauma bay to assess the damage. His patient's skin is cold and moist to the touch, and he is grayish in color or, in medical terms, cyanotic. Although unconscious, he emits noises that Merrick notes as "incomprehensible." His breathing is very slow.

Though a seasoned physician, Merrick is shaken by the condition of the man who lies before him. "My first impression was, 'Holy shit, we're in trouble,'" he recalls. "I was thinking to myself, 'I don't know if I can save this guy. I don't know if anyone can.' But we were the only ticket he had."

Merrick says that an ER doctor "lives and dies" by his nursing staff. "This is a team game, not an individual sport. That night I had excellent nurses on, and we spent a lot of time on that man."

One of the two nurses assigned to the case places an oxygen mask on Osborne, which delivers a high, constant flow of heated, humidified oxygen. Using scissors, Merrick and the other nurse remove Osborne's still frozen clothing and take off his boots. They insert two IV lines that will provide fluids warmed through a heater sitting near Osborne, part of the hospital's Active Core Rewarming (ACR) protocols for hypothermia patients.

Through the IV, they'll deliver sodium bicarbonate (salt) because severe lactic acid buildup occurs when a patient is starved for oxygen. In an effort to counter the perfusion of fluid into Osborne's system, they also use Lasix, a diuretic, to ensure that Osborne's kidneys can expel the fluid before his lungs get flooded. "If all the pieces don't fall into place, you can't make any one of them work, and we lose him," says Merrick. "If we can keep the fluids going in and out, we're winning, and that's what eventually happened."

Osborne is also given a heavy dose of sugar because his blood sugar levels are so low. He's been under enormous strain, and he hasn't had any food or fuel for a long time.

Portions of Osborne's feet have turned dark blue and purple, as have portions of his face and torso, indicating severe frostbite. A nurse places electrodes onto Osborne's cold upper torso and turns on the cardiac monitor.

"The job with a hypothermia patient is to keep the brain, heart, lungs, and kidneys surviving," says Merrick. "As you rewarm him, this guy's going to show stuff on the EKG monitor that's going to scare the shit out of you. And you're going to have to treat it, because that's just what a cold person does. You need to manage the airway and the cardiac arrhythmia while you're trying to rewarm him."

Because the tips of Osborne's fingers are frozen, they cannot clamp on a pulse oximeter to measure the oxygen saturation in his blood. His pulse and blood pressure are minimal but detectable. "A frozen person is only oxygenated in those places where he's moving blood," says Merrick. "As you get colder and colder, your body attempts to survive by bringing its circulation in tighter and tighter toward the core. He was maintaining his core but not his periphery."

In addition to Active Core Rewarming, Merrick and his team initiate Active External Rewarming protocols through the use of a Bair Hugger, a hot-air wrap placed around Osborne at a temperature of 100 degrees. They also use heating blankets and warm radiant lights to create warm air all around him.

At 9:06 p.m., Osborne's core temperature registers 76.28°F, which stuns Merrick and his team. Severe hypothermia is defined as a core body temperature below 82°F. At that level, death is considered imminent. At 77°F, the heart can suddenly stop beating. Osborne is the coldest patient Merrick has ever treated.

Shortly thereafter, Osborne is intubated by the anesthesiologist, a Foley catheter is placed in his bladder to help him expel fluid, and a triple lumen catheter is inserted into the superior vena cava of his heart. The three IV lines of this catheter will infuse Osborne's heart with warm fluids at a rapid rate over the next three hours. "I was using really warm saline going into his heart as a central rewarming technique," says Merrick.

Merrick and his team are closely monitoring Osborne and making adjustments as his physiology dictates. While much has been done, Merrick is experienced enough to recognize he could be missing something. "The job of the ER doc is to marshal resources," he says. "I called in as much help as I could find. When you have a train wreck like this, it's foolish not to grab whatever resources are available. That's why the man's alive today, because there were a lot of people at the right time with the right knowledge and skills to get the job done."

Merrick discusses other warming techniques with Dr. Gene Krisinger, the on-call surgeon. He also contacts his fellow ED physician, Dr. Campbell McLaren, who is at home. McLaren is the hospital's resident specialist in hypothermia treatment. "My questions for Dr. McLaren involved the risks of transporting the patient to a larger facility versus the advantage of getting him to a hospital that could provide additional warming techniques that we didn't have in Littleton," says Merrick.

McLaren soon joins Merrick at the hospital, and the two colleagues reach consensus that Osborne should go to a critical-care facility, so McLaren makes arrangements with Dartmouth-Hitchcock Medical Center (DHMC) in Lebanon. N.H. "What he really needed was to be put on bypass," says Merrick. "We were doing all we could to stabilize him. But we knew we needed to move him. I was grateful to have a colleague like Campbell McLaren there to confer with."

McLaren is put in contact with Dr. Horace Henriques, a now-retired trauma surgeon at DHMC, who will be the receiving physician when Osborne arrives. McLaren explains the situation and asks if Henriques can facilitate a helicopter transport so that Osborne can benefit from either extracorporeal warming by dialysis or cardiopulmonary bypass. Henriques tells him he'll arrange for transport by air if the helicopter can fly or by ground ambulance if the weather poses too much risk.

"He's terrific," says Henriques of McLaren. "I loved talking to him when he referred patients here because he'd have the care plan all set up for me."

It will be after midnight before the transport will begin, but Merrick, McLaren, and the hospital staff are happy to know it is in the works.

XXX
PIONEERS

*"For those who meet their match in the mountains of
northern New Hampshire—home of some of the world's
worst weather—deliverance from a cold death often comes in
the emergency room at Littleton Regional Hospital."*

—*Paula Tracy,* Manchester Union Leader

When Matt Stohrer arrives at Littleton Regional Hospital with a critically ill patient, Dr. Richard Merrick is curious about why the crew of the Black Hawk selected this hospital.

"Why did you choose us?" Merrick asks.

"Well, sir, my orders are that all hypothermic patients go to Littleton," replies Stohrer.

On reflection, Merrick realizes this is exactly the right place for James Osborne. "He was in a position of questionable survivability," says Merrick. "It's knowledge of the cold person that's going to save him. When I joined Littleton Hospital, I knew right away that these people were into cold."

The treatment Osborne receives at LRH that night stems from work done throughout the White Mountain region beginning in the 1970s and '80s. This work, which greatly increased the understanding of hypothermia, was pioneered in large part by the late Dr. Harry McDade Jr. and further advanced by his colleague at LRH, Dr. Campbell McLaren.

"Harry McDade was a Norman Rockwell painting, the quintessential gruffled surgeon," says Merrick. "He was very good at what he did and cared about his patients. And at some point, years before anyone else, he became fascinated by cold people."

McDade, who like Merrick, was an aviator and avid mountaineer, joined the surgical staff at LRH in 1959 and developed the hospital's first disaster management plan. The soundness of that plan was put to the test in 1967, when McDade managed the critical care response to the Cog Railway disaster, which killed eight and injured seventy-two. He recruited twenty-five doctors and forty nurses, who worked through the night on the historic mass casualty incident.

After McDade began to study and explore new treatment protocols for hypothermia patients, he soon became the go-to expert for other medical personnel in the region. "We'd call him even in the surgery room for advice, and we eased the pain of a lot of people in the mountains, and perhaps even saved a life or two, because we had Harry on the other end of the line," said Kent Olson of New Hampshire's Emergency Medical Services program, in a profile of McDade published on the LRH website.

In a Feb. 8, 1991 interview with Tom Oppel of *The Sunday Rutland Herald*, McDade discussed the unpredictability associated with treating cold patients. "Just as you think you're home free, you can have a whole lot of other things happen," he said. "It's almost like a [Charles] Dickens story, with a lot of little side plots."

According to Merrick, it was McDade who got his colleague Campbell McLaren interested in the work he was doing with cold people. McLaren worked in the Scottish Highlands in the 1970s, where he ran a nine-bed hospital with three nurses on staff. A frequent winter mountaineer, he found himself treating many patients presenting with hypothermia in the chill, wet Scottish climate. In 1976, he moved to the U.S. with his family and worked at Androscoggin Valley Hospital in Berlin, N.H.

McLaren had heard about Harry McDade and the 1967 Cog Railway disaster. He also knew McDade was the coordinator of disaster response for LRH, an area that also interested him. In 1979, McLaren began working alongside McDade in the Emergency Department at LRH, and the two worked together, off and on, for about eight years.

"My first case with Harry was a Green Beret who fell into a brook along Kinsman Ridge," recalls McClaren. "He was found the next day and came in with an astonishingly low core temperature: thirty-eight degrees Fahrenheit. We revived him after twelve hours of continuous CPR in the field and eventually got his core temperature up to ninety-three or ninety-four degrees. But his brain had frozen, and he didn't make it. After that, though, hospitals around the country were calling us for advice with hypothermia patients."

McDade and McLaren are two of a small cadre of medical experts who were driving innovative care for hypothermia and other cold-weather injuries at the time. In partnership with McDade, Dr. Frank Hubbell and Dr. Murray Hamlet put their focus on pre-hospital care, specifically in the area of wilderness medicine.

Hubbell, who in 1976 founded the North Conway-based Stonehearth Open Learning Opportunities (SOLO), the oldest wilderness medicine school in the U.S., recognized the need for a different approach to backcountry medicine. "When I took what I was taught for street medicine and applied it to the wilderness setting, it failed miserably," Hubbell says. "We had to start thinking through the process. Most of the time, we needed to allow patients to rewarm on their own, but there were those times when we really did have to be aggressive. We got them on a heart/lung machine, took their blood out, rewarmed it, and put it back in. But that's the exception, the extreme case."

Hubbell believes that McDade was out in front on cold-weather injury treatment because of the hospital's proximity to the White Mountains. "Harry McDade was a great man," says Hubbell. "He's the one who said that we were going to see hypothermia, we were going to see frostbite, and we needed to understand this process. He and Murray Hamlet and other folks really dug into it. What were we going to do to save a person's fingers and nose and toes? How could we resuscitate someone with hypothermia?"

For his part, Hamlet pursued the science and behavior behind hypothermia as it applied to military training. "Hamlet realized environmental factors—how heat and cold impact soldiers—are extraordinarily important for the military," says Hubbell of his friend and colleague. "He had a laboratory where he was developing the science behind it. So we took his science and applied it in the field when we were faced with hypothermia victims—sometimes with success, sometimes not. Then we'd assess what went right, what went wrong, and what we could have done differently."

Over the years, the science of hypothermia has evolved along with treatment protocols. "We used to look at hypothermia as a disease process," says Hubbell. "This person is sick, and we need to correct the ongoing disease process. Today we realize hypothermia is not a disease process. When a person is at ninety degrees core temperature, their physiology is perfectly normal for that temperature. The body is doing what it has to do to adjust. Not everybody has to be aggressively rewarmed, not everybody has to have thoracic or inter-abdominal rewarming with warm water poured into their chest or abdomen. They don't have to be submerged in warm baths. We've learned that most people do great if you allow them to rewarm on their own, so we've backed off a lot."

What Hubbell and his wilderness medicine colleagues have learned is that a person who's hypothermic is going to warm best from the inside out. When you are hypothermic, you are also likely to be exhausted, having burned through the glycogen stores in your liver, which usually last about twenty-four hours but are burned off more rapidly when your body is trying to stay warm. By the time you're hypothermic, says Hubbell, "you've got nothing to replace that glycogen. So your shivering mechanism starts to fail and that's when your core temperature starts to drop."

In most cases, treatment involves providing energy—calories to burn—in the form of sugar, which can be infused through an IV drip. "Once we get the sugar on board, it gives you the opportunity to shiver, and we want people to shiver, because if you're shivering, you're producing enough heat to warm yourself at approximately two degrees per hour. If a person is at ninety degrees core temperature, and you've got to bring him up to ninety-eight, that's just four hours, so you just let him shiver. But he's got to have calories to burn."

Besides learning from others' research, Hubbell and his colleagues did some research of their own, specifically targeted to search and rescue emergencies in the White Mountains. "With the help of New Hampshire Fish and Game, we were able to look back through the records of mountain rescues, and we came to realize that the vast majority of them, including many fatalities, were caused by hypothermia," says Hubbell. "We're not cold animals; we're designed for the tropics. When you throw us into a winter climate, we're okay if we can maintain our microenvironment, but as we cool off, we have no natural defenses against the cold."

One of the things hypothermia research has made clear, says Hubbell, is that "as we get cold, we get stupid. Errors start to happen. Once we get hypothermic, all of our experience is erased. We stop thinking clearly. Instead of going down the mountain, we go up. Instead of seeking shelter, we stay out in the wind. Instead of putting on a hat and jacket, we take off layers of clothing."

Hubbell recalls an experience on Mount Washington that

demonstrated the danger posed by cold weather even for veteran rescuers. "During one rescue we were on in Alpine Garden, we topped out on a ravine and stopped to plan our next steps," says Hubbell. "There were whiteout conditions, and I was listening to the conversation taking place about what to do next, and I realized I was listening to hypothermic rescuers. I thought to myself, 'We've got to get this under control quickly or we're going to have a real problem.' Everyone was so focused on searching the ravine. We were lucky we didn't kill everyone on the rescue that day."

Subsequently, the search and rescue community has used hypothermia research to help them stay strong, warm, and alert during missions. "I can remember going on a later major search and rescue mission in the middle of winter in Huntington Ravine," says Hubbell. "As we were preparing at the AMC's Pinkham Notch lodge, the cooks came out with pounds and pounds of bacon for us to eat before we headed up. We were drinking coffee with tons of sugar and eating all that bacon to get fats into us, so we'd have calories on board to stay warm while we're up there trying to rescue somebody."

But though the research and advanced knowledge and protocols have helped, hypothermia continues to be a critical problem in the White Mountains, which Hubbell attributes to the large numbers of people who flock to these accessible mountains in all seasons. "One quarter of the North American population lives within a day's drive of us," he notes. "Washington, D.C., is only ten hours away. So you have a lot of people who access our mountains, and the vast majority of them have no experience. They come up to go hiking and think they can pull on sneakers, put one foot in front of the other, and go up the mountain. They don't realize that with every thousand feet of elevation gain, you lose three degrees of ambient temperature. They don't appreciate the calories you'll need because of the energy you'll use up."

Hubbell's advice on how best to avoid becoming hypothermic is simple: know when to pull the plug on your plans. "What I want people to understand is that they have to respect our mountains," he says. "You have to be willing to go down. You've been planning your trip for four months, and you're coming here with your friends, and you hit the trailhead, and you start up. You stop to take a break and think, 'Wow, it's really cold!' You need to constantly assess your plans and your preparation. 'Do I go forward or do I need to go back? Am

I prepared to be here?' Unfortunately, people are very summit-minded. They think they can't go home and tell their friends and family that they failed to summit. That's a trap you have to avoid falling into."

XXXI
"WTF!"

"Experience is not what happens to you;
it's what you do with what happens to you."

—*Aldous Huxley*

Little Haystack Mountain
Monday, Feb. 11, 2008
9:15 p.m.

Mount Washington Observatory Surface Weather Observations (9:00 to 10:00
p.m.): Temperature -14°F; winds out of the west averaging 66 mph; visibility
1/16 of a mile, fog/blowing snow; windchill -55°F. Peak wind gust: 82 mph.

Black Hawk 031 still has more work to do that night. As planned, from Littleton Regional Hospital the crew heads back to Little Haystack to pick up the body of Fred Fredrickson. They also decide, given the frigid temperatures, to evacuate the six rescuers waiting with Fredrickson on the mountain.

"We went right to the summit," says Zach Lane, who is at the controls. "There was some risk involved in going back, but I can remember thinking that if we didn't, we'd be going back later for victims. They were so exposed up there. We needed to get them off the mountain. We all agreed there was no way we were not going."

"Risk mitigation for everyone meant taking the rescuers off the mountain," says Pilot in Command Pete Cartmell, who will again take over the controls for the approach and landing. "The alternative was for them to hike out all night."

Conservation Officer Jeremy Hawkes recalls his elation and relief when Matt Stohrer returned and told them, "You're all going!"

"I was so happy," says Hawkes. "In my head, I was hiking down that night, because there are so many times we do that. It seemed like summer inside the helicopter compared to where we were, and I could still see my breath in there. There was so much gear. I was on the floor next to Fredrickson, and Matt got out of his seat and said, "Sit here. You guys have had a really rough night."

Despite everyone's relief at being off the mountain, the ride is a difficult one. Fredrickson lies in the Stokes litter, and the rescuers are finding this up-close-and-personal moment emotionally trying. "There was no discussion; it was a quiet ride," says Stohrer. "Everybody looked tired. They were in their proper equipment, bundled up. It was a quick flight, but it was a time of reflection."

Alain Comeau, who's also in the rear cabin, is adding Fred Fredrickson to the gallery of victims he has found over several decades, some of whom, like Fredrickson, he couldn't save. "All of the fatalities, they're kind of like images on the wall; they don't go away," he says. "When I look back, they're all there. It's like a little room with a gallery. Every now and then, you kind of wander into it."

At 9:21 p.m., just south of Littleton, Lane is piloting Black Hawk 031 toward the hospital when his focus is suddenly disrupted.

"You've got to be kidding me," grumbles Cartmell. "I've got master cautions flashing."

He looks immediately at the Caution Advisory Warning Panel on the console in front of them. There are at least four caution lights illuminated in yellow, and each has a label to indicate the problem:

#2 Gen

MR (Main Rotor) De-Ice Fail

MR De-Ice Fault

TR (Tail Rotor) De-Ice Fail

The first caution indicates the most serious problem, the possibility of a generator failure. Warren Lyons, a rotary-wing flight instructor for the Army National Guard, explains what it would have been like in the cockpit at that moment. "Immediately, one of the pilots would have said, 'We've got a master caution,' which spins everybody up in these conditions. So now one guy's flying, one guy's pulling out the caution checklist or just acting from memory."

In this case, according to Lyons, Cartmell is going to have to try to reset the failed generator. If that doesn't work, he will have to do an emergency start-up of the Auxiliary Power Unit (APU).

Cartmell and Lane are understandably disheartened by this turn of events. "We thought we were out of it," says Cartmell. "We had everybody on board, and we thought, 'Let's get to the hospital.' But suddenly, there were a lot of lights flashing. It probably took me a couple of seconds to figure out what had happened, but it felt like a minute."

The first thing on Cartmell's mind is whether or not the aircraft is still flying. Fortunately, it is. "I always look to see if the rotor system is at one hundred percent on the display," he says. When he finds out it is, he relaxes a bit. "Okay, we're flying," he thinks. "We're not falling out of the sky. But what the fuck is going on here?" He quickly realizes that the generator must have failed and kicked off the electronics.

The generators on board produce electrical power for the Black Hawk's electronic systems, and each generator powers specific things. According to Lane, Black Hawk 031 has two main engines and a third engine of 90 horsepower that runs the hydraulics and electrical systems but is not strong enough to drive the rotors. Blade de-icing and windshield de-icing require a generator to operate. The APU will not kick on for an electrical problem, he says, so when generator two (Gen 2) kicks off, the main rotor de-icing, the tail rotor de-icing, and the windshield anti-icing all fail. But the caution indicators don't say specifically that a generator has actually failed, so the problem is not immediately obvious.

Once Cartmell understands what is happening, he attempts to reset the generator and turns everything back on, but it doesn't clear the problem. He and Lane decide to rely on the redundancy systems built into the aircraft and turn on the backup generator. Cartmell reduces the electrical load on the remaining generator, and they continue with the mission. "In the end, it was not a big deal," says Cartmell. "But those few seconds it took me to figure it out…."

Warren Lyons is more candid about a problem that could have become a big deal. "The aircraft is full of people in bad weather and poor visibility," he says. "Icing is a huge consideration in those conditions. You can lose lift quickly. A generator failure and three additional caution lights—that will put the pucker factor in you as a crew, guaranteed. But they continued with the mission. It speaks to their character and training."

Stohrer and Robinson, who are in communication with the pilots, are the only two in the rear cabin who are aware of any problem. The others are just focused on getting through the flight. At 9:28 p.m., Black Hawk 031 touches down at the hospital's helipad. Stohrer and Hawkes bring Fredrickson into a quiet exam room, and Hawkes sees Mark Ober in the hallway. It turns out that Ober has not needed medical intervention. To start feeling better, he's just needed to warm up and get hydrated. At this point, Osborne is still in the trauma unit awaiting transport to Dartmouth-Hitchcock Medical Center.

"How're you doing?" asks Hawkes.

"I'm good," replies Ober.

"How's that guy?" Hawkes inquires, looking into the trauma bay at Osborne.

"He's got, like, a one percent chance of making it, man," says Ober sadly.

"That's too bad; that sucks," says Hawkes.

Ober asks Stohrer and Hawkes if he can hitch a ride on the Black Hawk and follows the pair onto the aircraft.

After their departure, Dr. Merrick walks into the exam room where Fredrickson lies to make the grim but necessary determination: "Fred was beyond anyone's help," he says. "I pronounced him dead. You could not articulate his joints. You could not move him. There was no hope. I felt very badly for the man."

Lt. Todd Bogardus has directed Conservation Officer Sam Sprague to travel to the hospital to meet with Merrick. "Sprague's role was to gather as much information about the victims as he could," says Bogardus. "He worked with hospital staff to get medical status, collect evidence, and inventory gear to see what the victims had with them. He served as a combination of liaison and investigator."

Combined with the investigative work already done throughout the mission by Incident Command, Sprague's time at the hospital with Merrick and the victims allows Fish and Game to conclude definitively that James Osborne is the sole survivor. Sprague notifies Bogardus so that he and Goss can begin the difficult process of notifying family members.

Incident Command Post
Falling Waters Trailhead
10:10 p.m.

It is Lt. Jim Goss who calls Bette Fredrickson.

"Did he make it?" Bette asks. "No," Goss replies somberly.

"Are you sure?" Bette asks again. "Yes," says Goss.

Years later, Bette describes what it felt like to learn of Fred's fate. "It was like someone punched me in the stomach," she says. "When he said 'Yes,' I think I just hung up. I was on the ground on one knee, hunched over and trying not to cry."

Bette tells her sons, and they agree it is time to begin notifying the rest of the family. "It was like a hole getting knocked in my heart," says Fred's son Trevor.

"I do recall taking relief in the fact that everything happened very quickly from the time I learned of my father's situation to the news that he was found and had perished," says Trevor's brother Kyle. "If it had been days of searching and not knowing, it would have made the whole thing supremely agonizing. It was about six or seven hours, and part of me is grateful for the quickness with which it all happened."

XXXII
A NEEDLE ON HAYSTACK

"I would say: first thing, don't panic. Think before you do anything, and try not to make the situation worse. Be calm, assess the situation, and try to make a safe, thoughtful plan. Use what you have with you to try to stay warm."

—*Jim Surette, Mountain Rescue Service*

Incident Command Post
Falling Waters Trailhead
Monday, Feb. 11, 2008
9:40 p.m.

Mount Washington Observatory Surface Weather Observations (9:00 to 10:00 p.m.): Temperature -14°F; winds out of the west averaging 65 mph; visibility 1/16 of a mile, fog/blowing snow; windchill -54°F. Peak wind gust: 82 mph.

Before heading back to base, Black Hawk 031 takes one last ride to Franconia Notch, where it drops off the rescuers at the Incident Command Post. While Matt Stohrer and Allan Robinson help their passengers off the aircraft, Jeremy Hawkes makes his way over to the mobile unit to check in. On his way, he meets Conservation Officer Mike Eastman who, along with Conservation Officer Heidi Murphy, hiked out to Lincoln Woods in the Pemigewasset Wilderness in the early stages of the search. "I can remember talking to Jeremy in the parking lot when he got off the helicopter," recalls Eastman. "You could just tell it had become really stressful up there."

✳ ✳ ✳ ✳ ✳ ✳

Back on Haystack, MRS-3 members Steve Dupuis and Tim Martel, who have been trying for hours to make it across the ridge from Mount Lincoln to help the rest of the team, are unable to reach the summit before Black Hawk 031 takes off for the second time. "We were right under them on both trips," says Martel.

But though Incident Command called them several times to ascertain their progress and try to arrange for their pickup, the pair has found the going too rough to move with enough speed. "We kept thinking we were really close," says Martel. "We were hoping, because we really wanted that helicopter flight. But it was brutal. It was one of those kick-kick-kick-step slogs. You know, knocking down snow in front of you and stepping with snowshoes on. We were taking turns with the kicking."

When they reach treeline just below the summit of Little Haystack, Dupuis and Martel are informed by Todd Bogardus that the Black Hawk doesn't have enough fuel to fly back up the mountain a third time for them. They'll need to walk down Falling Waters Trail.

"As we wandered around on the ridge with our headlamps on, through the indistinct rocks, krummholz, and wind, we located the spot a couple of hundred yards above treeline where a body had clearly lain in the snow, melting it down to the schist underneath," recalls Martel. "Nearby, we found the imprints left by the Black Hawk and rescue crews. Then as we headed down, not far from where the trail goes into the woods, we found the impression left by the lower of the two victims. To me, he appeared to be just a few feet above treeline and to have almost made it to the relative shelter of the trees and deeper snow below. We had kind of lost the trail ourselves at that point."

The wind, blowing snow, and almost complete darkness are conspiring to make a proper exit off the ridge difficult. Dupuis and Martel are disoriented. The terrain here is, in Martel's words, like "a knobby pile of rocks without any real distinguishing features."

The two find themselves circling around, trying to find the elusive entrance to Falling Waters Trail. "We could have gone into some thick trees. It would have been a worst-case scenario, but at least we'd have had shelter," Martel says. "The thing with coming down off Little Haystack in poor visibility is that you can lose the cairns and end up in the trees. I'd been there before. You're only fifty yards from where the trail goes into the woods, but you can't find the entrance. If you were hypothermic and didn't have the wherewithal to think your way through it, you'd never find the trail."

As the exhausted pair moves along the treeline hoping they're on the right side of the summit, their headlamps illuminate the pick end of a mountaineering axe sticking out of the snow. They know immediately that they've located the trailhead. It is the axe that fellow MRS team member Charlie Townsend drove into the snow as he and his teammates left treeline for the summit of Haystack over two hours before. At the time, Townsend assumed they would use the makeshift signpost on their way back down, never imagining that they would end up being deposited at the trailhead by a Black Hawk helicopter.

"We had gone slightly the wrong way following rescuers' tracks down to Osborne's location near treeline," says Martel. "I remember losing the trail, because we were following the tracks from the crew that attended to him and brought him to the helicopter. We realized what we had done and then backtracked, reoriented, and went in the right direction. Then we saw the axe, which was a good symbol of affirmation that we weren't going to have to backtrack again."

Once they find the entrance to Falling Waters, Dupuis and Martel begin the downhill trek. They will emerge into the parking lot at 11:40 p.m., the last rescuers out of the woods. There, they'll be welcomed by Todd Bogardus and other members of the Fish and Game Search and Rescue Team, who are waiting for their return. "We didn't leave until everybody we sent into the woods was back out," says Bogardus.

XXXIII
HOME AGAIN

"It's the first time they've landed like that at night.
We were in the process of getting about thirty people together,
to get ready to go up there and carry them down. It would have
taken all night."

—Lt. Jim Goss, New Hampshire Fish and Game
New Hampshire Union Leader, *Feb. 13, 2008*

N.H. Army National Guard Aviation Support Facility
Concord, N.H.
Monday, Feb. 11, 2008
10:25 p.m.

Before the final pieces of the rescue mission have been put in place—but none too soon for the crew—Black Hawk 031 arrives safely back at the base, having completed its crucial role in the night's events. As sometimes happens in the immediate aftermath of a crisis, the flight back had produced a light moment. Pilot Zach Lane asked Pete Cartmell, an instructor pilot, if he had induced the generator failure as a training exercise.

"Pete, when that happened, I was thinking, 'Why are you screwing with me right now?'" Lane tells him with a laugh.

"Hey, Zach, you know there's no way I'd do that!" Cartmell protests.

In fact, Cartmell can't imagine having thought about messing with his crew that night. "It stands out in my mind as one of the trickiest missions I've ever done, and that includes tours in Afghanistan and Iraq," says Cartmell. "I heard someone say once, 'You don't want to put yourself into a position where you're using all of your skills, all of your knowledge, and all of your luck.' Well, I kind of did that here. We were right up against that edge."

Matt Stohrer, too, is feeling the impact of an unprecedented experience. "I think everybody was like, 'Man, did that really just happen?'" he says. "We did a brief after-action review on the flight back, but we were just smoked. There are things in my military career I won't forget, and that mission is one of them. I've been deployed to Iraq and Bosnia, but the mission we did that night was the most dangerous I've been on."

"Would I do it again?" Cartmell asks himself. "Probably. My piece of it certainly wasn't at the level of what Matt had to do. He showed unbelievable courage and commitment by leaving the relative comfort of the Black Hawk and venturing out onto the side of a four-thousand-foot mountain in unforgiving conditions."

While Black Hawk 031 was headed back to base, Todd Bogardus called Col. Frank Leith in Concord and told him what his crew had accomplished that day. As a result, Leith is there waiting for them when they arrive back that night.

"That was amazing, what you guys did," Leith tells them. "You guys are heroes."

To this day, Cartmell remains deeply affected by Leith's praise. "For Frank—a Distinguished Flying Cross recipient—to say that…. It was an emotional moment. I still get choked up."

In an interview with *New Hampshire National Guard* magazine following the rescue, Leith offered further assessment of the crew's performance. "With winds up to sixty-five knots, and freezing fog causing ice buildup on the blades, limiting the aerodynamics, it was the most extreme mission for a New Hampshire Army National Guard search and rescue crew in twenty years."

As time goes by, this mission will become a signature event in White Mountain search and rescue history. Both the ground rescue teams and the Black Hawk crew will be recognized for their outstanding service. But that night, the aviators know only the exhaustion, relief, and adrenaline depletion that follow a life-or-death effort. "We were all mentally drained, and Matt was physically drained, too," says Cartmell.

Still, as late as it is, and after all they've just been through, they will arrive the next morning prepared to answer the call if another emergency arises. In fact, during the same week, Black Hawk crews will participate in two additional search and rescue missions in the White Mountains. Using a hoist for both missions, the crews will rescue a stranded hiker trapped in deep snow on the eastern slopes of Mount Lafayette and, days later, two hikers lost in Dry Valley in Crawford Notch.

A Black Hawk helicopter flying in the shadow of the Old Man of the Mountain in Franconia Notch.

XXXIV
GAINS AND LOSSES

"You put thousands of people out there and every so often one's going to get into serious trouble. In retrospect we all try to explain it, but it just so happens they were there on that day. Really, it's amazing it doesn't happen more."

—*Steve Larson, Mountain Rescue Service*

Littleton Regional Hospital
Tuesday, Feb. 12, 2008
12:26 a.m.

Doctors Richard Merrick and Campbell McLaren and their medical team watch as the flight medic and flight nurse for the Dartmouth-Hitchcock Air Response Team (DHART) wheel James Osborne out of the Emergency Department and over to the air ambulance waiting on the helipad.

The three-person DHART crew went through a pre-mission assessment process similar to that of the Black Hawk crew. There was a risk assessment that included a weather check and a safety briefing. But unlike Pete Cartmell, the pilot of the DHART aircraft wasn't provided with any details about the patient, only his location. "In the civilian world, we do not want the pilots influenced by patient information," says DHART Operations Manager John Hinds, himself a former flight medic. "Our pilots make their decision based on whether they can get the aircraft there and back safely. Everything in our world is about safety, and if there's anything that's going to interfere with that, we're not doing it."

DHART, which averages between 1,300 and 1,400 flights per year, has a "four to go, and one to say no" protocol leading up to and during a flight. The pilot, medic, flight nurse, and dispatcher all need to agree on the mission parameters or it doesn't go on, even if they're in the air. "If you don't communicate well as a team, you run the risk of a fatality, and that's unacceptable," says Hinds. "If the hair is going up on the back of your neck or your gut is telling you there's something wrong, ninety percent of the time you're absolutely correct. Even if you can't identify it, it's telling you to slow down, stop what you're doing, and reexamine what's going on."

The DHART aircraft carries a great deal of medical equipment on board. "We take the first forty-five minutes of emergency or trauma care to the patient," says Hinds. "That means everything from surgical chest tubes to surgical airways to large-bore fluids and arterial lines. That's what we do. It is totally different than working in a facility. We have autonomy, and we're expected to do something for the patient."

Flight nurse in a DHART helicopter.

Stephen Jameson, DHART's clinical director, who started with the team in 1998 as a flight medic before becoming a flight nurse in 2005, recalls the care the team had to use to safely transport the critically hypothermic Osborne. "The pilot shut down on arrival, and we exited with our cot," he recalls. "We did know [Osborne] was on a ventilator, so we brought all of that gear in with us. We moved him over to our equipment, got the report from the physician and nursing staff about care management, and picked up where they left off."

Once Osborne is on board, the DHART crew continues to try to rewarm him, making sure his temperature doesn't slide in the wrong direction. They are also careful not to aggravate his arrhythmia, which would precipitate a new crisis.

One difference between the DHART aircraft and the Black Hawks flown by the Army Air National Guard is that DHART helicopters don't have hoists. "The insurance cost and risk involved in hovering over a place where we can't land are too great, " explains Doug Moore, a DHART pilot. "If we can't put the skids on the ground, we can't pick somebody up. We do transport. We're looking for first responders to be there before us, and they will have initially engaged with the patient."

The helicopter used to transport James Osborne from Littleton Regional Hospital to Dartmouth-Hitchcock Medical Center.

Another difference, says Moore, is that civilian medical aircraft operate with a single pilot. "The military operates with a six-man crew in Special Operations and a four-man crew with a rescue," he says. "It's easy to delegate tasks, because even though it's a far more complicated mission in the military, the pilot has a lot more help." When you fly with a single pilot accompanied by a medical crew, he says, the crew's responsibility is to the patient, not the pilot.

Moore, who has flown for DHART for sixteen years, has logged more than 8,500 hours flying rotary-wing aircraft, 5,000 of those while serving for twenty-two years as a pilot with the U.S. Air Force, flying helicopter missions with pararescue and other special operations forces. "In the military, you learn to adapt, improvise, and overcome—you press forward until you can't," he says. "You might be forced to the ground because of the weather, so you wait it out and continue the mission. Here, you can't do that. If you take a patient out of a hospital, and you end up having to land short of your destination, you've done the patient a disservice. The military aviator is worried about getting shot at, so he comes in fast and hot and gets the heck out of there. Civilians have to be much more concerned about limiting risk. That means taking it easy, coming in easy, and being aware of your surroundings."

Still unconscious and intubated, Osborne will arrive at Dartmouth-Hitchcock Medical Center nineteen minutes after leaving Littleton. Once on the ground, he will be wheeled directly to the Intensive Care Unit.

Dr. Merrick's narrative portion of the medical report he writes about Osborne's stay at Littleton Regional Hospital captures in stark detail the extent of the life-saving care he received in his short time there. While at LRH, Osborne received seventeen liters of IV fluids infused over three and a half hours. "The blood volume of the whole body is five liters," says Merrick. "I replaced that three-plus times. That means this gentleman underwent an exceedingly aggressive resuscitation process. You're looking at a man who, based on precedent, isn't going to survive. We were pulling out all the stops. We were not going to give up on this guy. And he held on. The more we did, the better he held on. He responded amazingly."

By the time he was airlifted out of Littleton, Osborne's core temperature had risen to 83 degrees Fahrenheit, an increase of 7 degrees. According to New Hampshire Fish and Game, Osborne's core temperature on arrival at LRH set a record low for a hypothermia survivor in the Northeast (07-09 Biennial Report, p.62). And Dr. Murray Hamlet says, "To my knowledge, he's one of the coldest people suffering from dry-land hypothermia ever to be revived in the United States."

Dr. Horace Henriques, the receiving physician for Osborne at Dartmouth-Hitchcock, believes he would not have survived had he not been taken off the mountain by helicopter. "I think if he'd been up there two more hours, he'd have died," says Henriques. "He was so close. There was minimal time to spend on his rescue up there."

At the time of the transport that night, Osborne's fate still hangs in the balance, and Merrick's report ends with a sobering comment: "Simply, this patient I feel is at very high risk for developing adult respiratory distress syndrome, and his prognosis was certainly quite guarded at the time of his arrival and at the time of his transfer of care."

Osborne's ultimate survival is, in large part, a testament to Merrick's passion for practicing medicine and his focus on patient care. "It was a wonderful thing," he says of the hospital's ability to help save Osborne. "All the pieces had to be there; they all had to work. James was as cold and as critical and as tenuous as any hypothermia patient I had ever seen. I needed to put every ounce of my resources toward saving him. It was a privilege to be part of that."

Littleton Regional Hospital
Tuesday, Feb. 12, 2008
2:30 a.m.

The fate of Fred Fredrickson presents a tragic counterpoint to the near-miracle described by Dr. Merrick, and it is a sad irony that the two friends were briefly reunited in Littleton for one last time.

After receiving the news that Fred has died, Bette Fredrickson, her two sons, Kyle and Trevor, and Trevor's future wife, Amy, drive to Littleton Hospital, where they've been told Fred has been transported.

"We got into Trevor's car and headed over there," says Bette. "I had to see him and hug him. It's like you believe it, but you don't believe it."

Shortly after their arrival, the four sit quietly in the Emergency Department's waiting room. A nurse approaches and tells the exhausted and dazed family they can see Fredrickson. "My mom went in first," recalls Trevor. "I think she didn't want us to see him."

Bette follows the nurse into the examination room where Fredrickson lies. She vividly recalls the moment she saw the man she considered the love of her life. "I sat there, I don't know for how long," she says. "His eyes were frozen open. He had the most beautiful blue eyes, but with his eyes open, he just looked so harsh. So I used my hands to defrost his eyes, and then I closed them."

Once Bette has had the time she needs with Fred, she returns to the waiting room and walks her two sons in to see their father. It is a brutal moment.

"My brother started crying, and I was sobbing," recalls Trevor.

Given the hour and the emotional exhaustion of the Frederickson family, a nurse has arranged for the four to stay at a hotel in Littleton. They get lost several times on the way but eventually arrive and check in. In the morning, after a mostly sleepless night, they are stirred by a knock at the door. A Conservation Officer gives them Fredrickson's still-frozen backpack and his ice axe. Later, Bette will donate all of his outdoor gear to her local rescue squad to help them and their patients.

The officer walks the family through what investigators know up to this point and tells them about Fredrickson and Osborne's failed attempt at self-rescue.

"It was distressing to hear all that," says Trevor. "But it was good to know what happened in the final moments. They were that close to making it. It was rough, but in a way that's hard to explain, it was good for us to hear."

In the days and weeks that follow, Trevor will not be able to shake the thought of how solitary his father must have felt up there on the mountain. "I will never not be sad about it," he says. "I don't really think about how or why it happened. I think about how alone he must have felt at the end."

EPILOGUE

"A man does not climb a mountain without bringing
some of it away with him and leaving something of himself upon it."

—Sir Martin Conway, British mountaineer

Concord Country Club
Concord, N.H.
Sunday, Feb. 17, 2008

A week after Fred Fredrickson's death, Concord Coach will hold a memorial service for him at the Concord Country Club. With one coworker dead and the other in critical condition, the company's staff is reeling with sorrow and disbelief. Former coworker Aubrey McPhail recalls the "stillness" of the memorial service. "Everyone was trying to fill the emptiness with something, and it was sad and uncomfortable," she says.

Trevor remembers how deeply affected he was by the outpouring of support for his father. "It was revelatory," he says. "He was really loved by the people he worked with. There were even commuters who found out about what happened and came to the memorial service. One said, 'Your father was the nicest person I've ever met, and I loved that he was my bus driver.'"

As family members walk out of the service, they spot an enormous snowy owl perched on the roof rack of a parked car. They view the owl's presence as a sign that Fred is there with them. "I swear it was my dad's spirit animal," says Trevor. As the majestic bird, a symbol of winter, launches from the roof and flies away, one family member murmurs, "There he goes."

Months later, Bette Fredrickson will walk with quiet commitment along the Alpine Garden Trail on Mount Washington. The contents of her backpack are precious to her and her three hiking companions: sons Kyle and Trevor, and Trevor's wife, Amy. Inside her pack is a small bag holding Fred's ashes.

Earlier in the day, at the Mount Washington State Park Visitor Center, the four were drawn to a wall that displays the long list of those who have perished in the Presidential Range. It is a haunting roster.

Bette is disappointed when she can't find Fred's name on the list, not realizing that it is reserved for people who died on this mountain range and does not include those who perished in the Franconia Range or other locations in the White Mountains. The Franconia Ridge Loop hike and the trails that link to it are seeing an increase of hikers and have become a hot spot for rescue missions. Given the hike's accessibility, steep, rugged trails, and fully exposed ridgeline, it is not out of the realm of possibility that the Franconia Notch State Park might one day host a memorial wall of its own.

After leaving the Visitor Center, the family descends the Auto Road to the Cow Pasture parking lot at 5,700 feet. The weather is surprisingly glorious. The sun is on full display, and the skies are a deep, cloudless blue. A warm, steady breeze moves gently across the lichen-covered boulders and massages the branches of fragile flora that have adapted over thousands of years in order to survive here. The pleasant weather stands in sharp contrast to the conditions that Trevor and Kyle's father faced, along with friend James Osborne, during their long winter ordeal in Franconia Notch.

Following a gradual descent from the parking lot, the Fredricksons reach a slight bend in the trail where they see a tall cairn. This is where Bette is intending to stop. She knows it is a place where Fred always liked to linger for lunch whenever he was hiking on Mount Washington. "He loved it because it was quiet and serene," Bette says.

Kyle and Trevor stand by silently, lost in their own thoughts. The last time they were here, they were much younger and hiking the Huntington Ravine Trail with their father.

The family forms a half circle in front of the cairn. Bette removes her backpack and retrieves the small bag that holds Fred's ashes. On the bag is the word "Love," which she inscribed not long after Fred was cremated. The months since Fred's death have been difficult for the whole family. But for Bette, his passing is especially hard. Even though they were no longer married, their love had endured. "I was so mad at him," she admits. "I couldn't miss him until I'd gotten through the anger."

Just before opening the bag and tipping it toward the cairn, Bette says, "I'm setting you free in a place that you loved. I know you'd want to be here."

Then she gently pours the ashes, which cascade down the meticulously placed stones of the iconic structure. There are thousands like it strategically placed throughout the alpine zones of the White Mountains to aid those seeking safe exit from perilous situations. Bette, Trevor, and Kyle are living with the sad knowledge that Fred Fredrickson had been beyond such aid. But they are comforted by the thought that they've brought him back up to a high place he cherished.

Dartmouth-Hitchcock Medical Center, Lebanon, N.H.
HealthSouth Rehabilitation Hospital, Concord, N.H.
February 2008 – May 2008

After three and a half hours of aggressive medical intervention in the Emergency Department of Littleton Regional Hospital, James Osborne will spend three months at Dartmouth-Hitchcock Medical Center (DHMC) in Lebanon and at HealthSouth Rehabilitation

Hospital in Concord. His survival is due in large part to his rescuers, the medical professionals who treated him, and to Osborne himself.

"He stopped sliding that night; he didn't get any worse," says Dr. Richard Merrick, Osborne's emergency physician at Littleton Regional Hospital. "James scared the hell out of us, but he was better when he left than when he came in. You have to give a lot of credit to James. There's something in him that just wasn't ready to stop. The power of the human mind is something not to be trifled with. We gave him the opportunity to live, but there was something in him to make the most of that opportunity. He was a real fighter."

Steve Larson, a member of Mountain Rescue Service who was on Little Haystack that night, wants to be sure the medical team accepts the credit it deserves. "The fact that he lived with a core temperature of seventy-six degrees is just unbelievable," says Larson. "That's a medical story, and it's really kind of earth-shattering to think about."

Rescuers, medical professionals, and Osborne himself also believe strongly that Fred Fredrickson was looking out for Osborne by choosing the outer position in their overnight shelter on Franconia Ridge, thus taking the brunt of the raging weather. Fredrickson's selfless act likely contributed to the preservation of at least some of Osborne's vital heat and energy stores overnight.

But the physiological insult the cold perpetrated on Osborne was still overwhelming. Fortunately, once he regained full consciousness on Wednesday, Feb. 13, it became clear that his cognitive function was intact. Research has shown that hypothermia markedly reduces the brain's need for oxygen. When the brain is cold, it can sustain itself for a long time before permanent damage occurs. He was still being monitored for traumatic brain injury because of his many falls, experiencing atrial fibrillation, and having respiratory failure. Because of his severe frostbite, his kidneys and liver needed significant support through dialysis to clear the toxins and debris from his bloodstream.

In the days and weeks following his rescue, portions of Osborne's hands and legs will succumb to frostbite, and he will develop periodic fevers, signaling serious infections. Surgeons at DHMC will be forced to amputate his right leg below the knee, half of his left foot, and a finger from his right hand. He will also endure additional interventions, including surgical repair of his femoral artery due to an aneurism; several skin debridement procedures to remove necrotic tissue from his hands, legs, and abdomen; and multiple skin grafts. Today he wears a prosthetic on his lower right leg and retains scarring over much of his body.

Osborne's nurses and physical therapists, along with everyone who supported him through his recovery, all highlight Osborne's openness, self-reflection, and positivity.

But for all his optimism and self-deprecating humor, he will suffer moments of emotional darkness. While hospitalized and in the months following his discharge, he will be plagued by a recurring nightmare. He is staggering down the mountain in Franconia Notch at night, wading through the snow, and stumbles out onto Interstate 93. When he tries to flag down an approaching snowplow, it nearly hits him, and no other vehicle will stop to help.

"James is reliving that experience of desperation, the feeling that no one will help him," says Ken Norton, executive director of the National Alliance for Mental Illness in New Hampshire and an experienced White Mountain hiker and backcountry skier. Norton intimates that, for James, survival may have been confusing, unsettling, and difficult to adapt to. "In his dream, he knows he's not going to make it without someone intervening, and yet no one is there to intervene," says Norton. "He's now down off the mountain. He's near society and needs help, but no one is helping him. I think these nightmares might have resulted from James's wondering why he lived, why he didn't die. He had made his peace with his impending death up on the mountain that day."

Grieving for his friend, Osborne will grapple with his guilt at being the sole survivor. Then, one weekend afternoon, Bette Fredrickson and son Kyle will appear at his hospital bedside. It is the first time he's met them. Bette can imagine Osborne's feelings of guilt and tells him, "It's not your fault, James. I'm not angry with you because you're here and Fred isn't. You're my link to him."

Osborne says Bette and Kyle's visit lifted a weight off him. "It was very important for me to hear that and know they weren't mad at me," he says. "I needed their reassurance that it was okay, that everything was going to be okay."

Ken Norton notes that Bette's empathy is a lesson for all of us and helped James's healing process. "If Bette had not said things that were helpful and supportive, or sent angry messages, or was even just silent, it would have impacted James's recovery," he says.

Norton also stresses the importance of self-forgiveness in the healing process. "There's going to be a searing sense of self-examination about what your responsibility was in this event. Did your actions contribute to your buddy's death directly or indirectly?" he says. "You have to be willing to forgive yourself for your human mistakes."

Osborne acknowledges that he has asked himself repeatedly if it was the right idea to shelter in place instead of going back that day. "It's a haunting question I still ask myself," he says. "Did we make the right decision? I also wonder if having sleeping bags with us would have mattered. There were things that happened that I think would have ended in disaster no matter what, so it may not have mattered. I used to beat myself up about the accident, but I've come to accept it for what it was: a series of poor decisions."

Throughout the intervening years, Osborne has not once shied away from owning his share of the tragedy. "I take responsibility for what happened to me," he says, resolutely. "I've never blamed Fred for this. I've always taken the tack that I made the decision to go on that hike. I should have been better informed and knowledgeable about the weather, the procedures, and the necessary equipment. About how quickly your life can change on the basis of one decision you make. But if that was the worst moment and the handful of worst decisions I'll ever make, it's also my greatest blessing, because I was rescued and was given a second lease on life. For that, I am grateful."

Since his recovery, James has been able to resume an active life in New Hampshire with his partner, Susan Paris. Together, they enjoy traveling in the U.S. and abroad. In 2010, James learned adaptive skiing through the New England Healing Sports Association, based in Sunapee, N.H. He now hits the slopes every winter and serves as a volunteer ski instructor. He is also an avid cyclist and logs several thousand miles per year in local and national events and on rides organized by the Challenged Athletes Foundation. He is currently working a "gig-economy" job in the metro Boston and Southern New Hampshire regions. Clearly, his optimism and never-quit ethos have remained strong.

James Osborne today.

Cannon Mountain Ski Area
Franconia Notch
May 9, 2009

One year after being released from the hospital, in May 2009, Osborne will return to Franconia Notch. Factoring in the windchill, it will be over 100 degrees warmer than it was the night he was flown out of the Notch by a Black Hawk helicopter. He is here to speak before a large group of search and rescue personnel at their annual training to recount his story and to thank those in attendance who were involved in saving him.

"He was very sincere," says Lt. Todd Bogardus, the Incident Commander for the mission that saved Osborne's life. "It was good therapy for James to be there and for the rescuers to have him there. Having an interaction with a victim they've saved is an affirmation of why they do what they do. The people who rescue care about what they do; they're deeply invested in it and committed."

Conservation Officer Jeremy Hawkes was also engaged in the rescue that night, but this is the first time he will actually meet Osborne. "I was happy that James was there," he says. "I just wanted to see him alive, because I never saw his face that night. He was covered up in the bivy sack the whole time. He was a very nice and a very grateful person. But his gratitude made me a little uncomfortable. I was just doing my job."

Chris Noonan, of Mountain Rescue Service, is pleased to meet Osborne as well. "It was cathartic to see him and meet him. In the back of your mind, you're always worried that if you find the victims you're searching for, they're not going to be alive. But you have to hope. We were surprised and happy that James was alive when we found him."

MRS teammate Alain Comeau has a similar reaction on watching the man he helped save recount the ordeal. "It was kind of emotional seeing James up there talking," he says. "It really made quite an impression. Thank God that helicopter was able to come in and get

From left to right: Mark Ober, NHFG; Alain Comeau, MRS; James Osborne; Chris Noonan, MRS; Jeremy Hawkes, NHFG, May 9, 2009.

him, because if we had had to carry him down, he never would have survived."

Gordie Johnk, who led his Pemigewasset Valley Search and Rescue teammates up the Skookumchuk Trail that night, says Osborne's talk was powerful to hear. "I can't imagine being in his place," says Johnk. "When you hear of people going through those experiences, it really drives home that you need to make good decisions in the mountains—in life in general—but particularly in the mountains."

In addition to speaking at the SAR training, Osborne will join Bogardus on several occasions at Hike Safe presentations to share his experiences with fellow hikers in hopes of helping them avoid a similar fate. Members of the search and rescue community, particularly those closely involved with the mission that saved him, hold Osborne in high regard for taking responsibility for the decisions he made and for his efforts to help educate hikers. "James really puts himself out there," says Larson. "He owns what happened. He is thankful and has said he will do anything he can to help, and he does."

N.H. Congressional Law Enforcement Awards Ceremony
Police Standards and Training Facility
Concord, N.H.
Oct. 23, 2011

James Osborne sits next to his partner, Susan, and listens to Congressman Charles Bass describe his and Fred Fredrickson's ordeal and the rescue effort that saved him. The large gymnasium is filled with members of the New Hampshire Congressional Delegation, other state and local officials, members of the military and the media, and friends and family of the first responders who are there to be recognized. Among these are some of the eleven men who saved James's life on Franconia Ridge three years ago.

From the moment the rescue mission ended, Todd Bogardus has felt strongly that the multiple acts of courage displayed on Little Haystack Mountain should be recognized formally—and publicly. Now, thanks to his efforts, the eleven rescuers are about to receive New Hampshire Congressional Law Enforcement Awards.

From left to right: Capt. Peter Cartmell, former Chief Warrant Officer 3 Zach Lane, James Osborne, Staff Sgt. Matthew Stohrer, Sgt. 1st Class Allan Robinson, October 23, 2011.

Black Hawk 031 pilot Zach Lane recalls Congressman Bass's summary of the actions leading to the honor he and others are about to receive. "It was rewarding to hear our story from another perspective," he says.

Osborne himself is deeply moved, because many of the details he's hearing about his rescue were previously unknown to him. He listens as each man who was with him on Little Haystack is named:

For the New Hampshire Fish and Game Department:
Conservation Officer Mark Ober Jr.
Conservation Officer Jeremy Hawkes

For Mountain Rescue Service:
Steve Larson
Chris Noonan
Alain Comeau
Jim Surette
Charles Townsend

For the New Hampshire Army National Guard:

Captain Peter F. Cartmell

[Former Chief Warrant Officer 3] Zach Lane

Staff Sergeant Matthew Stohrer

Sergeant First Class Allan Robinson

"It was a very formal event," recalls Black Hawk 031 Pilot in Command Pete Cartmell. "I was honored to be put in for the award. I usually shy away from the recognition aspect of our missions. When [Osborne] said, 'Thank you so much for all that you've done,' I wanted to say, 'It's really Matt [Stohrer] who deserves your thanks more than I do.'"

For Todd Bogardus, whose own actions in coordinating and leading the entire rescue mission were a significant factor in Osborne's survival, the event serves to honor an outstanding team accomplishment. It provides satisfying closure, for both Osborne and his rescuers, to one of the most challenging search and rescue missions ever executed in the White Mountains.

SEARCH and RESCUE ASSIGNMENTS

Incident Command:
Lt. Todd Bogardus, New Hampshire Fish and Game
Lt. James Goss, New Hampshire Fish and Game

Falling Waters Trail to Little Haystack Mountain:
Conservation Officer Mark Ober, New Hampshire Fish and Game*
Conservation Officer Jeremey Hawkes, New Hampshire Fish and Game*

Mountain Rescue Service (MRS-1)
Steve Larson
Chris Noonan
Alain Comeau
Charlie Townsend
Jim Surette

Old Bridle Path to Greenleaf Hut to treeline on Mount Lafayette
Conservation Officer Brad Morse, New Hampshire Fish and Game*
Conservation Officer Mark Hensel, New Hampshire Fish and Game*

Mountain Rescue Service (MRS-2)
Jeff Fongemie
Joe Lentini
Bayard Russell Jr.
Joe Klementovich
Rob Adair
Sam Bendroth

*denotes "Hasty Team"

Liberty Spring Trail to Franconia Ridge
Mountain Rescue Service (MRS-3)
Steve Dupuis*
Tim Martel*

Skookumchuck Trail to treeline on Mount Lafayette
Gordie Johnk, Pemigewasset Valley Search and Rescue Team (PVSART)*
Matt Glarem, Pemigewasset Valley Search and Rescue Team*
Irv Locke, Pemigewasset Valley Search and Rescue Team*
Allan Clark, Radio relay from Skookumchuck parking area

Greenleaf Trail to Greenleaf Hut
Conservation Officer Craig Jellison, New Hampshire Fish and Game*
Conservation Officer Sam Sprague, New Hampshire Fish and Game*

Lincoln Brook Trail into Pemigewasset Wilderness
Conservation Officer Heidi Murphy, New Hampshire Fish and Game*
Conservation Officer Michael Eastman, New Hampshire Fish and Game*
Officer Herb Karsten, United States Forest Service (Radio relay from Hancock pull-off Route 112)

Black Hawk 031 Crew
First Lt. Pete Cartmell (Pilot in Command), New Hampshire Army National Guard
Chief Warrant Officer 3 Zachary Lane (Pilot), New Hampshire Army National Guard
Staff Sgt. Matthew Stohrer (Crew Chief), New Hampshire Army National Guard
Staff Sgt. Allan Robinson (Crew Chief), New Hampshire Army National Guard
Conservation Officer Delayne Brown, New Hampshire Fish and Game (daytime flight)   *denotes "Hasty Team"

HIKER RESPONSIBILITY CODE

You are responsible for yourself, so be prepared:

1. **With knowledge and gear.** Become self reliant by learning about the terrain, conditions, local weather and your equipment before you start.

2. **To leave your plans.** Tell someone where you are going, the trails you are hiking, when you'll return and your emergency plans.

3. **To stay together.** When you start as a group, hike as a group, end as a group. Pace your hike to the slowest person.

4. **To turn back.** Weather changes quickly in the mountains. Fatigue and unexpected conditions can also affect your hike. Know your limitations and when to postpone your hike. The mountains will be there another day.

5. **For emergencies,** even if you are headed out for just an hour. An injury, severe weather or a wrong turn could become life-threatening. Don't assume you will be rescued; know how to rescue yourself.

6. **To share the hiker code with others.**

hikeSafe: It's Your Responsibility.

The Hiker Responsibility Code was developed and is endorsed by the White Mountain National Forest and New Hampshire Fish and Game.

HikeSafe, a mountain safety education program, was developed jointly by the White Mountain National Forest and New Hampshire Fish and Game.

Recommended Clothing and Equipment for Hikers

For Summer Day Hikes:
The Ten Essentials
  Map & Compass
  Warm Clothing
    Sweater or Pile Jacket
    Long Pants (wool or synthetic)
    Extra Socks
  Extra Food and Water
  Flashlight or Headlamp
  Matches/Firestarters
  First-aid kit/Repair kit
  Whistle
  Rain/Wind Jacket and Pants
  Pocket Knife
  Sturdy Footwear and Socks

Watch
Hat (wool)
Trash Bag (for trash or rain protection)
Light Plastic Tarp or "Space" Blanket
Guidebook
Insect Repellent
Sunglasses
Sun Lotion
Gloves or Mittens
Personal Medications
Cord/Rope
Gaiters
Extra Batteries

Add for Overnight Trips and Groups:
Sleeping Bag
Foam Pad
Tent or other shelter
Extra Clothing
Pots, Cup, Bowl, Spoon
Food
Water Purification
Toothbrush, Towel, etc.
Stove, Fuel

Add for Winter:
Extra Warm Clothing
  Insulated Parka
  Extra Mittens
  Balaclava
  Insulated Boots
  Overmitts
  Snowshoes

Add for Above Treeline:
Crampons
Face Mask
Ice Axe
Goggles

Add for Avalanche Terrain:
Avalanche Transceiver
Avalanche Probe
Snow Shovel

IN CASE OF ACCIDENT OR EMERGENCY CALL:
N.H. State Police 1-800-525-5555 or 911

https://hikesafe.com

Acknowledgments

As you will see in the list below, I was supported by many individuals and organizations in my quest to tell this story. I'm so grateful for their trust and time, and willingness to talk with and teach me.

James Osborne: Thank you for answering my inquiry and trusting me to tell your part of the story. Your humility and transparency throughout this process are a reflection of your strong character. Your optimism, strength, and resiliency are an inspiration to me.

Bette, Trevor, and Kyle Fredrickson: Thank you for your strength and courage in sharing Fred's story with me, for trusting me with it, and for sharing your personal memories and experiences.

The Law Enforcement Division of the New Hampshire Fish and Game Department: Col. Kevin Jordan, Capt. Mike Eastman, Lt. James Kneeland, Lt. Brad Morse, Lt. Delayne Brown, Lt. Heidi Murphy, Lt. Jim Goss (ret.), Conservation Officer II Craig Jellison, Lt. Wayne Saunders (ret.), Trooper Mark Hensel.

Lt. Todd Bogardus (ret.): Thank you for the time you devoted to sharing the story of the rescue mission, and for taking me inside your decision-making process.

Lt. Mark Ober and Sgt. Jeremy Hawkes: Thank you for your candor and transparency in sharing your stories. Your willingness to share lessons you learned will help others in the backcountry.

Mountain Rescue Service Board of Directors, with special thanks to team members Steve Dupuis (President), Rick Wilcox (Founder/Past President), Steve Larson, Chris Noonan, Alain Comeau, Jim Surette, Charlie Townsend, Bayard Russell Jr., Sam Bendroth, Rob Adair, Tim Martel, Joe Lentini, Joe Klementovich, and Justin Preisendorfer. Thank you also to Jeff Fongemie for facilitating the approval and interview process.

Pemigewasset Valley Search and Rescue Team Board of Directors, with special thanks to Allan Clark (Founder/President), Gordie Johnk, Matt Glarem, John Hansen, Chris Whiton, Thom Davis, John Tatone, Jamie Cunningham, and Pam Bales.

New Hampshire Army National Guard: Maj. Gen. David Mikolaities, Col. Frank Leith (ret.), Lt. Col. Greg Heilshorn, Chief Warrant Officer 3 Iain Hamilton. Special thanks to Capt. Pete Cartmell (ret.), and Chief Warrant Officer 3 Zach Lane, Staff Sgt. Matt Stohrer, and Staff Sgt. Allan Robinson. Thank you also to Warren Lyons at the Eastern Army Aviation Training Site at Fort Indiantown Gap, Pa. for an enlightening Black Hawk simulator experience.

Mount Washington Observatory: Krissy Fraser, Brian Clark, Rebecca Scholand, Ryan Knapp, Stacey Kawecki, and Brian Fitzgerald. Special thanks to Tom Padham for his painstaking research efforts and for helping me understand the dynamics of mountain weather.

Littleton Regional Hospital: Gail Clark and Natalie Kennett, with special thanks to Dr. Richard Merrick and Dr. Campbell McLaren for the lessons on emergency medicine and hypothermia.

Dartmouth-Hitchcock Medical Center: Jim Alexander, Kyle Madigan, Doug Moore, Stephen Jameson, Dr. Eric Martin, with special thanks to Dr. Horace Henriques (ret.) for his expertise in critical care and John Hinds for an inside look at DHART operations.

Lucille Stott: I'm so pleased we could work together again. Thank you for your perspective, candor, and guidance through the writing process. You are an exceptional editor, and I'm grateful for your friendship.

Ted Walsh: Thank you for providing a supportive framework for me to tell the story. I have thoroughly enjoyed our long working relationship and, more importantly, our friendship.

Brenda Dimick, Paul Parisi, and Max Leepson: Thank you for giving generously of your time to read an early manuscript and offer valuable feedback.

Thanks to those who played a part in helping me at some point in this process: Tricia Larson, Dick Martel, Kenneth Krause, Steve Smith, Chief Chad Morris, Caroline Alexander, Seth Cooper, Cecil Cooper, Paul Cormier, Cindy McLaren, Brad White, Lt. Gary Prince, Elizabeth Gruber, Russell Gates, Andy Knight, Tim Lucia, Darlene Deschambeaultlt, Jim Salge, Beth Farley, Gary Rasmussen, Ernie Brochu, Aubrey McPhail, Abbie Saffian, Christine Northrup, Ken Norton, Frank Hubbell, Murray Hamlet, Sandy Stott, Mike Cohen, Sheriff Jeff Stiegler, Tom Andross, Chief Jason Lyon, David Lottmann, Keith Watling, Nikki Becker, Tiffany Eddy, Gordon Giesbrecht, Jamie Cunningham, Carl Herz, Samantha Brady, Matt Sakakeeny, Mark Synnott, Jason B.A. Van Camp, Former U.S. Senator Kelly Ayotte, Former Gov. John Lynch, Jerome Maslan, David Lottman, Kimball Rexford, Dan Szczesny, Chief David Goldstein, Laura Waterman, Peter Fisher, Joe McQuaid, Lorna Colquhoun, Ron Reynolds, Michael Durant, and the Primex Board of Trustees and staff.

My wife, Debbie: I'm so grateful for your love, support, and friendship. Thank you for your patience throughout this project…again…and for a perfectly balanced mix of encouragement and nudging when writing took an unplanned hiatus. This truly was a team effort.

I assume full responsibility for any errors. Throughout my research I put forth my very best effort to tell this story accurately in hopes that readers might learn valuable lessons in decision-making, risk-taking, and empathy. I spoke with many technical and subject matter experts. If I got any of the details wrong, I own that.

Selected Bibliography and Further Reading

Allen, Mel, "Making the Final Choice on Katahdin," *Yankee Magazine*, 1980.

American Alpine Club (various editors): Since 1948, the American Alpine Club has issued an annual publication entitled *Accidents in North American Mountaineering*. Current and past postings are available online at http://publications.americanalpineclub.org.

Daniell, Gene, and Smith, Steven D. *White Mountain Guide, 28th Edition*. Boston, MA: AMC Books, 2007.

Giesbrecht, Gordon G., and Wilkerson, James A. *Hypothermia, Frostbite, and Other Cold Injuries: Prevention, Survival, Rescue, and Treatment*. Seattle, WA: The Mountaineers Books, 2006.

Gonzales, Laurence. *Deep Survival: Who Lives, Who Dies, and Why*. New York: W.W. Norton & Company, 2017.

Hamilton, George T. "The Katahdin Tragedy," January 31-February 1, 1974, *Appalachia* No. 159. Boston, MA: Appalachian Mountain Club, 1974.

Howe, Nicholas. *Not Without Peril: 150 Years of Misadventure on the Presidential Range of New Hampshire*. Boston, MA: AMC Books, 2010.

Hubbell, D.O., Franklin R. *Wildcare: Working in Less Than Desirable Conditions and Remote Environments*. Conway, N.H.: TMC Books LLC/Stonehearth Open Learning Opportunities, 2014.

Julavits, Heidi. "What I Learned in Avalanche School," *The New York Times*, Dec. 31, 2019.

Kick, Peter. *Desperate Steps: Life, Death, and Choices Made in the Mountains of the Northeast*. Boston, MA: AMC Books, 2015.

Krakauer, Jon. *Classic Krakauer: Essay on Wilderness and Risk*. New York: Anchor Books, 2019.

McCammon, Ian. "Evidence of Heuristic Traps in Recreational Avalanche Accidents," presented at the International Snow Science Workshop, Penticton, British Columbia, 2002.

   —"Heuristic Traps in Recreational Accidents: Evidence and Implications, *Avalanche News*, No. 68, Spring 2004.

Ryan, Jeffrey H. *Appalachian Odyssey: A 28-Year Hike on America's Trail.* Camden, ME: Down East Books, 2016.

Simpson, Joe. *Touching the Void: The True Story of One Man's Miraculous Survival.* New York., NY: Harper Perennial, 2004.

Stark, Peter. "Frozen Alive," *Outside Online*: https://www.outsideonline.com/2152131/freezing-death

State of Alaska. *Cold Injuries Guidelines*, Department of Health and Social Services, Division of Public Health; Section of Emergency Programs. 2014

Stott, Sandy. *Critical Hours: Search and Rescue in the White Mountains.* Dartmouth, NH: University Press of New England, 2018.

Szczensy, Dan. *The White Mountain: Rediscovering Mount Washington's Hidden Culture.* Concord, NH: Hobblebush Books, 2018.

Waterman, Laura and Guy. *Forest and Crag: A History of Hiking, Trail Blazing, and Adventure in the Northeast Mountains.* Boston, MA: AMC Books, 2003.

Weathers, Beck and Michaud, Stephen G. *Left for Dead: My Journey Home from Everest.* New York: Bantam Books, 2015.

Online Resources:

Hike Safe: https://hikesafe.com

Mount Washington Observatory: https://www.mountwashington.org

New Hampshire Outdoor Council: https://nhoutdoorcouncil.org

Mount Washington Avalanche Center: https://mountwashingtonavalanchecenter.org

Photo and Illustration Credits

My sincere thanks to those individuals and organizations who provided me with images for the book. They help immensely in telling this story.

Keith Watling
- Front cover
- Title page
- Pg. ii

Jamie Cunningham, Jamie Cunningham Photography
- Back cover
- Dedication page
- Pg. 41
- Pg. 171

Dave Lottmann, https://northeastalpinestart.com
- Opposite Prologue

White Mountain Images/Chris Whiton Photography, https://www.whitemountainimages.org
- Pg. 5
- Pg. 53
- Pg. 63
- Pg. 81

Fredrickson Family
- Pg. 7
- Pg. 13
- Pg. 14
- Pg. 25
- Pg. 26
- Pg. 265

New Hampshire Army National Guard
- Pg. 20-21
- Pg. 214 (Staff Sgt. Joshua Stephenson)
- Pg. 257
- Pg. 274

Ty Gagne
- Pg. 29

Mount Washington Observatory
- Pg. 31
- Pg. 94
- Pg. 116

Kimball Rexford, TrailsNH.com
- Pg. 42, 93, 143, 175, 223 (Ted Walsh, TMC Books, graphics)

Bruce Neff, New Hampshire Civil Air Patrol
- Pg. 54
- Pg. 57

James Osborne
- Pg. 60, 67, 72
- Pg. 61
- Pg. 71

National Oceanic and Atmospheric Administration (NOAA)/National Weather Service (NWS) Weather Prediction Center
- Pg. 62
- Pg. 82

Ted Walsh, TMC Books
- Pg. 97
- Pg. 124
- Pg. 129
- Pg. 139

Joe Lentini, Mountain Rescue Service
- Pg. 135

New Hampshire Fish and Game Law Enforcement Division
- Pg. 272 (Todd Bogardus)
- Pg. 278-279

John Tatone, Pemigewasset Valley Search and Rescue Team
- Pg. 154

Joe Klementovich, Mountain Rescue Service, http://www.klementovichphoto.com/
- Pg. 166

Courtesy of Tim and Dick Martel
- Pg. 168

Delayne Brown, New Hampshire Fish and Game
- Pg. 172
- Pg. 174

Charlie Townsend, Mountain Rescue Service
- Pg. 173
- Pg. 206
- Pg. 221
- Pg. 224

Dartmouth-Hitchcock Health
- Pg. 260-261

Mark Johnson, Ironstring
- Pg. 271

Kimberly Davis, Photography by Kimberly
- Pg. 286, author photo

About the Author

Ty Gagne is chief executive officer of New Hampshire Public Risk Management Exchange (Primex³), a public entity risk pool serving local governments in New Hampshire. He is a certified Wilderness First Responder and the author of the book *Where You'll Find Me: Risk, Decisions, and the Last Climb of Kate Matrosova*. Two of his essays, "Footprints in the Snow Lead to an Emotional Rescue," and "Weakness in Numbers: How a Hiking Partner can be Dangerous" were published in *Appalachia* journal.

CPSIA information can be obtained
at www.ICGtesting.com
Printed in the USA
BVHW090530191120
593591BV00001B/1

9 781734 930832